Merryland

Also Available from Eclipse Press

Merryland

Two Years in the Life of a Racing Stable

A DIARY BY TWO-TIME
ECLIPSE AWARD-WINNING AUTHOR
JOSH PONS

Photos by Ellen Pons

ECLIPSE
PRESS

Essex, Connecticut

ECLIPSE
PRESS

An imprint of Globe Pequot, the trade division of
The Rowman & Littlefield Publishing Group, Inc.
4501 Forbes Blvd., Ste. 200
Lanham, MD 20706
www.rowman.com

Distributed by NATIONAL BOOK NETWORK

British Library Cataloguing in Publication Information available

Library of Congress Control Number: 2007935988

ISBN 978-1-4930-8133-2 (paperback) | 978-1-4930-8134-9 (epub)

CONTENTS

To Mary Jo Pons

AUTHOR'S NOTE

Brigadoon

Twenty-five years ago, our family mulled over the wisdom of signing up for a down-at-the-heels dowager, Merryland Farm, a former queen among the many historic horse farms of Maryland. In her heyday in the mid-1900s, no farm could match the bluegrass of her fields, the white fences, the hunter-green roofs atop white training barns, the crystal-clear stream that flowed through the land.

As youths, we had seen Merryland at her best, and our recall was euphoric. As adults, we faced the reality of decades of deferred maintenance and indifferent ownership. We checklisted her points of beauty. Still just a quick eight-mile drive from our home farm, Country Life. Still a great swatch of farmland in a preservation quilt of six thousand acres known as the Long Green Valley. Still one hundred stalls for Thoroughbreds and a sandy five-eighths-mile racetrack and a fieldstone farmhouse dating back to the 1800s.

And . . . she still had her history. In the 1950s, yearlings prepped here for the Woodward family's dispersal of famed Belair Stud. In the 1960s, national champions Process Shot and Silent Screen trained here. In the 1970s, the stallion Rock Talk resided in the handsome two-stallion stud barn, his daughter Heartlight No. One to become, in the 1980s, a champion filly for songwriter Burt Bacharach, who was among the farm's many A-list clients.

* * *

With a four-month study period to decide whether to buy, we could see the fallen-down farm was an Augean stable, an endless cleanup effort of Herculean proportion. Clarity came one summer afternoon. As I drove a friend down the steep hill of Bottom Road, through overhanging oaks and ship-mast straight poplars, through virgin woodland opening onto a dramatic vista of low-ground farmland — there, from a sudden bend in Bottom Road four hundred feet above the farm — I quipped derisively: *"Thar she blows."*

All my friend saw was the lovely lay of the land, the natural beauty. He exclaimed, "Why, it looks like Brigadoon down there!"

I understood the term to mean a make-believe place. As we drove through the farm, neither of us could believe how overgrown and unkempt grand old Merryland had become. She was far from the pastoral retreat of one-time owner

William V. Elder, who had purchased the farm (then named The Willows) during the Great Depression and had renamed her "Merryland" in honor of his first Thoroughbred racehorse, a mare named Merry Land, foaled in 1920, out of the mare Merriment II.

The condition of Merryland surely would have saddened master horseman Danny Shea, who bought the farm from Elder in 1939 and thereafter plowed his life earnings into improvements. His indomitable widow, Betty Shea Miller, with a broken heart, had witnessed the sad, slow decline through the 1990s from her home on the hill opposite the farm.

By the summer of 2001, Merryland's fields were a jungle of prickly multiflora roses, and the driveway's lanes of privet hedges, gone wild, were too tall to trim. What barn roofs didn't leak, soon would. And neither plumbing nor electricity could possibly be up to code. But under all that overgrowth, never to feel a developer's claw, lay the beautiful bottomland of the Long Green Valley—a wannabe Brigadoon. All the old farm needed was a workforce, a loving family (the larger the better), and a few years of backbreaking, expensive renovations. Enter the posse: the Pons family, preteens to elders, aided immeasurably by the Gutierrez family of Michoacán, Mexico, who to this day return annually to maintain Merryland and care for the horses.

To bring Merryland back to a fully functioning farm, well, that effort filled a book. In a diary that appeared monthly in the trade periodical *BloodHorse* in 2005 and 2006, I chronicled the often not-so-idyllic reality of raising and training racehorses on a farm under renovation. That twenty-four-part series was republished in 2007 in book form as *Merryland: Two Years in the Life of a Racing Stable*, a bit of a bookend to my *Country Life Diary: Three Years in the Life of a Thoroughbred Farm* published in 1992. Both books happily sold out of print. A third book, *Letters from Country Life: Adolphe Pons, Man o' War, and the Founding of Maryland's Oldest Thoroughbred Farm*, was published in August 2024.

For this second edition of *Merryland*, I considered a world of changes since 2005. Most memorable to me personally have been family related. My father, Joe Pons, died during the first year of the Merryland diary, on October 12, 2005. My mother, Mary Jo Pons, died on January 1, 2017. And my older brother, Andrew, the best horseman of our clan, died on January 2, 2024.

When *Merryland*'s first printing appeared, my two sons, Josh and August, were sixteen and thirteen. They are now both married and well into adulthood, and my wife, Ellen, and I are one year into grandparenthood.

When *Merryland* first appeared, the Maryland Jockey Club had just spent $30 million to renovate the racing surface at Laurel. Now Laurel is doomed for development under a plan to concentrate resources on Pimlico as the home of the classic Preakness Stakes.

In 2005, the Thoroughbred foal crop was 38,000. For 2024, it will be about 17,000 — a 55 percent swing in the wrong direction. In the preface to *Merryland* that I wrote two decades ago, I imagined the book as a time capsule, but who could have predicted an industry sawed in half by attrition? I need to write faster.

Still, in all, the basics of taking care of horses and the land they live on have not changed. Here follows a lightly edited second effort at two years in the life of a Thoroughbred training farm — at times dreamily remote from reality.

It's been almost a century since The Willows became Merryland. The farm now hums with equine activity, once again a magical, mythical place, timeless and idyllic (well, most days). Whenever I drive down from the top of Bottom Road and view Merryland in the valley below, I see a bit of Brigadoon, that unforgettable farm I first saw in my youth.

Josh Pons
Merryland Farm
August 2024

PREFACE

Seen from the air, the oval of a racetrack suggests dreams. Look down into Louisville. There's Churchill Downs, sacred ground. Over the Pacific, Del Mar pulses with the tides. Belmont Park floats on the vast Hempstead Plain of Long Island. I don't fly often, but when I do I always look for racetracks.

On approach to Baltimore, as the plane banks north of the metropolis, the brown sand of the training track at Merryland Farm stands out amidst the lime-green cornfields of the Long Green Valley. It is spectacular Maryland geology. Valley and ridge. Valley and ridge.

In decades-old topographical maps of valley districts, the track is sketched in, a perfect oval amid squiggles of elevation, a landscape feature sure as a stream. The only manmade exception in the maps of the Long Green Valley.

Of course, from a plane, from a map, the tableau masks reality. Distance is a deception. At ground level, obstreperous young horses have resisted domestication since Danny Shea first broke yearlings here in the 1930s. On more than one occasion during our ownership of Merryland Farm, a helicopter has landed in the infield, to whisk away a fallen rider to a trauma center in Baltimore. Riders, high up, understand the fact: It's not *if* you fall; it's *when* you fall. And on the ground, same as it ever was, owners of racehorses face the economics: That most racehorses are simply hayburners, dream breakers.

So what? The nuances of racing are nothing new. Reality on the ground does not diminish innocent airborne excitement. Look! There's a track down there!

I love to find Merryland from the air. But there is danger in that illusion. So to get my head out of the clouds, I began keeping a diary of the lives of the young horses in training at Merryland and of our efforts to restore a grand old farm that for decades has launched racehorses, like so many jets off an aging aircraft carrier.

Two years. No time at all, really, in the great arc of this ancient sport. Just a little time capsule from a corner of the racing world, from a corner of a beautiful long green valley, suggesting some dreams.

Josh Pons
Merryland Farm
September 2007

WINTER
2005

January

Saturday, January 1

In 1939, restless trainer Danny Shea settled on a farm in Maryland's Long Green Valley. He changed the farm's name from The Willows to the playfully punned name, Merryland.

Shea envisioned a racetrack in the flat land between the fixed obstacles of Bottom Road and a magnificent bank barn a quarter-mile into the farm. Fitted stone walls of the barn stood resolute against a precise five-furlong track circumference; Shea's engineers designed an oval about 100 feet shy. Shea improvised. He set two finish-line poles. Exercise riders named the first line "Danny's selling pole," where 2-year-olds worked the time of their lives as inducement to buyers. He set the second pole farther down the stretch, at the true five-furlong distance. Before departing each season for Garden State, Atlantic City, Monmouth, and Rockingham, Danny clocked his 2-year-olds to the second pole to pick his traveling team.

By the time Country Life Farm purchased Merryland in August 2001, the twinkle in Danny's eyes had been gone from this earth for 42 years. His racetrack rail could be pushed over with a touch. Poison ivy climbed the bank barn's faded walls. Both the "selling pole" and the precise pole had long since toppled.

When Country Life bought Merryland, 9/11 was just the birthdate of a friend's son. A blink later, the Trade Towers fell, the Pentagon exploded, and a field in Pennsylvania became the grave of a friend. All that first autumn, chevrons of fighter jets ripped the afternoon air over Merryland on flight paths from Andrews Air Force Base 75 miles south of the farm.

It is a different world than when Danny plowed his life savings into these acres, but his island of merriment is intact. His barns have been painted, his hedges tamed, and his track has been restored—all but the "selling pole."

Officially renamed Country Life Nursery at Merryland Farm, it would please Danny to hear the van drivers skip the Nursery bit: "You want this filly dropped at Merryland?"

Horsemen respectfully remember Danny's farm and three decades of stewardship by his widow, Betty Shea Miller, where sets of horses trained over a perfectly corduroyed track. There were flower beds against white fences, hilly pastures where track-weary horses were refreshed and restored, wreaths on the stalls at Christmastime. Young horses schooled in a state-of-the-art, Puett six-stall starting gate. Young horsemen schooled as grooms and riders.

The farm was famous. When Danny died, Merryland was the largest commercial horse farm in the state. Marylanders remember a picture on the front page of the *Baltimore Sun*: 19 yearlings running at full tilt, strung out across a deep, broad hillside at Merryland. A spectacular photograph. The perfect image of a perfect farm in a state where people loved horses.

Sunday, January 2

One day into his yearling year, lost a boarder the hard way. Phone rings at 3 a.m. Clinic. "Intussusception of intestines. Telescoped."

What's the bill so far?

"About two thousand."

How much more for surgery?

"Including pharmacy? Maybe eight more."

Complications likely?

"Yes."

I do the math. We'll be at 10 grand for an ordinary colt with scar-tissued intestines. Abdominal surgery requires announcement at sale — he'll never draw a bid. How can I phone his 80-year-old owner at 3 a.m. to ask permission to euthanize the colt? It'll kill the owner just to answer the phone this time of night. I instruct the clinic:

Put him down, please.

Just like that. I lie awake another hour, maybe two, adrenaline pumping. Welcome to the horse business, a school of hard knocks, where it can all change—just like that.

Monday, January 3

At Arlington National Cemetery, good horsemen are on the wrong side of the Turf—under it. Today, they buried another one, Col. Arthur H. Wilson Jr. The obit in the *Washington Post* said: "He collapsed at his barn while caring for his horses." He captained the West Point polo team to three championships and coached polo at the university level. He also commanded the Battle of the Beltway, after his two-horse trailer lifted from the pickup's tow ball and careened down the slope where I-95 meets the ramp for Towson. An unmounted policeman said: "I don't know anything about horses. You take care of them. I'll take care of the traffic."

A nighttime evacuation, klieg lights on a movie set — that's the image I recall of horses against the backdrop of the roaring interstate, Col. Wilson calmly loading them like polo ponies back onto another trailer for the ride home to Free Union, Va.

At Arlington today, in the gift shop after the service, I read from *In Honored Glory, The Final Post*:

"For infantry officers of colonel rank and above, a caparison — or riderless horse — follows the caisson to the gravesite. The black horse, the solemn color of mourning, has a sword strapped to its English riding saddle, with boots reversed in the stirrups ... symbolizing that the soldier will never ride again to lead his troops."

The famous caparison horse of President Kennedy's funeral, Black Jack, died in 1976 at the age of 29. I wondered if the Black Jack of Harry Wilson's service would be exhausted tonight, if the war in Iraq would be straining the Caisson Platoon. I heard no other horseshoes on the cobblestones of Fort Myer Chapel. I heard only one 21-gun salute, saw only one flag folded, corners tucked tight, presented to family members.

Always one of a kind, Col. Wilson, even at your final post.

Tuesday, January 4

The Garrett Building in downtown Baltimore took its name from a merchant of finance, a railroad magnate. Ceilings soar overhead. Marble floors clack underfoot. Three-and-a-half years ago, lawyers in the Garrett Building passed around documents for our purchase of Merryland. Above the dark paneling floated ghosts of men who came to this building to secure financing for speculative ventures. Some hit gushers. Some hit dry wells. I took note.

An hour later and a world away, on rusty wrought-iron gates, wife Ellen and sister-in-law Lisa unfurled an orange-and-blue banner, as Mom and Dad and a passel of youngsters posed for a ceremonial photo next to the farm's new sign. "Country Life Nursery at Merryland Farm" opened for business.

Wednesday, January 5

Having a training track means not having to sell every young horse as a weanling or yearling. A dream thus came true of naming a racehorse for Country Life's version of Cal Ripken Jr. — ironman Richard Harris, who foaled Maryland's all-time leading earner Cigar here in 1990. Richard himself was foaled in the coal mining town of Jenkinjones, West Virginia.

A rugged bay colt trained with us until the rider's hands hurt holding him back, and today, just-turned 3-year-old Jenkin Jones climbed on a trailer for Flint Stites' barn at Penn National, 90 minutes north, in the mountains of Pennsylvania.

Thursday, January 6

With 61,000 slot machines on target to churn out millions in purse subsidies, Pennsylvania is an 800-pound gorilla. Every breeding farm in Maryland has received this fax from clients: "Please make arrangements to send my mare to Pennsylvania to foal."

Most mom-and-pop farms up there are nearing capacity to accept foaling mares. Commercial farms add staff, clean out machinery sheds, fit them with stalls.

Not the first silver dollar has fallen out of a slot machine in Pennsylvania, and already they've raised purses twice.

Kentuckians drive to Mountaineer for slot purses, toothpicks keeping eyes open on the six-hour drive home. We're lucky. We can get back and forth to Pennsylvania in 45 minutes to see JJ train.

Friday, January 7

The accountant is tracking the track: "For every mare that ships out-of-state to foal, if you add a yearling to break, or a 2-year-old to prepare, it's something of a wash."

How do you think we get up in the morning?

Saturday, January 8

The late Dr. Peyton Jones did a stint in a small-animal vet clinic. He encountered frantic poodle owners, crazy cat lovers. From hit-and-runs to hairballs, Peyton's line was always the same: "Well, Mrs. Worthington, I would be concerned, but not alarmed."

Peyton's bromide became my mantra. It works pretty well in life. It's not a blanket fix, though. On Christmas Day, we accompanied our best mare to the vet clinic, and a possible mild colic was rediagnosed as uterine torsion. Concern escalated into alarm. She's back now, stapled from stem to stern, flank to flank, but the foal is alive on ultrasound, due February 6.

Sunday, January 9

Today in Kentucky, at a stallion show that featured Malibu Moon, a former Country Life Farm stallion we relocated to the Bluegrass, excitement beckoned elsewhere for our 14-year-old son Josh.

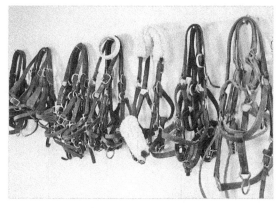

"Can I go play lacrosse with Will?"

Stallions aren't the only Maryland import into the Bluegrass. They play lacrosse there now, too.

Monday, January 10

At Pimlico these early days of January, racehorses displaced by construction at Laurel live in circus tents. All eyes are on the skies should snow be forecast, as canvas couldn't stand the strain. Thank goodness for a mild winter so far. Meanwhile, at Maryland breeding farms, interstate health certificates are drawn up for mares to ship to Pennsylvania, to West Virginia, to New York, and to New Jersey, where slots weave silk purses.

I watch the vans come and go, thinking of Michelangelo — Michael Busch, that is, patron saint of slots opponents, speaker of the Maryland House of Representatives, foe of pro-slots Gov. Bob Ehrlich. Proud traditions of horse racing and breeding are sacrificed to the squabble. It's as though Maryland horse people are partners in a restaurant with a reputation for fine food, but no liquor license. We watch our customers slip across state lines for a drink. Soon, with slots pouring into Pennsylvania, they'll be too loaded to drive home.

Maryland trainers shift tack to Charles Town and Philly Park, colorful silks in backseats of empty-coffee-cup-filled cars.

Here, on these two farms, we're lucky. We have two assets that level the playing field somewhat — a renovated track at Merryland in a region bursting with strong purses and an exciting young sire in Kentucky. We do all we can for the cause, but we can't sit around wringing our hands at legislators in Annapolis. That's a path to madness.

Tuesday, January 11

Brice Ridgely is built like Haystacks Calhoun. He feeds his young horses like prize show cattle. Declan's Moon looked bullish when Brice took him to the Timonium yearling sale, but Samantha Siegel grimaced when she looked down at her catalogue page to discover that Brice had had him gelded. Like raising steers. Easier to handle. Saves the next fellow from having to pay for it.

Samantha bravely bid for Declan, and in two weeks, she'll find out whether her unbeaten Maryland-bred gelding will receive the Eclipse Award as champion 2-year-old "male."

"You better get a tux," I told Brice today. "Get one of those country and western ones, with tails, the kind Garth Brooks wears."

"All right now," Brice said. "Be nice."

Wednesday, January 12

Am working on H-2A visas for a band of brothers from Mexico stuck below the border awaiting approval from the Immigration and Naturalization Service. Every season they return, belongings in a backpack.

Meanwhile, locals apply for work, loaded with baggage: dogs, kids, bills, gray hair. Just like me.

Young men around here have easier options than farm work. The locals these days are workforce veterans who sit in the office armchair reciting qualifications for work, chests swelling bravely, soldiering on through revelations of dreams they had of a life that didn't work out, and now they are back looking for work on a horse farm in winter, more arthritic than when they last asked. Just like me.

I want to name these good people here, register them for the sake of history, make a rock wall with their names on it. But I can't hire them. We don't have enough housing for men with families, and we're not that busy yet. I have to wait for the INS to process the brothers.

Thursday, January 13

Thrill seekers enter the horse business, get hooked on e-mail adrenaline: "Your horse is running today." They get out sometimes when misfortune reroutes the path to the winner's circle and points instead to the breeding shed.

"I'm sorry it didn't work out," he wrote. "I jumped out of airplanes until the preparation didn't match the thrill any longer. I jumped three, maybe four times."

Horse breeding isn't for everyone.

Friday, January 14

Threw the door open for a discussion of names for a 2-year-old. One partner suggested Maryland Monroe. Sorry, The Jockey Club wrote back, it's taken. Well, how about Merryland Monroe? Nope, sounds like the first name.

Christy Holden in our office lobbied online: The horse named Maryland Monroe is a foal of 2001. There's a mare named Hookedonthefeelin, and a racehorse named Hooking Thefeeling. Similar names abound. The chance of a racetrack announcer calling a stretch drive between Maryland Monroe and Merryland Monroe in a Maryland Million race is remote. Please?

Cyberspace smiled: name granted.

Merryland Monroe will be auditioning this summer, perhaps at a theater near you.

Saturday, January 15

This afternoon, into the broodmare barn's bowling alley of a hayloft, climbed four boys and a trio of men. The escalator started, and 100-pound lads pitched their bantamweights against heavy bales of Western alfalfa, sliding on a pine floor worn slick by field hands from Danny Shea's era.

Fresh-air breaks and soda stops never took the assembly line down, and within an hour, heads were leaning out the loft door, counting down the last 10 bales.

"How many left, Phil?" Michael's son had the last in his hands.

"One."

"That's the one we're looking for!"

Any other occupation but farming, such child labor would be exhaustive drudgery and probably illegal. But on a farm, it's fun when all hands join in.

Sunday, January 16

Church seats 30, maybe 40 for a christening. It rests in the corner of an old farm. It's intimate and quaint, like that last scene in *Shenandoah*, when Jimmy Stewart's sons come limping in from the Civil War. When the minister says, "Thanks be to God," we concur and file out in low profile.

"Hey, saw the story on your horse!" bubbles the acolyte. He thinks we own Declan. Suddenly, talk of horse racing spills over coffee in the meeting hall. The horse business is a unique occupation. Laypeople require clarifications. I quietly answer questions, all the while feeling like I'm about to be cast out of the temple.

Monday, January 17

J.R. Walsh is Nebraska-bred and faced many a cold morning at Fonner Park in his formative years, ice frozen glacier-thick in race-barn water buckets. He stoically managed one Maryland farm for a succession of millionaires until his boys got into good colleges. Then he couldn't wait to get back to training — horses and people. He's the head coach at the University of Merryland.

"What do you hear from Flint about JJ?" J.R. asks of his former pupil Jenkin Jones.

"Says he doesn't like other horses passing him."

"Can't teach that to a horse," he notes modestly. "They either got it or they don't."

Tuesday, January 18

Some days when responsibilities obscure the farm's beauty, I close my eyes and remember how I saw it as a young man, in Betty Shea Miller's day:

Racetrack harrowed neat as a plowed field. White fences like necklaces circling jade paddocks, cleaved by a shimmering brook. White barns trimmed hunter green. Privet hedges clipped waist high, save for gate breaks, where topiary climbed in a column to accent the entrance. Riders in red caps crossing wooden bridges on dancing horses.

We're getting there, Betty, but we sprayed the fences black. White fences, except plastic, are just about obsolete and cost four times as much to maintain.

Wednesday, January 19

A rule of thumb is that at any one time, half the horses in a racing stable will be laid up. Wintertime especially. Glance down the shedrow of patients recovering from surgeries or simply resting: knee chip, cracked cannon, ankle chip, throat, suspensory, ankles again, lots of ankle problems.

"How's everything today, J.R.?"

"Surviving. They're all surviving. They'll all make it back — I think."

Thursday, January 20

No foot, no horse.

No roof, no barn.

A horse is sound from the bottom up, a barn from the top down. We've reroofed the neediest of Merryland's fine old barns, in green asphalt shingles life-spanned to jibe with a 20-year mortgage.

Not so in the old days, when slate quarried from nearby Whiteford covered wooden Amish artistry for 100 years. Steam engines fed cables out over 100-foot holes to lift slabs blasted free by soft explosions of black powder. Welsh workmen in shanties sawed blackboards, sidewalks, doorsteps, tombstones, disks for farmers to cap creamery crocks and feed barrels, and they punched two tiny nail holes in quarter-inch-thick shingles. Stacked neat as new money then packed in straw, the slate shingles were loaded onto horse-drawn wagons bound for the depots of the Maryland and Pennsylvania Railroad, or shipped down the Susquehanna on canal boats. Barns roofed with Whiteford slate stood advantaged against the elements. Nails rusted off before the slate wore out.

Danny's old bank barn is a cathedral from the Middle Ages of America, thanks to its first roof.

Friday, January 21

At the December sale last month, he chain-smoked outside the pavilion between hips. Back inside, he sat and waited until the auctioneer's hammer poised in the air above the wood block — that's when Mr. Smoke waved excitedly.

"Get your bids in early," the auctioneer chided. Mr. Smoke slinked down in his seat, pulled his baseball cap down over his eyes.

The mare for which we outbid Mr. Smoke is due to foal today. She hasn't bagged up, and we are sending her to Pennsylvania, but snow is coming and so the van isn't. I feel like Mr. Smoke, waiting until the last possible moment, the hammer about to fall.

Saturday, January 22

At 10 a.m. in Baltimore, they deiced the wings as the first of eight inches of snow began falling. We ate peanuts for 3,000 miles, then had dinner at a restaurant called The Farm, a block off Rodeo Drive. The Beverly Hillbillies got nothing on us.

At 10 p.m. in Los Angeles, the moon was rising.

Sunday, January 23

Before Merryland, there was Malibu Moon. He came to us as a 2-year-old man-child, retired after two races in 1999. Back then, we asked: How many stallions bred as 3-year-olds had amounted to anything? Not many, brother Mike reported, just Raise a Native and Hail to Reason.

Malibu Moon bred mares at three, including a foundered old gal we pampered named Perfectly. Her son Perfect Moon made Moon a star. Maryland is a satellite to Kentucky. Every other state is, too. So we packed Moon's duffle and sent him off to the majors in the Bluegrass.

At Santa Anita the day after Christmas, Perfect Moon held the lead late in the Malibu Stakes, but the symmetry was too good to be true. He missed by a half-length. At Santa Anita today, he broke bad, and you can't spot California sprinters a whisker.

Perfect Moon started it all, a $4,700 Timonium yearling, a Maryland-bred whose second dam was by our old Turn-to stallion Big Brave. Sentiment plays a big part in this game. Old loves die hard. I'll never forget the role Perfect Moon played in my life.

Monday, January 24

Brice bought lunch for six. When the bill came for $250, he rubbed his eyes in disbelief.

"I can't stay in this town long," he said. "Between this lunch and having to wear a tux, we damn sight better win the Eclipse."

Declan obliged. When Samantha thanked Brice in her acceptance speech, I looked over and thought the studs in his tux shirt were going to pop out.

Tuesday, January 25

At the Fairplex fairgrounds today, had to hunt for a 2-year-old we just shipped from Merryland to Mel Stute, who trained Malibu Moon. Found Randy's Moon, another Brice-bred, languishing in the old Pomona race barns down the sandy strip from the new sales pavilion. Perfect Moon started here, I informed Randy's Moon, as he shook straw from his two-toned chestnut coat, trace-clipped to cool out quick in the brisk Maryland weather he had faced back home.

Meanwhile, the Barretts winter mixed sale droned on. Six hundred horses in the mainstream of California breeding averaged $6,000. It felt like a bad winter sale at Timonium, without the parkas. Shiny brass nameplates displaying fancy pedigrees that failed. Apparently, all that glitters is not gold in California, where even a strong state-bred program can't overcome the relatively small number of tracks or the high cost of horse living.

Wednesday, January 26

Gov. Bob Ehrlich is 0-for-2 in getting a slots bill passed in Annapolis, and in his third State of the State Address, he sounded too irritated to make a deal with opponents this year. I'm not wasting all spring watching every newscast on the slots issue. It's a bad marriage in the long run, one of convenience. In West Virginia this week, the legislature is reaching into the slots monies built up for racing's purposes, just a loan to shore up the state's workers' comp fund.

When $7,500 claimers run for $27,000 purses at Charles Town, horsemen should wander the maze of whirring machines in the OK Corral casino and thank every one of those folks with bar-coded cards chained to their necks. It's a thin chain, though, yanked easily by legislators looking for dough, and it'll always be that way. You don't really have it even when you have it.

Thursday, January 27

First foal of the year born today — in Pennsylvania.

Either the mare or the foal has to live in Pennsylvania for 90 days sometime during the year of foaling. I'll bring the mare back and breed her here, send her back up after weaning this fall to complete the day deal. The pragmatic side of me reasons that we should foal her where the baby can excel in inflated, restricted Pennsylvania-bred races. The contrarian in me says we should foal in Merryland's ocean liner of a broodmare barn, that the exodus to Pennsylvania will create a vacuum here, that in coming years we'll have a topflight stable of Maryland-breds competing against crops thinned by attrition to slots states. Heck, maybe we'll have slots?

It's a guessing game these days.

Friday, January 28

A farm covered in snow on a clear night glows. Barns float. Houses drift by.

Painted white, the surface of the track is out of character. It's always brown, except in snow, when it surrenders color quietly. You only know it's there because of the rails, which seem to rise on the turns as though ascending a great white staircase. The curved rails appear to lead somewhere, not just around turns.

There's no noise, unless you walk. Then the snow pads your footfall. It's eerie. It's peaceful. It's another world.

Everyone, at some moment in their lives, should stand still, in the center of a farm, on a snow-covered January night.

Saturday, January 29

A birthday card for Ellen:

Merryland, Week One. Ellen zeroes in on meowing coming from a feed chute in the vast broodmare barn, yanks out two decades of coffee cups and beer cans, and out tumble a half-dozen starving kittens, courtesy of feral parents from the prior regime. They leap into Ellen's heart and appropriate our basement. At the first crack of the kitchen door, out they pour, as though from a chute again, only this time into the waiting arms of sons August and Josh, who play with them before the bus.

I have never liked cats much, but these boys do, a gift from their mom, who is not indifferent to the plight of all creatures great and small. She neutered that litter and others, kept a striped kitten, named her Chuter.

Sunday, January 30

Kids. How you gonna keep 'em down on the farm once they've seen their friends' video games or made the travel team?

A snowy Sunday morning, when hired help can't reach the farm, is one way. Wheelbarrows of manure sped out of the barns this morning. Christmas penknives sawed through baling string. Let's get done before Teddy gets here with the plow.

Last I saw of them, they were knee-boarding on plastic sleds down snow-covered farm lanes, and the horses were all in clean stalls.

Monday, January 31

I kept a regular diary from 1989 to 1991. Then suddenly, along came two young sons who absconded with my evening time — just grabbed it out of the air. Dinner-time to bathtime to bedtime, when they wanted a story. I read *The Armadillo From Amarillo* and listened to one son stretch-spell words for me, then reminded the older boy to turn his reading light off, it was late. Just two more pages, Dad? These boys were puppies. Now they are 11 and 14.

Still, I kept an undisciplined, intermittent diary, more pages missing than Lewis and Clark journals. I noted Ellen's magical moods when she returned from lifting wheelchairs onto pony-drawn carriages as part of Driving for the Disabled, and the early morning Uncle Johnny died. I imagined his spirit hovering over the farm as though saying goodbye, and then — whoosh — he was gone, absorbed into some mythical afterlife where he leads a parade of Remount riders, yardstick straight in the saddle, past Victorian storefronts in Front Royal, Virginia.

Now Merryland Farm presents new discoveries a day at a time. And the boys can read themselves to sleep.

February

Tuesday, February 1

A handsome maple tree stands inside white curbing on a grassy oasis near the training track. Grooms and visiting railbirds gather on the four right-angled benches that frame the tree trunk in a perfect square.

From this perch in 1967, owner David A. Werblin and trainer J. Bowes Bond gazed at a sleek bay yearling filly named Process Shot. A year later, Process Shot became the first of a pair of 2-year-old champions to leave Merryland and carry Sonny Werblin's Elberon Farm silks to honors. The second was a copper colt named Silent Screen, 2-year-old champion male in 1969, one of the favorites in the 1970 Kentucky Derby.

Werblin was Frank Sinatra's agent. He ran the company that owned Madison Square Garden and Arlington Park. He founded the Meadowlands sports complex. Werblin set up a table on the sidelines of the Orange Bowl and signed Alabama quarterback Joe Namath to his football team, the New York Jets.

Werblin would arrive in a limousine to sit on a bench in the shade and eat chicken salad sandwiches with Bond, watching yearlings under tack, dreaming of the Kentucky Derby.

History is a fine distraction in February. We spent the day fixing sheared pins on the snow blower, the racetrack a whiteout. But, hey, we're one day closer to the first Saturday in May.

Wednesday, February 2

The 3-year-old gray colt P. J. Indy stands 17 hands. He reaches down to play. Today, he grabbed his groom, Loye Buckheit, in the back and bit down hard. Tears flowed but no cuss words. She's got heart. I think he does too, but that was a sneaky move, to wait until her back was turned. He'll remember that, and do it again.

Tonight, I wrote the partners: "P. J. doesn't need his testicles. I know some of you think he might win the Derby and be a stallion, but he's not our Derby horse this year. Another gelding is: Declan's Moon. Geldings keep their mind on business, not biting."

One partner wrote back: "Research shows that geldings carry 15 percent less weight on their front ends." Odd. We're talking about his hind end. Oh well, we're doing this for your own good, P. J.

Thursday, February 3

1939 to 1960: Danny Shea.

1961 to 1986: Mrs. Henry Obre.

1986 to 1992: Seymour Cohn.

1993 to 1999: Baltimore County Department of Parks and Recreation.

1999 to 2001: William Rickman.

2001 to present: The cast from *Arrested Development*.

Friday, February 4

Under the maple tree on a hot day in June 1999 sat Delaware Park owner William Rickman. In the turnaround stood the auctioneer hired by Baltimore County to dispose of the not-so-white elephant Merryland Farm had become since accepted six years earlier as a charitable donation.

The county's vision of a Maryland Horse Park similar to that in Kentucky vanished when estimates came back for fencing, electrical upgrades, plumbing, roofing, septic, paving, bridge repair, equipment, pasture renovation. Whose idea was this anyway? What were we thinking? Get rid of it.

Scent of development in the wind, the Long Green Valley Conservancy Association double-teamed with the Maryland Environmental Trust and insisted the county place an easement on the storied old property prior to auction.

Mr. Rickman outbid the local farmers but stopped just shy of the county's announced reserve. The auctioneer called a half-hour time-out and phoned superiors in Towson. I tried to estimate the take in a half-hour of slot machine operation at Delaware Park.

"The farm is not yet sold. The bidding will resume."

Mr. Rickman raised his own bid and took the farm off the county's hands. But he bought a horse farm, not a house farm. He immediately built a helicopter pad with a parking spot for the golf cart used on his quick visits. Two years and a ton of repairs later, Mr. Rickman sensed an opportunity. Mare Reproductive Loss Syndrome was rocking the Bluegrass. He phoned: "Boys, do you know what this means? People up here are not going to send their mares down to Kentucky. You need to buy my farm. I'm too old for this game anyway. What was I thinking?"

Michael and I were thinking Kentucky would survive MRLS and mares would return there. Even so, Merryland seemed an irresistible opportunity. A farm with almost 200 acres of lush pasture, 100 stalls, and a training track. A farm built for racehorses, just eight miles from the breeding shed at Country Life.

Saturday, February 5

Magna just spent millions widening the racetrack at Laurel. Not wide enough for Malibu Moonshine. Turning for home with a wall of horses outside him, Moonshine had no running room. With all of us riding him, he rated the High Occupancy Vehicle lane. Cowboy Steve Hamilton yanked the wheel, found the HOV lane clear, and broke new ground on the long Triple Crown trail.

Trainer King Leatherbury has won 6,000 races but no Kentucky Derby. Ninety-one-year-old hotelier Woodrow Marriott missed the $600 nomination for the classics. For $6,000 on March 26, he gets a second chance. Wonder if there's room at the inn for another Derby contender by Malibu Moon?

Sunday, February 6

Dutch doors on the yearling barn courtyard were closed up tight. Stall nameplates hadn't kept pace with the shuttle of young horses between the two farms.

"She's here somewhere," but not finding the black filly on a stall-by-stall search. "She's the best yearling at either farm."

"I'm sure she is, but the Super Bowl's coming on."

A horse is just a horse, unless you own a piece of it. Then it's the best horse, on any farm, and worth searching for on a cold night. That's the dream. That's every horseman's Super Bowl.

Monday, February 7

Timonium sales. Cell phone rings. I look down and read "Merryland."

"What? I can't hear you in the pavilion. Let me get outside. Not much better. What's all the noise there? A helicopter in the infield? A 2-year-old fell with

Rachael? Oh, no! OK. Keep me posted."

As a symbol of a frugal regime, we built a basketball hoop on Mr. Rickman's helicopter pad the very first day we owned Merryland. I hadn't anticipated we'd ever need a heli-pad again. I was wrong. We've got a rider down, and a MedEvac chopper settling on soft turf instead of reinforced concrete. It's a nightmare in progress. One of the hazards of horses and riders.

Tuesday, February 8

The morning after a horse sale. A desk of untended details. A stall with a just-turned yearling colt, hip number white as a new-car sticker. Went to the desk first, opened J.R.'s e-mails sent by cell phone yesterday. In grainy digital attachments, I saw J.R.'s daughter Rachael being taken by MedEvac to Shock Trauma, brown chopper lifting off brown ground, J.R.'s text reading: "Broken Collarbone, Possible Collapsed Lung, Nothing Worse."

"Bought a Pennsylvania-bred, huh?" Yeah. Wasn't thinking of the financial risks, but the physical risks posed by horses. Red flashing lights on an ambulance, whirring helicopter blades, frozen strobe-light images on e-mail.

Wednesday, February 9

"Got the right horse, Josh?" Dr. Willilam E. Riddle, Jr., asked me with a smile.
I glanced at the colt's markings, wiped the nameplate clean.
"This is him, all right."
Doc unwrapped a sterilized pack of stainless steel objects: "A carpenter has tools. A surgeon uses instruments."
The colt stood at attention, like in line for a crewcut. I considered my decision: This colt's not bred well enough to be a stud. And when he's done racing, he can't even be a riding horse unless we cut him today.
"This is the emasculator," Doc explained. He held out an instrument resembling a pair of vise-grips. The colt pulled at the shank.
"You only have 13 minutes to get the job done once we give the sedative," Doc explained. "I keep this stuff locked up at the clinic. Someone might steal it. In powdered form on the street, they call it angel dust. Strong stuff."

I held the colt still and spoke to him in quiet tones as Doc found the jugular.

"In the old days, tranquilizers weren't as smooth. Horses flopped around when they came out from under anesthetic. They didn't regain motor ability at the same time they regained consciousness. That's when they broke legs. That's what happened to Ruffian. The newer stuff doesn't abolish all reflexes. The horse can blink his eyes, swallow. Now, when they stand up, they've regained most motor skills.

"Now just give him the shank, Josh. Just steady him. But stand back a step."

The colt began to sway like a treetop in a breeze, this way and that, then seemed to faint in slow motion, pitching forward onto his knees, dropping back onto his hocks, rolling onto his side in the courtyard grass — as soft a landing as I had ever seen a horse make. Asleep on his side, eyes wide open. Doc quickly calf-roped his hind legs, hitching the right leg back. He scrubbed the surgery site clean.

"The tunic covers the testicles," Doc said as he worked. He slit the tunic and folded the skin back. He click-locked the emasculator into place. With deft scalpel strokes, Doc plucked out a pair of baseball-sized testicles and set them on a white feedbag.

"You want to throw them over the barn for good luck?" Doc asked. I thought about that ritual: Seems every old horse custom has its root in sound husbandry.

What's gained by throwing them on the roof? "It's a pretty steep roof," I answered.

Doc left the surgery site open to drain after he released the emasculator. The horse awakened from the anesthetic. We watched him pull up onto his sternum and sit sphinx-like for a long moment. Then he rocked himself onto his feet, swaying only momentarily.

"Let him get his sea legs under him for a second," Doc said. "OK, now you can lead him to his stall."

Doc collected his instruments. I stared at the colt's stud career on the white feedbag and thought: Short of putting a horse down, ain't no decision as final as gelding.

Thursday, February 10

Crabcakes are for Rachael. Oh, she got bored? She's back at the barn?

Standing there holding a horse with her right arm, her left arm strapped in place to keep the collarbone immobile.

Friday, February 11

A good stallion is a rising tide lifting all boats: The racing stable, yearlings, mares in foal. It's quite a weight to lift, but such is the strength of a good stallion.

Of a bad stallion's foals, a hardboot once said: "I've got a barnful of them, and I've got a belly full of them."

A bad stallion will sink you.

Saturday, February 12

On the Paris Pike 15 miles from Lexington, the Kentucky Fried Chicken outlet is now a Mexican restaurant, an apt metaphor for the changing face of labor in the heart of the horse business. A friend of mine ordered a chimichanga with a familiarity once displayed for extra crispy.

Then we drove past the famed stone walls of the Bluegrass: some old, some rebuilt with the widening of Paris Pike. Myth attributes the rock fences to slave labor, but most were constructed in the mid-1800s by Irish immigrants escaping the potato famine. Irish stonemasons tutored the slaves. After the Civil War, freed slaves built many of the stone walls. The Bluegrass is a savanna: timber scarce, rock plentiful just inches below the topsoil. Geology met an abundance of labor.

Horse work is as hard as a rock fence. The faces of the caretakers change with time. The work doesn't.

Sunday, February 13

On a rainy Sunday morning at Spendthrift Farm, ghosts hovered nearby. After Man o' War's groom, Will Harbut, perhaps the next most famous stallion handler was Spendthrift's Clem Brooks, who enthralled tourists from Cincinnati or Singapore with tales of the Turf.

Before the buses arrived, Clem would rummage through the pickup beds of farm blacksmiths, pilfering discarded race plates. Hours later, Clem would declare to visitors: "I'm holdin' here a set of shoes worn by Nashua in his last race. Do I hear any bids?"

Clem was the eBay of his day.

Monday, February 14

A filly named Moon Thistle won the 2004 Russian Derby and Oaks — the first filly in four decades to accomplish that feat — so the Russians informed me as they arrived at Merryland in October last year, intent on buying her 2-year-old full brother Pocomoonshine. He shipped down that morning from Pennsylvania to gallop on the training track as part of the Russian inspection. They bought him before he cooled out. As I signed over The Jockey Club registration papers as agent for Poco's owner, I stared hard at the identification line. A light bulb went off: Dark bay or brown colt.

That was then. This was now. Holy cow! I didn't check under the hood. He'd been gelded!

With great embarrassment, I broke the news to his owner. "Deal's off. Russians can't import geldings. Only breeding stock."

He phoned today: "Thank you for screwing up that deal. He just won by five at Philly. With breeders' awards and all, I made just what I had him sold for — and I've still got the horse! Thank you, thank you, thank you."

The lesson? Always check hardware on male horses, and don't worry if every deal doesn't go as planned. Some work out for the best, despite you.

Tuesday, February 15

A memorial service was held today for Snowden Carter. Tagged Nick Carter (after a dime novel detective) by wags in the newsroom in early days at the *Baltimore Sun*, the name stuck. He used his writing skills and love of horses while editor of the *Maryland Horse* magazine. Michael worked for Snowden, who transformed that publication into the *National Geographic* of state trade publications. Just as Marge Finney Dance followed Humphrey Finney to the magazine, Lucy Carter Acton followed in her father's footsteps. She is now the editor. Snowden trained her well.

Wednesday, February 16

Racehorses are as individual as high school kids. Just ask the folks who groom them, lead them to the track, ride them, cool them out. Watch the way Loye moves around them as she tacks them up. Each horse different. Listen to the way Jeff speaks as he gives Troy a leg up. "Easy now" to one horse. A stern "stand now" to another.

Nicknames attach, often not flattering. Sometimes confusing to me when I ask about a horse. Oh, Donkey? Now, that's a runner. Oh, Butterbean? Don't worry, she'll be ready by Colonial.

Racetrack halters all look the same, but the faces peering out from yoked screens are not interchangeable, not fungible. I could stand all day and watch Loye and Jeff lavish attention on their oh-so-individual four-legged high schoolers.

Thursday, February 17

Three years ago the appraiser who determined Merryland's value placed no dollar amount on the training track. He lumped it with a 20-year-old house trailer as "value undeterminable."

But that's how Betty Shea Miller stayed in the black all those years, the training track. In Florida, such tracks are ubiquitous, comparable values easily established. In Maryland, appraisers apparently asked: What's this thing?

Friday, February 18

In this business, someday you'll sell a horse that goes on to great things for other people. You might keep a photo of that horse in a drawer you look through once a year with nostalgia, resignation, pride. The day Ellen photographed sales youngsters loading on the van, that weanling filly stuck out like a fifth-grader in kindergarten.

We set a reserve for the leggy Citidancer filly, a chestnut with a blaze. Kevin McKathan bought her for $38,000, scuffled back to the barn mumbling: "Didn't think I'd have to give that for her."

Three years later, she won a grade I in California for Bob Baffert. Six years after Timonium, she sold at Keeneland in foal to Deputy Minister for $1,525,000.

Last night in the foaling barn, her mom, Prospective Joy, delivered another fifth-grader. A chestnut colt with a blaze, a neck so thick you can't feel his withers. Joy was our Christmas crisis seven weeks ago, alarming us with emergency abdominal surgery for uterine torsion. Came home stapled shut like a box of Christmas apples.  How she survived that day to produce such a foal is a testament to the dedication of New Bolton veterinarians and staff, and the fine care of our broodmare manager Val Kilby and Ironman Richard Harris.

First time we've ever named a foal before it stood up: Malibu Miracle.

Saturday, February 19

The most unpleasant part of managing a racing stable is changing trainers.

If a Maryland trainer repeatedly ships to Charles Town, she might come home to find a note on her stalls. Or no stalls! Understandable. The racetrack pays all the expenses on the facility. Why shouldn't you be expected to fill races at the track where you train?

Because you can't win. Some horses need softer company. Not every Maryland outfit wants to race at 11 o'clock at night. So we ducked those outfits and sent a mare to Charles Town, where she's 2 for 4 in allowance company. Was fourth tonight. Not her distance. Beaten a half-length, a neck, and a nose. She thinks she's Ruffian under those halogen lights. When she cools out in the squalid darkness of an old Shenandoah barn shedrow, she is a singular beauty, a runway model posing on a tenement sidewalk.

Citi State has always been all heart. Now she's full of confidence. We just had to change zip codes. The parties concerned understand it.

I hate making that call.

Sunday, February 20

Fastest of 22 in February 3 work. Fastest of 18 in February 9 work. His first seven-furlong breeze underneath him now. In between buckets of rain in sunny California, Declan's Moon is on target to run twice before the Run for the Roses. In the Santa Catalina March 5, then in the Santa Anita Derby April 9.

Dad came into the office today and handed out winter-book tickets he bought at Pimlico, a $2 futures bet at generous 9-1 odds.

I don't want to tempt the racing gods by even thinking about the Derby. Hall of Fame trainer Charlie Whittingham said racehorses are like strawberries: They're beautiful, but they bruise easily. We all respect that. Still, when the first wave of 131st Kentucky Derby merchandise appeared in the Laurel gift shop, I bought Dad a twin-spired, red-rosed mug for his tea, and rubbed my fingers across the futures ticket, absorbing the great dream it represents.

Monday, February 21

Our band of brothers—our family of farm employees from Mexico—are en route to Guadalajara, then to the embassy in Monterrey, on their annual migration north to Merryland. They work in this country on 10-month H-2A visas. For two months over the holidays, they return to their families in Mexico.

On this exciting news, Merryland's harried home team takes heart as they take shifts hot-walking and night-watching and stall-mucking. Hang in there. The cavalry of Sergio, Armando, Maurilio, and Gerardo are on their way.

Tuesday, February 22

Famous black-and-white racing photo: champion jockey Eddie Arcaro in the 1959 Belmont Stakes, off Black Hills, crumpled facedown in the mud, unconscious, about to drown in the soupy track until the photographer lifts his head to breathe. That picture is in my mind as Rachael describes the fall:

"Not the filly's fault. Just stumbled. I thought I could pick her head up, but she fell. I went face first into the track. It was real sloppy that day. Her withers caught me in the back when she rolled. I knew I broke my collarbone, just like before on the other side. I was conscious and everything. When I arched my shoulders to get my face out of the mud — it's like eating sandy oatmeal — I pulled some muscles in my neck. So I couldn't move my head much. But I could move my feet and all.

"Didn't seem like any time before the ambulance was there. A medic tried to fit me with a neck brace, but I knew my neck wasn't broken, so I hit her with some profanity and she finally stopped. She called the helicopter. If you have to go to the hospital, that's the only way to travel. No curvy roads. Ten minutes from liftoff and you're at the emergency room, where they hit you with morphine. I thought they'd release me that night, but a scanner said my lungs had fluid in them, so they held onto me for a day. That was a drag. I wanted to come home.

"I hate being off work. I hate TV. I like to sew but that gets old, too. I couldn't wait to get back on a horse."

Rachael is lucky, and brave. Hollywood stuntmen plan it all out. Falls just happen. A filly stumbles. Bang. Down. Brave people, these riders. Unequivocally brave.

Wednesday, February 23

Sent a friend cost projections raising a weanling up to its 2-year-old season.
Weanling/yearling: $6,000.
Breaking to first race at two: $15,000.
Mortality insurance: $3,500.
Liability insurance: $500
Van/blacksmith, etc.: $1,500.

A bit more than $25,000 to get in a starting gate, and that doesn't include the purchase price of the weanling.

He wrote back: "No, thanks."

Is it any wonder folks fall out of their box seats to rush to the winner's circle?

Thursday, February 24

It's a magnet, this training track. It draws the grooms out of the barns to watch their athletes practice, proud parents on the sidelines. It draws owners, who dare to dream of afternoons at Monmouth, Saratoga, Laurel, Colonial. Along the back-stretch that parallels Bottom Road for three furlongs, a UPS truck slows, then stops; a commuter figures what's the rush and pulls over; a walker heels his dog and whispers, "Sit."

Some ancestral nerve is touched at the sight of riders on racehorses, in such proximity that you can speak to them, smell the racetrack sand warming in the end-of-winter air, hear the rhythmic da-dum da-dum da-dum da-dum of hooves on packed dirt, feel the air vibrate from the gallons of air exchanged in every fire-breathing gasp from the pounding beasts. This is your grandfather's racehorse. This is the way we lived before cable TV, cell phones, the Internet, air-conditioning, wall-to-wall people.

This racetrack is as old-timey as a wraparound porch.

Friday, February 25

The House approved a slots bill today, by the absolute minimal number of votes necessary for passage: 71 yeas. The 66 nays didn't have to go on record as voting for something they didn't like. A few yeas have broken arms tonight.

Yes, they passed a slots bill, but the bill's dead on arrival back in the Senate.

I don't even like slots. I just want to keep the horse business going in Maryland. To me, it's all about farmland preservation. Give us good purses, and we'll preserve farmland. The heck with Program Open Space. They've taken all the dough out of that anyway, just added it to the general fund.

In 20 years, you'll be able to walk on rooftops from D.C. to Delaware over land that once was Maryland horse farms. It just gives me the fantods.

Saturday, February 26

In the farmhouse's retro kitchen, Ellen decoupaged documents onto the round table inside the semicircular booth nestled in the bow window overlooking the track. She discovered the paperwork in trunks stowed next to Christmas wreaths in a room in the hayloft of the bank barn. You might have found Mickey Rooney on a cot reading the *Morning Telegraph* in such a room.

"Look, here's a 1930s piece in *Maryland Horse* by Humphrey Finney called 'The Editor's Saddle Bag': 'July 17. Inspection of yearlings offered for sale took me to Merryland Farm, then up to Country Life.' Isn't that funny? He left here to get there. Danny Shea bought brooms made by the Blind Industries, $1.55 a broom in 1959. Here's a training invoice from August, 1963: $3.25 a day to train a horse."

She found a bill for the green awning over the patio, where Sonny Werblin sipped juleps. She found receipts for a Bull Stud breeding, for racetrack sand — the famous "Campbell Mix" John Passero favored. Came from right over the hill in White Marsh, now a giant mall. Bills for fire extinguishers, tractor repair, electrical wire, plumbing, heating, fertilizer, lumber.

The trunks had domed lids, brass locks, wooden staves. Treasure trunks. Much gold had to be earned by horses to finance the services, the goods, the labor these records evidenced. Immutable is the financial challenge of owning a horse farm, then and now.

Sunday, February 27

Declan's Moon worked seven furlongs yesterday for the March 5 Santa Catalina Stakes. Weekend well-wishers who own pieces of young prospects have caught

Derby fever. They reason: If Declan can come off a farm 30 minutes from here and become a champion, the Derby favorite, why can't we?

The training track is a special place because the young horses haven't disappointed anyone yet. They haven't been tested and found wanting. Eight of 10 will be just hayburners, won't break even at the track. But that's ahead of them. Right now, it's all good, this moment in their lives. It's all good.

Monday, February 28

The living room of the main house is 10-feet long and 15-feet wide, smaller than a foaling stall. This is not a grand manor house. It's an early stone house with wooden wings added on. A modest farmhouse whose charm derives from high ceilings and generous windows with vistas of the farm.

When we did a walk-through after settlement three years ago, the house's random-width pine floors were covered in wall-to-wall carpet enjoyed by a herd of incontinent cats. The frames of five-foot-high, lead-weighted windows and the plastered walls carried coats of paint from the last six owners, decorative tastes varying from stencils to pencils.

Enter Lisa, the Sister Parrish of this eclectic farm family. These days the house is in the homestretch of three years of fixer-upper efforts. Drop cloths shield furniture from spackling dust. A giant wall clock ticktocks the minutes into history.

Discovered in the trunks were two framed Richard Stone Reeves prints of champions Silent Screen and Process Shot, commissioned by Werblin. He had the originals in his Waldorf Towers apartment. Lisa hung the prints on the staircase walls of the Merryland house.

As the late-winter sun hits the floor of the Long Green Valley outside the west windows, you climb the staircase awash in orange light. Your feet leave prints in the drywall dust. The curious would know that you stood and stared into the backgrounds of the paintings: Silent Screen posing at Saratoga, Process Shot perhaps on a farm in the flat New Jersey farmland near Colts Neck.

Throughout the house, ticktock, ticktock. In the barns, racehorses stir from afternoon naps, foaling mares drip milk. Vapor lights buzz to duty. Night falls on February. Now's the promise of March.

March

Tuesday, March 1

Goals for the 2-year-olds.
Dancer in the Citi: Laurel in August.
Haldy: Philadelphia Park in May.
Merryland Monroe: Delaware Park in June.
New York Moon: Saratoga in August.
Yeager's Jet: Monmouth in June.

The 2-year-olds aren't reading this plan. They're conspiring to buck shins, pop splints, catch colds, get loose, spook at starting gates, pitch fits — generally mock the hubris of a decision to take an immature 1,000-pound animal, stick a rider on its back, and ask it to run in a circle so fast it outraces the herd. We take our time with the babies, but the joke's on us.

Wednesday, March 2

Naming horses for people is quicksand. The people are so memorable; their namesakes likely not. It's not bad luck, it's actuarial certainty at work. Most horses are slow. Most races are claimers. Racing is a school with a lot of flunk outs.

Three years ago we named a filly Betty Shea Miller in honor of Danny's wonderful widow. Archival farm photos show Betty marching past the cupola of the stallion barn with a stream of inner-city children in close pursuit. Imagine being a fourth-grader in a city school and being told the field trip is to a horse farm named Merryland? Who could sleep the night before? Might as well tell 'em it's Disneyland.

The namesake filly wasn't so fortunate. Winless after four starts, she contracted severe arytenoid chondritis that required an emergency tracheotomy. Breathing like Darth Vader through a plastic tube in her windpipe.

"What would you do?" I asked the vet.

"If she were mine?" he answered. "I'd put her down."

Thursday, March 3

Four-year-old maidens in the racing stable are like employees who always have an excuse. Benefit of the doubt wears thin. Still, Rasta Dancer seems worth waiting for on her china doll looks alone. She broke her jaw in a paddock accident at two; New Bolton wired her mandible. Dr. Riddle took out an ankle chip at three, after she'd run second twice.

Sitting on a win tonight at Charles Town, 4-year-old Rasta Dancer had another excuse, out of her control.

"They called off racing," Flint Stites phoned in.

Friday, March 4

Winter and spring overlap and arm wrestle over who owns the weather. This morning on the farm, I heard the dull thump of winter's wrist pinned to the table by no more strength than that of a bird's voice.

Saturday, March 5

In the post parade before the Santa Catalina, jockey Victor Espinoza stood Declan's Moon at attention on the track, a long, dramatic frozen moment, the horse absorbing the scene. It was the same entranced stance Declan might have taken as a yearling back home in Howard County, Maryland, on the gentle hills of Brice Ridgely's Spring Meadow Farm, watching a herd of deer cross a corner of his field, or a fox trot by.

Brother Michael stared at the TV as Declan stared at the Santa Anita crowd.

"That's the way Cigar looked," he said.

How lucky to have had two such champions touch our lives.

Declan ran his record to five for five, still the undefeated Derby favorite. Left in his wake was a colt named Snack, pulled up permanently, euthanized. Whistling past the graveyard, our thoughts jumped ahead: What if Declan runs the table like Cigar did?

Sunday, March 6

The Sunday crew: part-time atoms circling a nucleus of regulars.

Angie — hospital nurse weekdays, equine caregiver weekends. Molly — senior in horsey Sunday school, received OK to host high-school graduation party at Merryland in June; she's that mature. Kate — vet school someday, can't wait to get to work, knows every horse, indispensable. Jonathan — nightwatches Fridays, sleeps Saturdays, shovels Sundays, odd-man out, a teenage boy who likes horses.

Average age Sunday crew? Twenty?

Average age regulars? Fifty-something — old enough to need once-a-week recharging.

Monday, March 7

"I'll do anything. Drive the bus. Clean Declan's stall. Anything! Just take me to the Derby with you."

Think of *The Far Side* comic, cows standing on hind legs, conversing, then back to all fours when they hear a sound, whispering a warning to each other: "Car!"

Jonesy moved out from Baltimore in the seventh grade. He had never seen a horse up close, but he imagines their thoughts. When I explained the role of the teaser to

him, he shook his head like Mr. Ed and said in a gravelly voice: "I made a *bad* career move."

If I had a Derby ticket, first I'd make sure Dad went. The Derby is his Holy Grail, a fountain of youthful dreams. If I had two tickets, Jonesy'd be driving Dad (maybe crazy by then), playing Springsteen's "The Promised Land" full blast at the end of the 600 miles.

Tuesday, March 8

Van drivers carry news like Pony Express riders, edit their own copy, polish headlines between stops. Late-night runs to Charles Town and Penn National make them caffeine freaks. Mountain Dew bottles fall out of cabs as the stories start:

"Jocks were out on the track at Penn last night for the first race before they canceled. Salt clumps hadn't melted. Salt won't work below 20 degrees — everybody knows that. What about all those horses who arrived early to be treated with Lasix? Who pays for that? What about the van expenses? Ever fill up a dually? It's one hundred dollars if you have two tanks. Who pays the owners and trainers for the track's mistakes? No one."

"So many horses broke down at Charles Town one night last week that racing was scratched the next day with the sun shining."

Van drivers' versions are reliable hearsay. I checked the Equibase charts, hit the "find" command on the toolbar, typed in three dashes (—) to find points of call never reached. A half-dozen "did not finish."

How lonely is driving an empty van home? No wonder they talk so much.

Wednesday, March 9

Walking the track. It's work you can measure, like mowing a lawn. It's a five-eighths-mile walk on an oval beach 30 feet wide. You walk the track clockwise, against the grain of the harrows, against the way the horses run.

How deep is the sand near the rail? Too deep. On the turns? Just right. In the center? Not quite enough. Track guru John Passero told you to carry a simple garden trowel, bend down every 100 feet, scrape away the cushion, measure the sand to the base. You forgot the trowel and just started walking, jamming your heel backwards like planting a football for a kickoff with no tee. Kick down to the base; should be four inches below the cushion and packed hard as a clay tennis court.

The cushion of sand moves in winter rains that wash and cut and channel where water finds weakness. You order four truckloads of new sand to stockpile for a dry spell this spring when Teddy can spend a Sunday feeding it out from a dump truck, adding an inch of material over a five-eighths-mile swath.

Beach replenishment, training-farm style.

Thursday, March 10

Robert is blind. When he visits the farm, he bear-hugs the maple tree to feel its size. He leans his cheek against the rough bark as though he can hear sap rise. Riding in the golf cart, he says he can feel gravel under the tires as though he's walking barefoot.

Tell me what you see, he will ask me. Just stop and feel it. Tell me what it looks like. Tell me from the moment you see the farm from the road.

Well, you can arrive from either end of Bottom Road. Driving out from the city, two farms flank you on the approach. One farm raises cabbages in perfect rows, and you see lights in the fields at night during spring planting as Salvadoran workers drop seeds in. The other farm is built up with greenhouses, poinsettias for the city, a flower farm.

From the other end of Bottom Road, you drop out of a great hardwood forest that folds back to reveal the valley floor, white rails of the racetrack running off into the distance, barns like a village. It's magical.

Robert's eyes are the color of the creek after a storm.

Friday, March 11

8:45 a.m. EST:

"Hey, just wanted to tell you before you hear it someplace else. We're off the Derby trail. He had some heat in his knee. Found a small undisplaced chip. I'm standing here looking at him."

It's 5:45 in California. I think about the disappointing day ahead of trainer Ron Ellis, his own Derby dreams dashed. His wife, Amy, a Louisville girl from a racing family.

By 11 a.m. our time, it's all over the Internet, quotes and all: Declan's out.

Saturday, March 12

Eight fillies ran in the $50,000 Conniver Stakes today at Laurel.

Five finished.

Three fell. Of those, two walked off. Citi State, hurdling horses, broke her neck on landing. Never knew what hit her.

One moment we're all in the merry-go-round of the paddock, jockeys in fabulous silks leg-upped onto fashionable fillies as trainers whisper last words of advice. The next moment, we're live at the crash scene, jocks on stretchers, jocks propped against inside rails, jocks standing bloody-faced, dazed, shaking. Ambulances driving on the wide dirt track — three for riders, one for a helpless horse. Mayhem.

I used to watch this filly out of my office window on brisk days when the weanlings would race up the steep hill to silhouette against the sky. We picked her for the broodmare band when she was a weanling. In between, she had to be a racehorse. She'd earned enough, won two of her last three, and, if third in a Maryland-bred stakes, would have black type. Hence, today.

The stakes was the last race. No urgency to clear the track. There was time to absorb priorities. Alive were the jockeys, fathers of kids, husbands of wives. They'd walk back into their living rooms without wheelchairs. They'd speak. Could anything else possibly matter?

I knew where they were taking her and found her in the morgue that fences dead racehorses out of sight until the renderer's truck arrives on Monday. I lifted the gate latch, pulled back the blue tarp off her pretty dish face, undid her tongue tie, stuck the wet flannel in my pocket, tried to close her eyes. *I am, we are, responsible.* I can barely see these keys right now.

Sunday, March 13

E-mails from partners and friends, who watched tiny images on video streaming from computer betting sites: Is she all right? The chart just said three horses fell. No details. What happened to Citi State?

Christy answered by Internet, uploaded a photo of the filly in full gallop from a better day, typed a banner that read "Tribute."

Orange silks still on dashboard of car. After the track cleared, with impressions of horses' shoulders raked out of the brown loam, I saw silks blowing against the inside rail. Those orange silks that went skyward like a spike in a graph, like a flare.

A trainer, Ferris Allen, called: That fellow that drives the horse ambulance, Joe Miller, best man in the world. He's from up near you. You *know* his heart breaks every time. But he does it because somebody has to, and he should be thanked for that.

I hadn't thought of him. You're right.

I watched foals at play then sat through a sermon.

Sorry about Declan, the acolyte said.

Oh, well, that's racing. He'll be OK. Thanks.

Monday, March 14

What's it like for her groom, Flint's son Owen, to walk past her empty stall this morning?

You shouldn't fall for horses. You can't help falling for horses.

Tuesday, March 15

The 2-year-olds come down from the training barn strung out in a line behind J.R. on his 12-year-old lead pony Timmy — Rockingham warrior of old, babysitter of late, tranquil in a hackamore, no bit necessary. J.R. sits atop him in a trade show Western saddle with silver medallions that glint in the sun. It quit squeaking about the third month of use. So did J.R.

The babies bottleneck at a wooden bridge above the swift stream that adds shimmering elegance to the farm. Still wary of the hollow thump their hooves make on the oak planking, the 2-year-olds tense up and stare down through thin gaps at water running below. Bravely they continue, trusting riders' hands, legs.

Past the house and onto the track they file, turning counterclockwise, the direction races are run. Ears pricked, they ease off into a trot, moving like gaited horses. Riders lean forward and sink weight into heels. The young horses feel the silent signal, and on cue their heads fall forward into a jog, their binocular vision focused on the vast track ahead.

Through *my* binoculars, they are cantering carousel ponies, heads forward and down, back and up, riders gyroscoped on shifting centers of gravity. Foreshortened against a background of produce farms and greenhouses, the young horses appear the way Toulouse-Lautrec might have painted them. They are sensual, hypnotically attractive, art. They come at you three abreast, filling up the binocular lenses until they are right on top of you, then they blow past in a strobe image you can't freeze-frame or separate, young horses hammering the deep sand, pumping, working, roaring past. You stare at their haunches as they bank into the turn for another circuit.

Wednesday, March 16

To draw a horse, you draw a circle first, add a neck, then stick legs, stick head, stick riders.

Animated, it's symmetry in motion.

Thursday, March 17

In Baltimore, where city school children jumped on buses for field trips to Merryland 40 years ago, son Josh on jayvee lacrosse played an away game — a *world-away* game.

Two blocks from the school, I bought a Coke and spoke through three-inch-thick bulletproof glass to ask for directions. Litter blew in the streets like dry snow that would never melt.

Living on a horse farm, every day is a field trip, and don't you forget it, Mister.

Friday, March 18

White legs delicate as porcelain, Rasta Dancer won by 6½ lengths Wednesday night at Charles Town. At four, a maiden no more. Worth the wait, picking up where Citi State left off. Symmetry at work.

Saturday, March 19

"Ready for some bad news?"

"J.R., they're horses, not people. We care for a critical mass. Who's critical today?"

"Merryland Missy."

"*Oooh* . . ."

"She re-bowed. You know how bows are? The first bow heals, but the fibers go sidewise, aren't elastic. Puts pressure on the rest of the tendon. A high bow heals, then they low bow. Ever really look at a photo of a horse in stride with all that weight on the tendon of one front leg? It's *gotta* be elastic!"

Six months ago, Merryland Missy won a Maryland Million stakes. Now she's off to the breeding shed.

Regarding sentimental names, she's the exception that proves the rule. Could a foal named Merryland Moon be as exceptional?

Sunday, March 20

Fear of fire on a horse farm is the greatest unspoken nightmare. Clicking down through digital images from Ellen's camera this month, I stared at a photo of two dozen fire extinguishers lined up for annual tagging by the Fireline inspector, red canisters with black hoses at attention, charged with saving lives.

It scares me to even write about fire.

Monday, March 21

Jenkin Jones is back at the farm with sore shins. Shock therapy was prescribed to accelerate healing of the periosteum that covers the cannon bone. Two weeks ago Dr. Riddle steadied the ray gun and fired off shots that sounded like a transformer shorting out in the next neighborhood.

Injudicious use may have given this resource a bad name. JJ's shins look a lot better to my eye and feel a lot better to the touch.

Tuesday, March 22

To stay in training shape, J.R. rehabs a claimer at a time. He winks with self-deprecation.

"Got to go. Got to get the 'Big Hoss' off the walker."

He's playing with a salvage horse named Maudy, plucked for a grand from racing-age rejects at the February mixed sale.

"If she doesn't make it back and I gotta breed her, I'll name the foal 'Good Gaudy Miss Maudy!'"

He almost *dances* back to the walker.

Wednesday, March 23

The sound of four shoes on pavement: clip-clop clip-clop clip-clop clip-clop. It's like the bells on the Sno-Ball truck. It's your best friend calling you out to play. A blind man could hear it and see.

WINTER 2005

Thursday, March 24

Route 340 to Charles Town drops down out of the Blue Ridge Mountains and descends to rock beds gorged by the confluence of the Shenandoah and Potomac rivers. It's mountainous and beautiful and majestic at dusk. A brown National Park sign tempts diversion: Antietam Battlefield. Over two bridges in three minutes, you leave Maryland, touch down in Virginia, then climb out in West Virginia, above the heights overlooking Harpers Ferry.

A Civil War buff in a six-seat minivan informs you: It could have turned out so different. In the fall of 1862, Lee invaded western Maryland and wrote out plans to capture the Union garrison at Harpers Ferry, putting the railroads in Confederate hands, part of a grand maneuver into Pennsylvania to cut the Susquehanna bridges at Harrisburg. An officer wrapped three cigars in a copy of headquarters plans, but lost them on a Frederick street. A Union soldier discovered the cigars *and* the plans. General McClellan moved with uncharacteristic boldness and speed, sending 100,000 troops to engage Lee at Antietam Creek, near the town of Sharpsburg. Lee was caught with his forces divided. Why did McClellan attack without hesitation? Lee wondered.

We won on a disqualification tonight. In this rugged country, history is on the side of the lucky.

Friday, March 25

Deep Throat is on the phone from Annapolis: "The bill's dead. Miller and Busch don't even speak to each other. Ehrlich's a referee. Slots? Folks don't want it in Frederick. Rickman owns the airport there; that's where it would go. Three years ago the first bill put slots solely at the racetracks. What a great idea. But that came 'off track' because it seemed like unjust enrichment for De Francis. '06 is an election year, too hot. '07? Depends who's still here. It's all politics."

No kidding.

Saturday, March 26

Anyone at Laurel today who didn't box the two Malibu Moons in the Private Terms Stakes paid the lack-of-faith penalty: missing the $273.20 farm exacta.

What a crazy game is horse racing. Two weeks ago the sky fell on our Derby dreams when Declan stepped aside. Now Dad is doling out dollars from his exacta so we can drive to Virginia for Easter with spare change, the March wind at our back. Makes me smile at this sport's twisted sense of irony. Is anybody in charge here?

Sunday, March 27

Cell phone voicemail Easter morning, sent last night at 10.

"Hi, this is Dr. Donaldson. Sorry to phone so late. The foal rallied yesterday, then crashed today. We think he had a perforated ulcer. I'm sorry. Please contact me on Sunday. Need to get the mare back to you."

I have a mild case of compassion fatigue for the things that happen to horses. It's Easter. They're supposed to roll away the stone, not fall under it.

Monday, March 28

Almost too good to be anecdotal. Merryland in the '60s was famous for its parties. More than a few ex-jumping riders have asked me: "Did you know we used to have Easter egg hunts? Not for eggs, but for miniatures."

Grown horse folk rooting through privet hedges for tiny bottles of liquor. I wouldn't have believed it if not for our first days of ownership, when we walloped the 15-foot privet jungle down to knee height, uncovering erstwhile Easter eggs of yore like archeological findings, jewels of the Tipple Crown.

Tuesday, March 29

Two late nominations to the Triple Crown at $6,000 each: the exacta boys Malibu Moonshine and his biologic half brother Hello Jerry (pronounced with malice aforethought, à la Newman from the *Seinfeld* show), keeping options open for the Preakness.

Wednesday, March 30

Spring peepers chorus from the pond. Baby frogs climb up onto the dike and make the causeway a cause for grief in miniature, unless you're a frog. Then it's a big deal.

Ellen can't stand it. I tell her we're making food for nocturnals. She doesn't buy in. Sends son August out ahead of her car with his lacrosse stick to scoot lucky amphibians back to water. Next farm sign, for horses and frogs alike: No Croaking.

Thursday, March 31

Go figure.

Citi State never takes an unsound step and she's dead on the track.

It rains *buckets* in sunny Southern California, tracks sealed then opened, sealed then opened. How hard is that on Derby hopefuls?

We hit a $273.20 exacta, and it's not as big as news of new Moons rising.

They finally pass a slots bill, then kill it.

An officer drops his cigars and the war lasts three more years.

I get it now. Nobody's in charge here. You just keep soldiering on, smiling at demons, praying you don't flunk out. Oh, well, that's racing.

SPRING
2005

April

Friday, April 1

Can't call the 2-year-olds "babies" any longer. Ninety days of 1½-mile jogs have sculpted muscle, on display now that winter coats are thrown off. Like hearing the first deep note in an adolescent voice; the end of one stage, the beginning of another.

Racetracks open for the season. Indian names — Pimlico, Delaware. Tribes of horsemen migrate north, lured by condition books.

Spring breezes through opened doors. Behind full-length screens in the foaling barn, heat lamps throw an amber glow. Postcard of a night scene; silhouettes of restless mares in yellow stalls, awaiting deliverance.

Redbud trees compete with white dogwoods at woods' edge.

April in Maryland. A series of unbroken gestures, like Fitzgerald said about personality. Same as it ever was.

Saturday, April 2

The starting gate is an incongruous presence on the vast sand. Think of the scene in *Blazing Saddles*, when Slim Pickens and his motley mob ride up on a tollbooth in the desert. Incredulous, Slim acquiesces to authority: "Somebody's gonna have to ride back and get a hat load o' dimes."

With Rachael and Troy on board, a pair of 2-year-olds approach the gate: What's this thing doing here?

They wiggle sideways, buy time, searching for dimes, excuses.

J.R. rides pony Timmy through the gate and back again. No bells sound. No doors clang. Yes, it's exposed architecture, pipes and bars — a frightening request to make of a young horse. But trust us. Today. After you've raced a few times, you will not trust us. Trainers say almost all horses will backslide and require re-schooling. The starting gate will come to mean a controlled explosion, sometimes painful. But not today.

Sunday, April 3

The Maryland Horse Breeders' awards dinner will be held April 21 at the Walters Art Gallery in Baltimore, where a fabulous exhibit of the 18th-century painter George Stubbs is on tour. Stubbs' portrait of the undefeated champion Eclipse (18 for 18) served as the model for Adalin Wichman's bronze statue, this sport's Oscar.

Cigar and Declan's Moon are Maryland-bred Horses-of-the-Year (Declan to be crowned at this month's dinner). Cigar won a mantel-full of Eclipse Awards for winning 16 in a row. Declan's Moon is five for five, in flawless emulation of Eclipse while earning the namesake award.

The horse business reveres ancestry.

Monday, April 4

What's it like in the saddle on a horse in such excitable wind?

In an instant on the backs of 2-year-olds, Rachael and Troy are flung from the inside rail to the middle of the track. How quickly a horse can duck out from underneath you! In this wind, anything is everything to a horse. The snap of a saddle towel on a clothesline, a plastic lawn chair blown over on its side. Terror everywhere.

Horses see the slightest movement, except perhaps high in the air. They don't look up well. They look down at everything. Prayerfully, not their riders.

Tuesday, April 5

What's this orange thing with all the spikes?

It's a Larcom & Mitchell track conditioner.

Where'd you get it?

At a yard sale. The "yard" was a former training track, now a golf course. We bid $400. It's 10 grand new. It has carbide-tipped teeth that resist wear — track sand is so abrasive.

What's the plow for?

It's a grader blade. Angles at an offset to retrieve sand under the rail.

What's the big flat thing?

A float. Just a heavy sheet of steel that drags behind the tractor. Seals the track before a rain, packs the cushion, smoothes out hoofprints. (John) Passero's favorite track tool.

How about that yellow box thing?

Snow blower. Throws it to the infield, so snow melts *off* the track — not on it. The thing about equipment, some of it just sits there. It'll come in handy some winter; it just didn't this winter.

What's the thing with scrolly tines?

A harrow. Riders say the pattern gives them motion sickness. Some things you can't predict. We've cobbled together an equipment shed of auction stuff that does who-knows-what.

We had to learn what.

Wednesday, April 6

Trainers trot horses on a hard surface, cocking their ears for the sound of unsoundness.

I asked Loye to trot 5-year-old lay-up Astana a few strides on the pavement. Astana was atonal — stifled by stifles. Last spring Dr. Riddle injected her chronically loose cartilage with an internal blister and, trained light by Flint Stites, Astana sprinted through her conditions in $4\frac{1}{2}$-furlong blasts at Charles Town. Out of conditions, worn and torn, she'd face fireballs at Chucky Town this year. No way to wind up.

It's April, Astana. What say we dance on over to the breeding shed? You did all we asked of you.

Thursday, April 7

When I stand outside Jenkin Jones' stall, riffs play in my head, roiling roller-coaster lyrics, something about trying to hit the big one, something about wildest dreams coming true. Everybody succumbs to the fantasy of "The Big Horse." It happens the way comets appear—very, very rarely.

Friday, April 8

George Stubbs' drawings in *Anatomy of the Horse* were published in 1766. To depict the muscling of horses, he hung carcasses in his cottage in Lincolnshire, England, sketching horses in layers familiar only to skinners.

Horse folk famously overlook odors of the sport. Kings and queens feel at home in stables; smell of manure sort of a woodsy thing, like mulch. We all get immersed in our work. Don't notice it until we sit with showered folk.

Still, I think Mrs. Stubbs — Mary Spencer — should have an award named in her honor.

Saturday, April 9

Near the Laurel receiving barn today, I stood at the rail on the turn where Citi State fell in March. All the money in the world (well, $30 million) spent on that beautiful brown track, and our filly is the first fatality. A distinction she could have lived without.

Sunday, April 10

When Mom and Pop married in 1950, the steam engines of the Maryland and Pennsylvania Railroad — the "Ma and Pa" — carried farm products, mail, freight, and passengers to 54 rural communities — Baltimore linked to York by a crescent necklace of farming villages. Unusually sharp turns, actual and fiscal, characterized the picturesque rail line.

I picture Mom as a young woman composing a letter at her typewriter, pausing to listen to the slow passage of that train, while a spring wind spread white apple blossoms like confetti in seasonal celebration over a countryside of nothing but farms — *nothing but farms.*

On a Sunday, on my mother's birthday, I type for her, for our own private Ma and Pa, for holding the line together through the turns, through the years.

Monday, April 11

To level the new racetrack sand at a four-inch uniform depth, Bob Warfield welded two steel runners onto his bucket loader. Sand higher than four inches falls into the mouth of the bucket. Sliding over the packed-clay base, he unearthed a relic: the 30-inch brass links from a chain shank, the leather long since dissolved away. Precious metal from God-knows-what era in this farm's long history.

Like finding an arrowhead, or touching the cover of a rare book. Hiding a story. A tough colt led to the track? Or ponied? Did he bolt, step on his shank, tear the leather, pull off his bridle? A rider down? An injured horse? A great escape? Or just a shank falling out of a truck cab?

Passero's seen the sand of many racetracks worked up and turned over. He told alarming stories of finding slivers of broken harrows, bolts sheared from tractors, foot-long wrenches bounced from tool boxes, all capable of devastating a horse's sole — a mere five inches across, thin horn supporting half a ton of galloping mass, thousands of pounds of down-thrust pressure. *Coffin bone killers*, he matter-of-factly described them.

But this chain seemed so animate. Like a horse, it resisted capture, and flowed like a gold necklace out of my hand.

Tuesday, April 12

Office manager Cheryl Clark commuted to Ellicott City, battling beltways to and fro. Now she leaves a neighborhood called Camelot and arrives at a farm called Country Life to coordinate business at a farm called Merryland. Good karma in those names. Cheryl carries it through her day; clients feel it.

Broodmare Whisperer Val Kilby was a pharmacist. Fresh out of the Racetrack Industry Program at the University of Arizona, she addressed accountability: "Well, I *did* fill nitroglycerine prescriptions for heart patients."

You're hired.

She's the girl you should have partnered with in high-school chemistry labs. Can you possibly guess the beneficial effect of precise medication on aging broodmares, the factories of reproduction? Grade I-producer Cruella, the dam of 2-year-old Merryland Monroe, this spring had the best foal of her life — at 23 years of age. It doesn't just happen. Val knows what the old gal needs: Regu-Mate, Thyro-L (thyroid supplement), trimethoprim-sulfa (antibiotic), vitamins C and E, Cosequin for arthritis, and a feed supplement named Hard Keep, for late pregnancy.

We've dismissed men (mostly stallion men, naturally) whose egos prevented them from taking orders from women. If Cheryl or Val say jump, you better jump.

Wednesday, April 13

Inside white rails gracefully circling the track are three paddocks. Good fields for yearlings of opposite sex. Can't touch each other, since the center infield paddock is double-fenced.

Jackie Wilson lives in an end paddock, adolescent male hormones eliciting comment.

"Might want to geld him early," everyone tells me.

"He's not even a full year old!" I counter, trying to buy some time, in defense of Jackie's horsehood.

"What if he chips an ankle running the fence line?"

Jackie Wilson is, for the moment, named in honor of the soul singer of the '50s and '60s whose anthem "Higher and Higher" energizes even the most reluctant dancer. However, our official name request was turned down. The matter is on appeal, pursuant to Rule 6F (7) of *The Principal Rules and Requirements of the American Stud Book*, which states that names of famous people no longer living must be approved by the board of stewards of The Jockey Club. The singer Jackie Wilson deserves a good horse named for him. He was buried in an unmarked grave until resurrected to dignity when voted into the Rock and Roll Hall of Fame in 1987.

The colt is by Citidancer. He's got two white feet — flashy dancing shoes. He just looks like a Jackie Wilson. Come June 11, the morning of the Belmont Stakes, the board of stewards will pause to consider the whimsical matter of this name request.

When the 2-year-olds gallop in sets, yearling Jackie follows in imitation, rounding the turns of his paddock until stopped by the double fence. Then he preens for the girls. The scalpel is looming.

Keep it up, Jackie, and you'll be singing higher and higher, too.

Thursday, April 14

No uplifting soul music, just the blues today. A phone call from New York. An Irish voice. He said: "Two months old, big enough to take care of herself. No idea how the foal died. She was a lovely Malibu Moon filly. Just found her dead in the stall."

After a long pause, I said: "Well, it's a dead horse. I'll need an autopsy report for insurance purposes. Can you get back to me with cause of death? Thanks."

What a business. A couple years of planning, selection, expenses — gone, no idea how. Stud fee wasted. No yearling to break. No Moon to race.

What a business some days.

Friday, April 15

The 3-year-old filly Straightforward just won a New York maiden special weight for Rich Horwitz. He's sentimental, breeding and racing an unbroken parade of foals from his late father's stakes winner Plain all Over. Heat in a knee was discovered by trainer Allen Iwinski, and Straightforward is headed home for Merryland.

"It's not a slab fracture," Dr. Don Baker said from Aqueduct, "but it would have been had they not stopped on her. Stall rest for 30 days, maybe a light blister, sand pen for another 30 days, then X-ray it again. When it's clearly healed on radiographs, give her another 30 days."

Earning power of a good runner makes the downtime sufferable, but not every owner or trainer would have stopped on her.

Saturday, April 16

Track kitchen, training-farm style. Ten spinning stools face a Formica countertop right angled to surround a waitress. A nod to the timelessness of the scene hangs near the window: a photograph of Betty ladling soup in the '60s. Farm workers on stools across the counter. One leans his head back, eyes closed. Soup of the gods, he must be thinking. Another face is rapt with childlike gratitude. A third man wears a tie, a cardigan, and a bonhomie smile.

In the photo, a silver cake cover conceals fresh dessert.

This photograph is a time warp. Sit down. Close your eyes. They've just left, seats still warm from the last shift, from folks who dedicated the prime of their lives to this farm in the '60s.

Sunday, April 17

The old walk-behind Graveley mower is a self-propelled widow-maker. At full throttle, it makes enough noise to fool the farm into thinking you're working instead of escaping. Below the vast dirt dike of the racetrack turn, the Graveley mowed multiflora rose, whacked wheat grass, blasted buttercups, sliced seedlings, and cut all communication to the outside world.

Monday, April 18

Irish voice from New York: "Autopsy report said the foal broke C-2 and C-3. Mare may have kicked her. Maybe she just ran into the wall. Won't ever know."

Two broken necks exactly four weeks apart. The flavor of the month. Go figure.

Tuesday, April 19

The facilitator rolled the Magic Marker between his hands, anxious to reduce the issue of unwanted horses to bullet points on butcher paper.

What is an unwanted horse? It's not the same as unusable. At the February sale at Timonium, perfectly functional broodmares, young or old, were unwanted. The summary-sheet euphemism *Reserve Not Attained* threw a curtain over a herd of "no bids." Upset at the upset price of $1,000, slaughter boys sat on their hands; no money in meat at that price. Under the shedrow later? Deals made.

Sentiment doesn't attach to every horse: The February catalogue listed a 26-year-old mare.

This is no answer to a complicated issue, and certainly health officials (water flowing underground) object to burying dead livestock. But when Cruella's day comes, we're leading her to a clay overlook under towering beech trees in the woods, where indentations in the ground are monuments. Same as it ever was.

Wednesday, April 20

Maypole Dance once ran five furlongs in :55⅗. It took less than that for newcomer Larry O'Laughlin to decide a 6-year-old stakes winner of $233,000 in 33 races was worth $15,500 at Timonium.

Inattentive agents attacked him: "I'll give you twenty for her!"

Beginner's luck vaporized when he took us as partners. Maypole resorbed to Malibu in 2004. An aborted return-to-racing campaign followed. Back to Moon in 2005.

"It's smaller than it should be," Dr. Ruel Cowles remarked with trepidation over the phone today, assessing the viability of a 15-day vesicle, "but Maypole's pregnant — again."

Hard-run mares are a genuine risk in the breeding game.

Thursday, April 21

This day blew by:

Ellen escorted a busload of second-graders on a tour of Merryland, breaking them out of the gate, cooling them out on the walking machine. Babysitting, training-farm style.

Declan's Moon's trainer Ron Ellis flew in for the awards dinner.

"Without Maryland, there'd be no Declan's Moon for me to train. He's doing great, and we may bring him back for this fall's Maryland Million Classic. Might be his first race back."

Cheryl stood transfixed in front of a Stubbs oil.

"Great stuff, sure. But I don't get it. What's with the lion clawing on the white horse's back?" She gave me that cross-eyed, broken-jaw look.

Something's always attacking horses, one form or another. It's art. Don't ask.

Friday, April 22

"Damn fence is sharp," Val says. "She doesn't get hurt on the old fence, but a week in the new field? Sliced the hide off her cannon bone. Tough place to stitch but we did. Might leave a scar."

Throw some scarlet oil on it. Keeps hair from growing back white.

"They took it off the market."

Vet upcountry mixes it in five-gallon buckets, then bottles it. Sorry about the filly's leg.

Fenced a small front field in new boards. Not as safe as diamond-mesh wire. Horses slice themselves on boards; bounce off woven wire. The choice is based on the impression a handsome wood fence makes. After the boards season in the weather, we'll spray them with asphalt-based black paint. For the moment, after a rain, with spring sunlight slanting on them, the boards appear golden, as though dipped in honey, a moment to savor before the cribbers, before the years, claim the beautiful wood fencing.

Saturday, April 23

At Pimlico today we finished last in a stakes named for the farm. Son Josh, with teenage self-consciousness, blasted the decision to run: "That was embarrassing!"

I wanted to answer, "Hey, that's racing. Some days you get the bear, some days the bear gets you. Some days the bug, some days the windshield. Some days the hydrant, some days the dog." But I said nothing, vagaries of racing so hard to explain, harder to accept.

Ellen collected custom-stenciled saddle towels, salvaging excitement where she found it.

All's well that ends well. Malibu Moonshine collared Hello Jerry in the Federico Tesio Stakes, another farm/Moon exacta. Next start Preakness?

Tryin' to hit the big one, all of us, still dreaming of horses ...

Sunday, April 24

Help's an issue everywhere. Father Ray drafted sons Josh and August as acolytes — cross carriers, candle snuffers. Entry-level roles; hotwalkers to God.

These boys love lacrosse, a sport Indians invented. French Jesuits named the stick resembling the cross.

Dad eased into the back of church today and whispered to white-robed Josh as he exited stage left: "Hey, Snuffy, is that a long-stick crucifix?"

Monday, April 25

"Come out with your hands first!" the sheriff called up to the boys' tree house. The homeless man stuck out his head, covered in wool caps. *"Hands first,* not head first," the sheriff repeated, fear of the unknown in his voice.

I tried to accept the homeless man as a romantic, a Dust Bowl victim, Woody Guthrie lyrics playing in my head. But I couldn't quite sing "This Land Is Your Land," not with the kids lined up behind me in fascination. When frisked, out fell discharge slips from the Harford County Detention Center.

"Let's drop him off in Baltimore County," the officers decided.

"Great, he'll be at Merryland in the morning," Mom said.

In the old days, Dad told me, they'd jump off the Ma and Pa, and your grandmother would pay them to rake the yard, then feed 'em dinner.

Dad, he's cracked. He's been in the tree house for six days. He speaks German and says he's from Texas. He *can't* stay.

Forged in farm memory, this is the day the homeless man came to play.

Tuesday, April 26

Jenkin Jones rapped his cannon bone on the bottom of his stall screen. His leg filled to twice its size. I couldn't sleep. "Another Horsedreamer's Blues."

J.R. rushed to apply a Cool-Cast, an astringent concoction of calamine and menthol, zinc oxide, and gelatin. An antiphlogistic poultice. What a difference that soft cast made. Still, we vanned our dream horse to Dr. Riddle's clinic yesterday, where Dr. Amy Woodford passed an ultrasound over the tendons, took digital X-rays of the cannon. She pronounced: "He's good to go. No problems. Shins look great too."

I drove him straight to Flint's barn at Penn, and watched JJ buck and roll in fresh shavings. He's guileless. I'm manic.

Wednesday, April 27

Urgent phone call from a vet school one year ago.

"This filly is very arthritic," the young vet explained. "I don't think she'll ever race. We could do surgery on her ankles and make her more comfortable if you'd like."

Something in his voice. How many racehorses had he seen in his brief career? Wear and tear is the price horses pay for pounding hard sand atop a bed of crushed stone or packed clay. Of course they have arthritis. So does everyone who works with them.

No, just send her home.

Dr. Riddle sees dinged-up Thoroughbreds every day.

"Looks better than most horses at the track," he said after X-rays, after passing a heat-sensing wand over her legs. "Inject her ankles with hyaluronic acid, give three intramuscular shots of Adequan over six weeks, then put her back in training."

Mrs. Vanderbilt won her conditions last year after Dr. Riddle's therapy. She is out of the last mare owned by Alfred G. Vanderbilt, who was blind late in life. That didn't stop him from coming to the races. Arthritis — accepted, treated, lived with — hasn't stopped Mrs. Vanderbilt from coming to the races, either.

Thursday, April 28

Away they go, 2-year-olds we got to know this winter.

To the racetrack this week went Patty's Punch Line, here for 90 days with instructions to "let us know if she has any talent." She does. To Peggy Pruitt at Pimlico.

Heypenny, $4,000 weanling bought as paddock mate for a filly who then died. Promoted to first string, like a pace-setting rabbit that beats the stablemate: unintentional promotion. To Kathy Dibben at Bowie, aiming for $34,000 Virginia-bred maiden races at Colonial in July.

Smoke N Numbers — RNA'd at Timonium, slight imperfections magnified in a 500-horse yearling sale. She'll smoke in the barn of Donna Lockard at Pimlico.

Christy worked up a diploma of sorts on the computer, mailed it to proud parents: Graduate of the University of Merryland.

Friday, April 29

A guest book entry on the farm Web site, hard to get out of mind:

"I fell in 1998 and had a spinal cord injury, my neck partially broken. I have permanent nerve damage in my legs and hands, but I can get around. My therapy is to walk every day which I do around your farm with my little Maltese dog Tucket and my daughter Elizabeth; she is almost 2. I miss riding very much but feel I was gifted to be able to walk again and have a child. I started riding when I was 2. Anyway, I am so happy for you all that you purchased this property and I wish you the best with your breeding and racing. We often pick up bottles and trash as we walk and are amazed how much people throw along your road; it is sad that people would do this. Thank you for making so many wonderful memories for my daughter and me (my dog too). Kindest regards, Diane."

Saturday, April 30

A vantage spot at the 17th fence of the Maryland Hunt Cup, in the rain, under the eave of a hardwood forest. Detached. Like watching a race at Saratoga from the backside, against the rail, where you can hear whips slash, riders cuss, dirt land. The essence, not the outcome.

Ellen shot a photo of a rider standing vertical in the irons, his horse captured in the moment before liftoff. Strapped to a rocket. You could make a bronze of the photo and nobody would believe it was an actual pose. By the second lap, loose horses were crashing through panels of oak. Eight minutes of sheer peril for horse and rider alike. Their courage obscured by the gentility of tailgate candelabras. Gentry in tweed.

Fans dashed across a mulch-covered road to witness the drama at the 13th, then ran in their Wellingtons and greasecoats back to the snow-fenced homestretch to cheer the finish. Rabid behavior — like newsreel clips of the Pimlico infield during the match race between Seabiscuit and War Admiral, 20 miles and 67 years from here.

They've been running the Hunt Cup for a hundred years. You have to be crazy as a stunt pilot to ride in it. It's the most beautiful horse race in the world.

Same as it ever was, the personality of life with horses in Maryland, in April — a series of unbroken gestures.

May

Sunday, May 1

One moment deep in the universal family tree, tribal members stood in awe as a horse first permitted a clansman onto its back. This is not *Stud Book* lineage, a breezy 300 years to three foundation sires. No, this is repressed memory, squared. This is the moment a jut-jawed jockey on the Eurasian steppes plopped atop a tamed horse — about 5,000 years ago. Maybe a moment as simple as a child, tired from walking, being lifted aboard a small horse, a foal perhaps, packed down with cooking pots.

"Come see! Kung's riding!"

"Unbelievable!"

What a perfect fit. A long-legged animal, hooves but no horns, domesticated to carry belongings, joins up with a short-legged hunter with migrations to make, wars to fight, sports to practice for *more* wars. In a flash: Olympic chariot races, Caesar's imports, James I's racecourses, Charles II's stallions, George Washington's visits to Annapolis races, the Triple Crown. Six degrees of separation, stretched.

When Sunday drivers see Merryland's horses, they pull over and reach through the fence, touching a memory they can't put their finger on — as though they hear the cascading horn notes from the movie *Patton*, trumpets in triplicate, signaling contact with ancient battles, ancestral spirits. We have all been here before.

Incurably romantic?

Not here! Signs on fences remind weekend warriors: All Horses Bite.

Monday, May 2

Gerardo steps out from the training barn and turns his chiseled Aztec face to the sky.

"Four days in one," he says, English words on Mexican tongue. "Sun, wind, rain, sun again."

"*Sí*," I answer. "*Agua caliente.*"

Gerardo looks at me like he's host of the Math Show and my answers are absurd. Am I talking about hot water or the racetrack in Tijuana? I give a light punch to his washboard stomach. "You are thee *rock*," I say, pretending to be Mexican pretending to be English.

He raises his hand for emphasis: "*Contento* here. *Mucho contento*. I love working here at Merryland. *Gracias, amigo.*"

"*De nada*," I muster.

In his eyes dance the figures of his family back home in Michoacán.

Tuesday, May 3

Horse breeders in the Bluegrass this week blearily navigate I-64 to greet clients in Louisville, find foals born back home. Our time is a fortnight away.

Demands of Kentucky Derby week, Preakness week. Indispensable cultural activity in the most testing time of a farm's season. Like going to rehearsal dinners and weddings during final exams.

Wednesday, May 4

Scent of a Triple Crown blew in the air in 1961, after Carry Back won the Derby. His sire, Saggy, stood at Country Life. Thursday of Preakness week, Mom invited some press to the home of the Derby winner's dad. The swallows have returned on the same day every year since.

Tomorrow is two weeks to the 45th Preakness Party. My stomach knots when I see not one but two farms in need of spring cleaning.

Thursday, May 5

Gerardo's brother Sergio parks the farm pickup in the Merryland turnaround, crawls under the bed, pulls loose hay off the muffler, and hands it to me. It's warm.

He points to the gap between the bed and back window, where hay falls to the muffler. "I should clean this," he says.

"Sergio," I say. "It's *Cinco de Mayo*. Do it *mañana*."

Mom is sensitive to the sacrifices made by the Mexican men. She admires their stoic dignity, their quest to assimilate, their relentless attention to the horses, the farms. We all do.

"I want to buy the men some beer, a case of *cerveza* in honor of *Cinco de Mayo*," she told me today. This date in 1862, Mexican cavalry, the finest in the world, defeated an invading French army.

Cortez brought some 20 horses to Mexico in the 1500s. He burned his ships so his men would not be tempted to return to Spain. He stole the Aztec riches but left horses as a legacy. Delivered them into the hands of natural horsemen.

Friday, May 6

Patton's horn notes blew over the Bluegrass farm where Malibu Moon now lives. Dad and Mike heard the bugles yesterday, and side-tripped off I-64, en route to the Derby.

In 1893, James R. Keene bought Castleton Farm. Domino stood there, sired only 19 named foals in two crops, but eight (42 percent!) became stakes winners. Domino died at Castleton, but his ghost toots its own horn.

Without Domino, there'd be no Commando, Peter Pan, Pennant, Equipoise, Swing and Sway, Saggy, or Carry Back.

Without Domino there'd be no Equipoise, sire of Crepe Myrtle, fourth dam of Seattle Slew. So, no Slew, A.P. Indy, *and* no Malibu Moon, to pose proudly at Castleton Lyons for Dad and Mike.

Saturday, May 7

It's dark in there. My sides will hit the wall. Every instinct tells me not to go into that big green monster. I won't go.

Before John Shirreffs trained Derby winner Giacamo, he imagined insecurities in the mind of the flighty mare Radu Cool, by pensioned farm sire Carnivalay. Petrified of starting gates until Shirreffs asked her: "Would a blanket over your flanks make you feel safer?"

Stubbs' lions sunk teeth into this vulnerable spot on horses. It's ancestral fear all right.

And so Radu Cool wore a security blanket behind her saddle as she loaded into the gate for the 1997 Breeders' Cup Distaff. When the gate opened, an attendant held onto the blanket.

That kind of horsemanship makes it easy to admire Shirreffs. In purely selfish solace, we read his quote: "Knew we had a good one when he ran second to Declan's Moon."

Sunday, May 8

Pop songs bounce down the shedrow as head groom Paul Drake delivers the gospel according to Murphy's Law. A refrain sings: "How will I know?"

"Started using Captan, a plant fungicide, to clear up skin disease," Paul says. "Good stuff, but we're disinfecting girth covers and saddle pads between every ride. You *do* know the Moon filly tried to jump her gate? Annie heard metal crunching and found the filly loose. Sutures are holding great. New York Moon is a lot kinder since we gelded him. Nothin' But Heat? Wow, he's well named. That's him hollerin' now."

Owners will phone about young racehorses. Thanks to Paul, I'll know.

Monday, May 9

In this supremely self-interested sport, the Derby outcome is specific.

"The mare I had in foal to Holy Bull just slipped at nine months," Flint told me yesterday. "What a bad year to lose a foal by Holy Bull, when he sires a Derby winner. Well, at least I guessed right who to breed to."

Tuesday, May 10

"Howdy, stranger," hired gun Troy might say, ready to draw on Sly Moon, sent here barely broke, a 3-year-old with a hair trigger. Troy draws side reins through a surcingle instead. She resists, backs into the shedrow wall, cracking a course of block. With Troy holding long lines, she's a plow horse run amok. The older they are, the harder to break. So headstrong by age three.

Troy learned to ride from his uncle, Charlie Whims.

"Riding's easy," says Troy. "Thing he taught me was how to fall."

Wednesday, May 11

"What'd ya hear 'bout JJ?" Richard asks every day.

"Flint's looking at June 19 at Colonial. You're going."

Richard can flip the legs of a cast horse easy as pulling the rope starter on his push mower. He'll Indian walk to dose an uncatchable Regu-Mate mare. He'll tell you a maiden's going to kick the stallion, even though she let the teaser jump her.

In the movie *Coal Miner's Daughter*, Loretta Lynn's Kentucky hometown looks like Jenkinjones, West Virginia, Rich's birthplace. Red brick company store. Coal tipples. I call Rich every time the movie plays. He says:

"Where you been for 20 years? I've seen it a hun'ert times!"

Everything Flint tells me about JJ, I already know. Of course he's workmanlike, stubborn, smart, dependable. I named him for the best man I've ever known.

Thursday, May 12

From Kentucky comes word that Maypole Dance is holding in foal to Malibu. That's enough good news for a week.

Friday, May 13

Ten years ago. A variation this evening.

Above the tree line drifts an orange moon of silky fabric. Movement in the wicker basket, fire *seen* before heard, two quick bursts of ignited gas. *Whoosh! Whoosh!*

Grazing horses hear the flame-thrower. Broodmares with foals swing into full alert. Single mares dance like ballerinas before a leap. Shielded by the hill, yearlings have no chance before the intruder is upon them, eight fillies moving so fast they look twice that number, red filly leading the way, others swinging in a chain behind her. The image is evolutionary in collective fright. *Not again!* Ancient man hunted

horses, bones piled at cliff walls, herds driven over by flaming torches. *Let's get outta here!*

They stream down the fenceline. The red filly stops but the others shove her onto the pipe gate. She somersaults, hind legs kicking the sky. She spins up through the top board of the next field, half falling, half jumping. The other fillies prop at the downed gate and consider escape but the pipes lay on the ground like a cattle guard and instincts warn of broken legs.

All this, in a blink. By summer's end, horses tolerate nightly flights of commercial hot-air balloons over the watershed. Life during wartime. Every year, same fear.

Saturday, May 14

No rain since the Hunt Cup. Lost-and-found hound Woody paws at door handles as heat lightning sparks the night sky. No rain to melt the late fertilizer applied this week, and the grass in the best fields just might burn brown before it grows green.

Sunday, May 15

Carry Back was conceived in Maryland, foaled in Florida. Ditto Malibu Moonshine, local interest in the Preakness. Carry Back ran in heart-stopping, last-to-first style. Moonshine, too.

The "People's Horse," Carry Back was a favorite in the grandstand, less so in the clubhouse, so sparsely bred. What business winning classics? By Saggy out of Joppy! Like being by Truck out of Texas.

Malibu Moonshine's mom might not have drawn a bid at Timonium before she had this big red colt. I know he's no Carry Back, but maybe he doesn't.

Monday, May 16

The *Sun* headlines scream: "Magna Threatens To Move Preakness. Says No More Dough On Pimlico."

Deep Throat says: "Editors put the word out to write about Magna's troubles. The paper's against slots, wants Magna the problem, not slots in Pennsylvania, West Virginia, Delaware, New York."

He says: "Never mind that Magna just spent $30 million at Laurel. No credit for that. Read between the headlines. It's politics, in print."

Tuesday, May 17

"We're 40-1 last week. Jock takes my mare out of the post parade, tells the track vet she feels unsound. Vet scratches her. Jock gets forty-five bucks without having to ride the race. He saw her past performances! She had no form because she took a year off to get bred. That's why she hadn't run since Hector was a pup! I'm not right often, but even a broken watch is right twice a day. Now I gotta sell the stewards on my story, work her to show she's sound before I can enter again."

Wednesday, May 18

Two-year-old Yeager's Jet takes his name after the legendary test pilot Chuck Yeager.

Gelding didn't relieve obstreperous behavior. Yeager's Jet still throws his head up into Troy's face as they jog. Riders hate that — the nose smasher. He still balks at the starting gate. Troy is patient, though uncomplimentary. J.R. says Yeager's Jet is made of the right stuff. If a boom is heard over the Jersey Shore this summer, Yeager's Jet has either broken the Monmouth track record or kicked the paddock wall. Odds on the latter.

Thursday, May 19

WVOB, the Voice of Bel Air, set up a microphone on the Country Life porch during the party in '65. A tape preserves the evening. Crops of foals in the newly minted Maryland-bred Fund heard the mellifluous voices of sports commentators Win Elliot and Jack Whitaker, background music by Joe Nichols, rinky-tink piano cover of "Peg o' My Heart."

"They talk about the Bluegrass," began Elliot, "but I enjoy the green. May it forever remain as verdant as it seems here tonight."

"Driving in here," continued Whitaker, "the fences so white, a full moon tonight. Anybody not having a good time, it's their own fault."

Red Smith said, "There's more bluegrass in Tennessee than in either Kentucky or Maryland, but I love this area."

Mom threw a great party in '65. Still does. But the area has changed in 40 years. Country Life is now the last undeveloped parcel on Business 1. When the party is over, I drive the farm lanes after blowing out the tiki lamps, after flipping on the breaker for the electric gate that keeps crazies out.

In '65, Whitney Tower observed from the porch: "This is the fastest-growing *Thoroughbred* community in America."

Take out *Thoroughbred*. Coming soon: Wal-Mart, Sheetz, Wawa. A culture of cars jamming Old Joppa, Route 1, air redolent of fried food. What chance of stopping "progress"? Good horses our only chance.

Friday, May 20

Bred mares in a grateful rain all day at Country Life, then drove eight miles south to Merryland.

"This farm's in land preservation," I explain to Walter Hillenmeyer, in from Kentucky. "I don't know the future of horse racing in Maryland, but this place will still be a farm. No McMansions."

Walter cautioned: "If you turn this house into a guest lodge, careful not to let 'em go into the barns after hours. Folks have gotten far away from any sense of animals, of agriculture. But they all want to pet a horse."

Saturday, May 21

Navy SEALs parachuted to pinpoints on the Turf course. Deafening silence as the black chevron of a stealth bomber passed over the Pimlico stretch. Followed closely by an eardrum rip that certainly spooked horses in the Preakness stakes barn.

Staged theatrics. Recruiting tactics. Nothing to match the real action of battle on horseback. The Preakness would have exploded in flames if not for Afleet Alex pulling himself out of a nose dive, if not for Jeremy Rose flashing reflexes of a biplane ace.

Malibu Moonshine lumbered home like a cargo plane, beat six, lost to seven, no match for Rose's jet. No Black-Eyed Susans to carry back home tonight.

Sunday, May 22

Phone call from Kentucky. Maypole Dance resorbed, again. An annual ritual now.

SPRING 2005

Monday, May 23

Chuck Merrick attended McDonogh School when it was a military academy. He was a cavalry kid. When he says that, at the age of eight, he showed Welsh pony-Thoroughbred crosses at "The Garden," he's quick to point out that it's not where the Knicks play. That's Seventh Avenue and 33rd Street. He means the old Garden, at Eighth and 50th, but not the *oldest* Garden, at Fifth and 23rd. He does not apologize for being precise. He is partial to gray horses.

"Yes, I like grays. I like to see substance in a horse, a smart eye, a swan neck, a short back — where all the weight is loaded — and a straight hind leg. You can't have too straight a hind leg."

At today's 2-year-old sale, Chuck bought a gray filly named Heavenly Creation.

"Sounds like an ice cream," he scoffed. "Bad luck to change it now, I suppose. All these 2-year-olds have had their heads scrambled. Take her back to Merryland; let her relax."

Tuesday, May 24

It's dizzying, watching 20 TVs replaying workouts of 500 2-year-olds in the two-day Timonium sale. A year ago, if you had a crystal ball, or Tim Ritchey's eye, you could have selected Afleet Alex off these TV tapes, and maybe have bought him for $75,000. And won the Preakness. And come in third in the Derby, second in the Breeders' Cup Juvenile. And be worth millions.

From watching TV. The trick is knowing what you're looking at.

Wednesday, May 25

Sunlight dances through leaves the size of dinner plates, to land on my desk in reflections that easily distract me from office details. The morning sun has moved center stage in the sky, and clear spring air asks for a curtain call: Come out from behind those curtains and see this day.

Thursday, May 26

Three-year-old Nothin' But Heat is named for a pitcher who throws fastballs, not for estrous behavior of fillies he swoons from two fields over. So in love he sent a broken-bat sliver of fence into his forearm.

"You sure he's gelded?"

J.R. flicked his hands, open palmed, like a knife on a whetstone. "*Sí.*"

Paul said: "Maybe they missed something?"

Phone call to the vet in South Carolina:

"I do 60 or 70 castrations a year, but I remember that colt. He had one undescended testicle, about one-fifth normal size. I fished for it and teased it right on through. Thought I got it all. But tell you what you do. Pull blood, check his testosterone. That'll tell you whether he's firing on one cylinder."

Friday, May 27

Yeager's Jet. Cresty neck with a scalloped mane rising straight up like a drawing of an Etruscan horse. Shoes clacking as he slips and shies en route to the track. Two seconds on loose sand, he's revving his engine. I say out loud: "He'd be like riding a dirt bike."

On cue, a motorcycle throats up Bottom Road, just as Yeager sets his jaw into the bit.

"I don't mind those Harleys," neighbor Billy Deitz once told me. "What I hate is those reckless kids on those crotch-rockets. They're noisy as hell, and they don't give a damn about nobody."

I watch through binoculars as the rocket speeds up the road that parallels the track, Friday afternoon freedom rider in mock "Willie the Shoe" crouch versus Cool Hand Troy on wild-child Yeager. I could see it all coming apart, see it faster than the speed of sound. Why doesn't that bike clown slow down?

Because he's clueless. So is Yeager, flashing past at a full gallop, under insistent urging, Troy so smart, just sending, sending, sending him past the roaring rival.

Saturday, May 28

In 25 years of coming to Dad's anniversary AA meetings, never heard the story from last night, why he declined the Derby invitation from colorful Jack Price, breeder/trainer/owner of Carry Back.

"I love the Derby," Dad told the Friday night group — hard-hat types, recidivist DUIs, Pimlico regulars — his kind of folks, big hearted, a little mustard on their shirts, repentant, sort of. "But I didn't go. I was afraid of myself in all that partying. We stood the sire of the Derby favorite, and I didn't go. That's how powerful alcohol is. It takes away the things you love."

In 1980, Dad entered treatment at a blue-collar facility on a grassy knoll a few lengths from Pimlico. He asked son Andrew to bet $2 on Temperence Hill in the Belmont Stakes. What a hunch bet! It paid $108.80 to win.

"Ombeleevobul," he said when Andy handed over the dough. First evidence that good things might happen, a day at a time, if he quit.

"Ombeleevobul," he said over and over last night.

Surrounded by nieces, grandchildren, sons and daughters, and a wife made of the right stuff, Dad laughed when the kids presented him his 25-year chip.

"Hmmm. Might have to go to Delaware Park tomorrow and see if it fits in a slot machine."

Sunday, May 29

Rachael is grounded again, a new broken arm to match the old ones on X-rays she holds to the sun: wrist bones opaque, except where white pins and plates fuse old breaks.

Monday, May 30

Truths:
Memorial Day as a holiday is a nonstarter — a joke — on horse farms, at tracks.
Maypole went back to the breeding shed today.
Not every day is paradise on a farm.

Tuesday, May 31

A training farm in full swing is a fine thing. Paul tacked up Heavenly Creation, and the battleship-gray filly, freshened with a week in the sand pen, paused at the bridge to consider walking on water, then bravely bowed her neck and proceeded. In white polo bandages, she looked every bit the show horse. When Troy broke her into a jog, she embodied the dream four years ago when we bought this old farm: Beautiful horses expertly prepared on a fine track.

Paul hustled down the shedrow, throwing saddles on the next set, stopping the walking machine to pull off cooled horses — kids too long at the fair. Riders ducked door lintels and 2-year-olds appeared. Watch your backs.

Barn to barn, the riders shuttled, just far enough to drive, their limber exercise saddles spread-eagled on the tops of cars in slow procession.

And in this way has gone a cool May. Balloons and bombers and bikers. Alex's acrobatics. Dad's 25th. The merry-go-rounds of Merryland.

Unbelievable.

June

Wednesday, June 1

The days grow long now, summer marching ever nearer like footfalls of a distant army. It's early morning at Merryland. Casement windows in the farm kitchen, cranked open toward the training barn, amplify soft sounds of feed tubs rattling, horses speaking, help arriving.

The barn is 160 feet long. In the shade of the woods before the day heats up, it rests languid on the hillside, muffled activity giving it life. Summer memories surface. It's a camp dining hall before the breakfast bell. The smell of coffee from the tack room clocks through the cool, heavy air to mix with the aroma of rhododendron on the run. It must be work, but it looks like vacation.

Thursday, June 2

"My eyes are going."

J.R. strained to see across the width of the track to iron markers Teddy posted at one-eighth-mile intervals. J.R.'s wife, Laurie, grabbed Stan the Fix-It Man to barbershop orange and blue tape on PVC pipe to fashion poles. Not quite the color-coded tradition of Belmont Park.

Sixteenth poles, *black and white.*

Eighth poles, *green and white.*

Quarter and half poles, *red and white.*

Yet, suddenly, the orange-and-blue poles assumed dominion. No longer was the track a mere oval of dirt. It had become a measurable test of a horse, divided into heats of 220 yards — each eighth-mile a furrow of a plowed field long, a furlong.

"Let's call Equibase," J.R. said. "Get workouts published again, like the old days, when they ran right off the farm."

The old abbreviation *Mry* was still on file at Equibase.

Friday, June 3

On a wager in 1873, railroad magnate Leland Stanford and photographer Eadweard Muybridge answered yes to the question of whether all four feet of a running horse are off the ground at the same time. Muybridge devised a variation of an optical toy called a zoetrope, a revolving cylinder with slits in its circumference, into which he placed photographs taken at close intervals of Stanford's prize trotter, Occident, in a collected canter. The magic lantern projected an image so lifelike that dogs barked at the screen.

The museum at the Kentucky Horse Park displays Muybridge's photos, a button activating the revolving cylinder. Seen from above (not the optical illusion through slits), the trotter canters in reverse, backing up counterclockwise. Viewed through the slits? He canters forward in the palm of your hand.

Through binoculars, I watch the 2-year-olds with gnawing skepticism, Muybridge in mind. Is their progress an illusion?

Saturday, June 4

Awkward moment with seventh-grade boys at Merryland this afternoon. End-of-lacrosse-season party. Eleven-year-old son August the only farm-raised team member.

One colt foal with accelerated hormones obviously displayed interest in an unsettled mare. (Yes, a *foal*.) Mrs. Robinson kicked at The Undergraduate. Questions flew.

A month ago, in the same situation, quick thinking deflected second-graders' curiosity: "Oh, why, yes, children, you're so right. Some horses *do* have more legs than others. Some even have more toes. When the world was a swamp, they had four toes on their front feet and three on their hind. Imagine that! Horses with toes!"

Today, with cynical seventh-graders, distraction provided escape.

"Guys, real quick, let's hop in the Eurociser!"

Sunday, June 5

So sweltering hot now, mares and foals aren't turned out until 7 p.m. Son Josh at 14 leads a well-behaved foal as I school him on paranoia.

"Watch for everything! A door opening. A car in the driveway. Cats. Dogs. Anything will spook a horse. Be prepared."

Woody the dog hears the whoosh of the hot-air balloon on a Sunday night cruise, barks suddenly, spooking the foal. The young horse gallops away. Josh hangs on courageously, sliding through the yard as if he's water skiing. The pair comes to a standstill at the wide trunk of an ancient sugar maple.

Val is behind us coming up the hill.

"Next time that happens, Josh, aim the foal at a mare's arse. That's usually closer than a tree."

Monday, June 6

"Time for a breeze," J.R. declares. Troy and Tim schedule a match race at one furlong between blocky Yeager's Jet and lanky Mister Keen. The farm crew makes book as the 2-year-olds jog slowly toward the backstretch straightaway to break into a breeze with no turns. Troy and Yeager jog along the rail, where sand accumulates from the camber of the track. Tim gallops Keen near the center; the highest part, sand thinner.

They hit the furlong pole as one body doubled, eight hooves off the ground at once. Then Keen's long stride separates the single image. The breeze, like most match races — through strategy, talent, or disaster — is not a close contest.

Troy felt the affair inconclusive. Requests a rematch next week. You're on, says Tim. A nascent rivalry, Domino and Henry of Navarre. My horse can beat your horse. The fundamental underpinning of all horse racing.

Tuesday, June 7

Arrived at Merryland after dark, yearling filly on the trailer. Spectacular fireworks of lightning blew out electricity at farm. J.R. parked his truck with headlights aimed at the trailer ramp. Off safely.

When Baltimore County owned this farm, mercury vapor lights glowed on every barn, on every lane, like a minor league baseball stadium. Teddy bought a telescoping light bulb changer and unscrewed the bulbs. The meter sighed in relief as the farm fell back into the valley's beautiful darkness.

Tonight, as lightning raced to the ocean, the name Spectacular Malibu suggested itself for the yearling, in homage to ancestors and evening alike.

Wednesday, June 8

Rainwater pools in low-lying infield paddocks. Bottomland on Bottom Road. The fillies have dug a mud hole that would swallow a Volkswagen Beetle.

Mosquitoes breed in standing water, vectors of venom. It never ends, the list of projects to maintain a horse farm. Cell phone message for Warfield, Bob:

"Need a little backhoe work, a few holes filled, some drain tile in the infield."

Thursday, June 9

Efforts to automate horse farming can't count to 10. Manure spreader. Hay elevator. Automatic waterer. *Hot-walking machine.*

At Delaware Park, where they'll run the $1 million Delaware Handicap in July, backstretch improvements skipped a page. Incongruous mechanical walkers from

the days of $2,500 claimers (read: pre-slots) still blot the refurbished barn area. High-end horses tethered to low-tech carnival rides. Shackled, they rear up in protest, front feet flying in rebellion.

The very first improvement we made to Merryland was the installation of a free-walking exercise machine. What a light bulb idea by the inventor! Let's make the stall move with the horse inside it. No chain on his halter bending his neck. A free head for balance, for stretching spinal columns, for unfettered exercise in both directions at any speed.

J.R. spins silliness out of fractious trackers before riders arrive. On his way home from Pimlico, Dad observes: "That *walking thing* was full of happy horses." Six stalls moving in a circle of sand. Six less paychecks for hot-walkers, historically unreliable help. J.R. compliments it: "Shows up every day. Dependable as electricity."

New York Moon ships out to Delaware this month. An admonition for Departure Papers: no tilt-a-whirl at the amusement park.

Friday, June 10

Alleged Moon carves notches in her stall doorpost for exercise riders she's tossed in the hay. A workers' comp claim waiting to happen. But Troy talks pretty to her. Tells her to forget her mama was by the mauler Alleged. To keep her settled, Troy jogs her the wrong way around the track — clockwise, the direction they ran at Belmont Park when it opened 100 years ago.

In *Belmont Park: A Century of Champions*, peerless Turf historian Edward L. Bowen describes the original layout of the Belmont track in 1905, an emulation of the variety of English courses — where right-handed racing was prevalent, the Epsom Derby the leading left-handed exception.

Alleged Moon's broodmare sire won the right-handed Prix de l'Arc de Triomphe twice, then made a career out of ending stallion grooms' careers.

Careful, Troy. She's got demons in her genes, coursing in both directions.

Saturday, June 11

Afleet Alex made the entire field look like it was running backward in Muybridge's zoetrope. The Belmont Stakes, when viewed from above, was not an illusion.

Sunday, June 12

At Belmont Park from 1905 through 1920, horses ran clockwise, the rail on their right. The 1921 meet followed a major renovation, and the direction of races changed to conform to the American custom.

Man o' War ran and won seven times at Belmont. He competed in 1919 and 1920. So, he must have run clockwise at Belmont, counterclockwise at other American tracks. Nowhere in literature could I find it stated that Man o' War went both ways, or won a third of his 21 races coming down the stretch with the rail to his right. An odd question I've reserved for the great beyond, a question to ask a grandfather gone before my arrival. Adolphe Pons managed the Turf affairs of August Belmont II, presided over Belmont's Nursery Stud dispersal in 1925. I'll betcha he saw every one of Man o' War's races at Belmont Park, though I'm in no hurry to collect that bet.

Monday, June 13

Harford Road to Baltimore County chokes with Monday morning commuters. Exit. Get to Merryland by Laurel Brook Road through the Gunpowder State Park. In the cool river that slices the counties, trout fishermen wade in hip boots under the stone bridge abutments of the abandoned Ma and Pa railroad. Up out of the park, farmland on either side. The oldest tractor on earth straddles a row of beans, the driver a farmer so doughty he'd be cast out of the movie — too improbable.

Why don't you live at Merryland?

What? And miss this marvelous ride every day?

Tuesday, June 14

Without begging for slot machines, Colonial Downs has quietly built a first-class meet, relying on purses stockpiled from attractive OTBs for their 40 days of racing, sure to increase in coming years.

Maryland's strategy of putting OTBs in failed crab houses? Well, *it* failed.

Wednesday, June 15

Everybody's buzzing about Jenkin Jones' first start on Sunday. From California comes a partner and wife, stopping in Texas to pick up grandchildren for a summer trip to Colonial Williamsburg, so happily close to Colonial Downs. From North Carolina will arrive another multigenerational entourage. Horse racing undersells itself as family entertainment.

From Maryland, of course, Richard maps the four-hour drive with Val, early risers too impatient to wait for the team bus. As mares and foals are led to fields this evening, hands slap like basketball players coming on and off the court, asking: *"How you think JJ's gonna do?"*

Thursday, June 16

"Haaay. That old mare of yours is back in foal!" Dr. Ruel Cowles sings over the phone.

Maypole Dance is only eight.

"Well, that's old for a broodmare carrying her first foal. Market doesn't like that, or the late cover. Gotta keep her now."

Cerebral Turf statistician and editor Joe Estes wrote that the value of a brood-mare as a producer is in direct proportion to her class as a racer. Time to get out the videotape of Maypole's races. That Keeneland stakes where she set the pace *might* assuage me.

Friday, June 17

Sometimes I watch Troy ride, as if he'd been born to it.

Poetic license not excused. That's how Troy appears, on a horse in motion, four feet off the ground.

Saturday, June 18

At Charles Town tonight, 6-year-old gelding Mr. V. cocked his head sideways just as the gate opened. Off balance, he lunged forward, hind legs recoiling like springs from the thrust of takeoff, overreaching, grabbing the bulb of his right front heel. Like tripping on your shoelace. His nose pecked the ground. Incredibly, Mr. V. recovered. Jockey Dale Whitaker had lost his stirrup irons. First time past the stands, he rode bareback style, legs straight down, back straight up, warrior-like. He jump-roped both feet into the irons just in time for leverage in the sharp turn. But the race was over the moment the gate had opened.

In a game of such random physics, sometimes excuses must be witnessed to be credible.

Sunday, June 19

In the first instant of Jenkin Jones' race, track announcer Dave Rodman shouted: "*And Jenkin Jones ...*"

In a nanosecond, we filled in the blanks: "... is leading the field ... is on top by five ... is moving like a tree-mendous machine!"

But Dave exploded our delusions: "... *walks out of the gate.*"

Eighteen hours apart, starting gate stumbles take away all chances for Mr. V. and JJ. A lost weekend.

Monday, June 20

"How'd JJ do?" the phone asked all day.

"He *dwelt.*" Chart notes are triumphs of euphemism.

Never hit a wrong key in recital practice. For an audience? *The Gong Show.* Partner Lucy Howard suggested he might make a jumper. Me first.

Tuesday, June 21

Chuck Lucier is a foot detective. He's been halfway upside down for long minutes, pinching clinches off Wahoo Moon's old shoes, searching for clues to re-shoe her properly. He straightens up and leans on her shoulder as his head clears.

"St. Croix Forge," he guesses the maker's stamp inside the toe of the old shoe. "Made in Minnesota. Good shoes, but I don't carry them. Any shoe will wear down sharp as a knife from dragging in coarse racetrack sand. I'm putting a Queen's Plate back on her."

You could slice baling twine with the worn shoes. Chuck bends over, lifts her foot to brace it above his knees, studies its shape. He rubs a 14-inch rasp sharply against ragged holes left in her hoof wall by nails. He's deft as a shoeshine boy. Walks to his truck. Taps a Queen's Plate on an anvil. The job looks so primitive. It is — and it isn't. Wahoo's eyes never leave Chuck at the truck.

Moments later, Wahoo's in new shoes. Case closed. Next horse.

Wednesday, June 22

Blood chemistry results for testosterone indicate that the 3-year-old gelding Nothin' But Heat may still be intact. Apparently, an undescended testicle is whispering to him: "Find fillies."

A veterinarian in Lexington suggests to the owner: "Put him on Regu-Mate. I recommend it to clients who have well-bred, studdish colts they don't want to geld."

So now we've got Nothin' But Heat on Regu-Mate. My mental jukebox plays a song about how it's a mixed-up, muddled-up, shook-up world.

Thursday, June 23

Accountant Dave Callan:

"This is a resort hotel. Horses here for 60 days, here for 90, incurring expenses. You're not like the trainer at the track. He gets 10 percent of purses *plus* day money. He makes his money when horses run, not when they eat.

"You? You're mailing a bill at the end of the month. What if the horse left at the beginning of the month, then got hurt at the track? That's a risk. Why not get a credit card number on arrival? Kentucky vet clinics do. Tell folks to use bonus points to fly here to see their horse. You run a horse hotel. Manage it like one."

Friday, June 24

Betty Miller, two years shy of 90, lets August drive her motorized scooter down the halls of Mercy Ridge. She only recently traded the jockey-in-silks hood ornament on her car for a fox head on her scooter. She ran Merryland with that same stylish hand for decades. She dearly loved husband Danny Shea, one of three she lived past. She says: "Sometimes at night I wonder what I'll think about." She smiles at the mischief of a memory. "No, better not think on that. I've had *quite* a life."

In the hallway, a recent arrival refuses to accept his fate at the old folks' home.

"Come with me when we visit my old farm," she melts him with kindness. "I'll introduce you to Merryland Monroe."

Sure you will, lady, says the look on his face. She'll tell me later the fellow took off — thought everyone was daft.

Saturday, June 25

Ninety horses in 90-degree heat when the ancient galvanized pipe from the well burst under the driveway at suppertime, water percolating up like Jed Clampett's oil field. Water on a farm, valuable as oil. Horses in hot weather can drink 20 gallons or more a day. Automatic waterers foiled without water.

Creative hose work backfilled the system. The charm of an old farm returned as horses drank heartily. An offset come Monday, when a herd of plumbers arrive to fashion a costly new line.

Sunday, June 26

In the sweltering heat of the Maryland Horse Breeders Association's yearling show, August pondered conformation of 20-some yearlings in Class IV, filled in the numbers of his top five on the amateur judging contest card. For most closely corroborating judge Ben Perkins Sr.'s picks, he won a julep cup. And the admiration of elders: What a nice young lad! What a natural horseman! Company man Aug loaded his card with home horses, including Spectacular Malibu, second in the class, red ribbon on halter.

As though frozen in a Muybridge photo, August's feet have not yet touched the ground.

Monday, June 27

Purple sky from a Munnings painting today at training time, 2-year-olds on edge in raindrops that stopped and started regular as a traffic light.

"Reminds me of the Custer County Fair meet," J.R. recalled of his formative days with Quarter Horses in Broken Bow, Nebraska. "Tornado country. See a sky like today, run for the basement."

J.R. laughs easily as he pushes the horn of the Western saddle and spins pony Timmy back to the barn to accompany the next set.

"Had a gelding named Sneaky Jack at Fonner Park. Ran somethin' like 116 races. Not all for me, of course. Had an ankle as big as my head ..."

I lost the rest of the story in the rain, swallowed in a sudden summer shower.

Tuesday, June 28

Warrfield lifted ground with his backhoe, pushed stone into the trench, laid down perforated plastic pipe, covered it with sediment screening cloth, then graded and rock-hounded the surface.

"Hey, ought to see this before I cover it up," he said when he reached a springhead 50 yards from the old Puett starting gate. Unearthed was a clogged line of terra-cotta pipe from Danny Shea's days. Water running down through the ages, connecting our stewardship to his. A sense of mortality shivered my bones.

Wednesday, June 29

"I shoed yo' mama," Chuck chants.

He fondly slaps the rump of a juvenile delinquent. A tough mare to shoe has produced a tough yearling to trim, and in that circular motion that pervades this game, Chuck is back underneath another generation. The family podiatrist. He wipes his forearm across his bandana, reaches down for the foot, maintains his grasp as the yearling engages powerful haunches to shake his leg loose.

"Just like yo' mama," Chuck chuckles, incremental victory in hand as the yearling sighs. The life of a journeyman blacksmith: refusal, and then surrender.

Thursday, June 30

Thoreau wrote he'd seen many a man dragged down by the weight of 100 acres. But horse farmers? A triumph of optimism over reality, indulgence over income. Hal Clagett is near 90, still bales his own hay, raises stakes winners every crop. It's that

good hay, he'll tell you, his thoughts warmed by the quiet memory of a field cleared of bales.

A local poet, Julia Wendell, wrote:
"Not the race, exactly,
But the before and after, the hush
On either side of desperation ..."

Hushed moments in the margins of farm life. Ellen's tiger lilies in bloom. Deer snorting before they bound off. A hawk harried by a mockingbird. Nine yearling fillies at dusk, the pecking order at work: newest gal last in line. The training barn like a great ship on the hill, ferrying young horses to the races. Buckling the padlock each night on wrought-iron entrance gates the former owner picked up from some vanished Turf club.

What compels us to open the farm gates tomorrow morning, to accept the wildly speculative life with horses? Maybe it's the before and after. Maybe it's the hush.

SUMMER
2005

July

Friday, July 1

Summer travel day, minivan halfway to Colonial Downs. Tomorrow, Jenkin Jones may atone for "dwelling" last out. Sunset stop at sister Norah's house near Point Lookout, Maryland. A peninsula between the Potomac River and Chesapeake Bay, Point Lookout was the site of a Union prison camp for Confederate cavalry unseated at Gettysburg. Diaries of captured scouts tell of a liberation attempt.

"Rode 80 miles at a stretch," wrote a Southern general who forayed a mile from Merryland Farm before turning south toward Point Lookout. "When a man's horse gave out, fresh horses came up. The horses we left were well-bred from Virginia and far better than the fat Maryland horses who could not stand 20 miles march."

These days, it's not Maryland horses that can't stand the march, it's the horsemen, railing at the hardship ride to Colonial Downs.

Saturday, July 2

Mutuel tickets for farm employees proved worthless as Confederate greenbacks when JJ stopped badly in mid-rally.

"He bled!" one partner exclaimed in almost delighted relief, excuse revealed by endoscopic exam. "He bled!"

Is there another sport where bleeding is good news?

Sunday, July 3

"That 2-year-old filly East Jet drew in for Tuesday night. I can't find her papers! You have them?"

The day is coming when a silicon chip embedded in a Thoroughbred will scan vital information, pet technology hastened by mad cow tracking. Occasionally until then, whereabouts of The Jockey Club certificate of registration will pose a minor crisis, especially with 2-year-olds.

"They must still be with the sale company," I answered. "She was scratched from the sale last month. What time's post?"

"Twilight."

The horse identifier can get her markings online for her tattoo. But it's a claiming race. Ownership could change. Can't run unless papers are handed over before she walks into the paddock.

"She's sittin' on a win."

We'll get the papers.

Monday, July 4

Kentucky from the air in July is not the lush land of Derby time. Thin topsoil over limestone loses moisture quicker than loams of home. Soft bluegrass is a fair-weather friend. Romance of horse country this day appreciated most in air conditioning of the Kentucky Horse Park museum, or in the shade of the Hall of Champions.

"A million visitors a year here," began the enthusiastic emcee of the parade of champions, "and surveys say 90 percent ask to see Cigar."

Clips of 16 straight wins flash on TV screens, the Dubai World Cup (UAE-I) in such dramatic relief, under lights, when he reaches deep into his soul to defeat Soul of the Matter. The greatest Maryland-bred ever, the world's leading earner, the main attraction for a million fans a year, the incomparable Cigar!

On to the Calumet trophy collection, a dynasty begot by Bull Lea. Equine taxidermy of battles between Moors and Knights. Herbert Haseltine's bronze of high-headed Man o' War. A meditation garden honoring erudite editor Kent Hollingsworth. The stately barns of the former Walnut Hall Farm retrofitted with open arms to the public.

The Bluegrass region is famed for its hospitality, but by necessity, gates of many farms swing open by appointment only. The Kentucky Horse Park is a brilliant solution.

Tuesday, July 5

9 a.m. Fasig-Tipton office.

"What'd you do? Spend the Fourth in Lexington? Those papers are still in Maryland. Call Mike at home, see if he can get to our Fair Hill office in time."

He did, then on to Colonial. Sitting on a win, East Jet sat behind the pace, all the way to the wire. A new excuse to add to the litany: The grass was too slick.

Wednesday, July 6

E-mails from horse-watch services shot through cyberspace moments after J.R. uploaded yesterday's works to Equibase. I realize it's just a brown horse running from one orange pole to another. But hey! It's a published work! What a moment to savor, after three years of hard-fought track renovation: an eighth-of-a-milestone.

Thursday, July 7

No farm manager can stare at a field of foals in summer without searching for signs of stress, straddling that fine line between vigilance and madness. This evening at turnout, Val kept her cool in the heat as she wondered about a foal.

Take his temp. Hmmm, 103. Fightin' sum'pin. Hold the hose on his neck. Jugular veins. Cool them, cool him. Much better. Leave him in tonight, fan on. Do blood work tomorrow.

Friday, July 8

At a client's farm today. An unloadable 3-year-old filly.

Cole stood in the center of the sand pen and chirped the filly into a loose trot. Round and round and round she went, sweat breaking out on her flanks, on her muzzle. He switched directions with her just by stepping forward in her arc. He would not let her slow down or speed up. She stayed close to the wall, as far away from him as she could. After a long period of trotting, she seemed to resign herself, the effort in heavy sand lowering her resistance. When he turned away, her eyes followed him. She took a step toward him.

The step-up gooseneck trailer was backed up to the sand pen gate. Cole slipped a chain shank over the filly's gums, gentle as pulling a light switch. He applied pressure to back her, then released the pressure to walk her forward. He asked her to follow him onto the trailer. She refused. Again. And again.

"How many times you try to load this filly?" he called over the fence to her owner.

"Fifteen, maybe 20 times. She's three years old, you know. Never been broke. Never been off this farm."

He turned her loose again in the sand pen, started all over. You could feel her spirit subsume into his. You saw it in her eyes. Her ears moved forward. The next time he walked her toward the trailer,

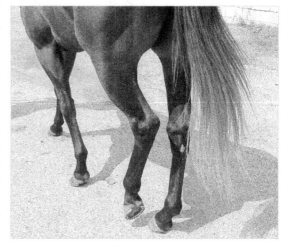

chain shank gentle on her gums, she followed him. He stepped briskly up into the trailer with her head beside him, her feet rumbling on the wooden floorboards.

There are books about this moment. All I know is what I saw: Years of tryin' came down to a couple of hours of knowin'.

Saturday, July 9

P. J. Indy's steel-gray coat and imposing height suggest a gentleman's hunter, but that's not Plan A. Every inch of his 17 hands tests our resolve. Throat tie-back operation. Hind ankle chip removed. Hind suspensory injected. Winter and spring off. Yet riders say he's still not right behind. Blood titers for EPM and West Nile negative so far. Another chip?

"X-rays are clean," declared Dr. Amy Woodford in Riddle's clinic. "Bones of the hock stack like building blocks, take a lot of concussion. That's when curbs pop. You see those bumps below the hock? Stress to the ligaments, aggravating tendons."

Dr. Woodford injected Depo-Medrol into his hock joints.

"When the joints are puffy, they're easy to hit," she said, "but joint capsules are very narrow. Always the risk of scarring the cartilage, of infection, if we're not *super* careful. Do him up in alcohol bandages for five days, hand-walk a few days, then apply a light blister of Doc's paint."

Plan B? Not yet.

Sunday, July 10

First time in collective memory when not all vans at the end of breeding season are taking horses away. Some bring green-broke 2-year-olds, layups, yearlings for early schooling. Without a training center, this family operation was a river with a dam in it. The addition of a sandy oval to our services tore down the dam, opened a stream of commerce. Boarding horses is hardly lucrative work, with the high cost of labor, feed, straw, but it creates an illusion of productivity that eases anxiety.

Mom fielded a call today for a van to pick up a mare and foal, drop off a yearling. "That's a switch," she said, history upended.

Monday, July 11

Child is father to the man.

I think that means if grown-ups took you to the track as a child, you're likely to return as an adult. Racetracks miss this point, view kids as a nuisance, per-capita betting a short-sighted guide. No seeding for a distant harvest.

Retiree Bernie Gugerty, Pimlico-goer at 10, marveled at Merryland's works on the Equibase site.

"Now that I've got a horse, I guess I need a computer. How do these things work?"

Tuesday, July 12

Be certain to return call to mare owner who's either irate or apologetic, after his van driver arrived at 10 o'clock Saturday night to pick up his mare and foal.

"They were turned back out after dinner," I'd told driver. "We can't disturb a herd in a big field at night. We hadn't heard from you. I'm sorry about the miscommunication. Can you come back tomorrow?"

Guess not, by the way the phone bounced down. I should have been more understanding of summer traffic, jammed highways, client satisfaction.

Wednesday, July 13

Only piece of equipment at Merryland settlement four years ago was a small water tank on a decrepit wagon. We've used it as a water truck all spring, but it's primitive and insufficient. On hottest of days, by the time riders arrive, the track can be as dusty as a bad Western.

Luck favored the prepared when a local racetrack returned our call: "Got a '75 International 1700, Gas — a 30-year-old truck with only 11,000 miles on it. Mounted with an 1,800-gallon water tank with a Vanguard pump that'll broadcast a 30-foot arc. It ain't pretty and it only turns right — just kidding — but it's what you're looking for. We're going to diesel."

Thursday, July 14

Colonial Downs' grandstand rises like the Governor's mansion in Williamsburg. Handsome Jeffersonian architecture, collegial, inviting: Come study here, nine classes today in the sport of Thoroughbred racing.

Could we wide-load this grandstand up I-95 to replace Pimlico's, a warehouse whose charm vanished when the Victorian clubhouse collapsed in flames in 1966? The point of call in a race, the "Clubhouse Turn," derives from that stately yellow structure, with its wraparound porches, its shutters opened on windows looking upstretch to the finish line. An iconic image preserved in paintings by Vaughn Flannery, Franklin Voss. Oh, and on a miniature cupola in the Preakness winner's circle, painted annually with the silks of the winning owner.

Friday, July 15

Half-hour late picking up Betty Miller for a promised day at her old farm. From a bench at Mercy Ridge, she waved off my apology: "Don't you think I know how hard it is to get off that farm!"

Parked in a Chevy minivan at railside to watch Merryland Monroe breeze, she could have been Mrs. Markey of Calumet, the limousine at Keeneland's rail, admiring Alydar the day of his Blue Grass Stakes.

Saturday, July 16

Sittin' on a win no more. East Jet broke her maiden yesterday at Colonial. Satellite feed in the office like being there for partners, wild cheering in that out-of-body experience acceptable at racetracks and rock concerts — except for Dad. I mouthed the question: *Claimed?* His eyes said: *Hope not.* Phone call to trainer catching the replay. He started into a joke, caught our silent anxiety. "No, just kidding, nobody took her. Thanks for running her where she could win."

Can't waver about putting a player on waivers, but it feels like Sophie's Choice if you know your baby can win.

Sunday, July 17

Streams of Merryland feed into the vast Chesapeake Bay watershed. Brooks accessible to horses will one day be entirely fenced off. Good news for the Bay and for fence contractors. Bad news for thrifty farmers and thirsty livestock.

Crabs, oysters, rockfish — victuals of this land of pleasant living — all prosper when farmers back off streams, fertilizers, manure. There's no free lunch in farming.

Monday, July 18

Across from the Berlin, Maryland, marshland where Samuel D. Riddle broke and trained Man o' War rests Ocean Downs, humble trotting-track grandstand anchoring vast flatland where casinos may one day lure Ocean City beachgoers off hot sand. It's the only reason why the land hasn't been developed yet. Meanwhile, Man o' War's training track is a golf course bearing his name, amid elegant beach homes in the Glen Riddle development.

From Ocean Downs, I watch the second race from Colonial Downs on simulcast, JJ, going from grass to dirt, second half of daily double, short field. All *good signs*. So bet the double? Wallet fat with losing $2 tickets from last race. You're no handicapper. Sit tight. Buy the kids an ice cream on vacation instead.

"Your attention please: The second race on today's card has been taken off the main track and moved to the turf course."

Whadesay? Taken off the dirt, put on the grass? Never heard of such a thing! JJ hasn't gotten out of a gallop on grass. Snakebit again!

JJ runs like Man o' War. The double pays $777.80. I don't have it, of course, but the win photo is satisfaction galore.

Tuesday, July 19

Meanwhile, in Kentucky at the Fasig-Tipton sale, Dad wore his orange-and-blue Jenkin Jones cap, missed the double, too, but not the race.

"Got to Keeneland, but they don't simulcast on Mondays. Drove back to the sales, turned on TVG, had a crowd next to me cheering like mad. Everybody down here knows how hard it is to get a winner. Ombeleevobul!"

Trainer from out west hopped on the phone.

"They do that at Turf Paradise sometimes, take a race off a sloppy dirt track to run it on well-drained grass. Safer."

Wednesday, July 20

Summer reading: biography of the Marx Brothers, vaudeville a family business like farming. Groucho was wiped out in the stock crash of 1929. The idiot Harpo had the first cent he ever earned. Chico played the ponies, made deposits into Santa Anita's purse account. Whenever they needed money, they made another movie.

Broadway, Hollywood, horse racing — all home-run businesses. For every *Cats* — for every Storm Cat — there're 1,000 strays that don't purr. You make ends meet between innings, games, seasons, until the home-run horse arrives: the stakes winner, the prepotent stallion, the breakout sales yearling, the 2-year-old pinhook. It's the Marx Brothers' *A Day at the Races*, in real time.

Thursday, July 21

Condition books tell nosey owners when exams are, but not the questions. Like: Who else is running? In the $50,000 Wine Country Handicap for New York-breds last Saturday at Finger Lakes, a tiger shipped in to run in 1:08 and change. Mr. V. ran like he'd been into the grapes.

"Thanks for trying, Flint. Sorry I ever made the suggestion. Just got all these fillies back here related to him, and some black type would've improved a lot of pages."

Friday, July 22

Disappointing descent of stakes competitor Cape Cosmo into claiming ranks. We've tweaked all we can: tracks, trainers, distances. Tonight at Colonial, she loomed boldly in midstretch against $25,000 claimers, only to flatten out and finish third.

"Jock just said he lost all horse, hit a wall," Flint reported. "We scoped her to see if she bled, and she *did* have some mucus, but during the exam, she displaced her soft palate repeatedly. I think she needs a Llewellyn (procedure)."

Vets say 60 percent success rate. One step up and two steps back, such a common refrain for racing stables.

Saturday, July 23

Home from vacation, new fencing so beautiful still, critical eye comforted by improvement, not dragged down by overwhelming list of repair projects. Morale of the troops high in such surroundings. Now: Find and keep good horses in these lovely fields.

Sunday, July 24

Cumulus clouds constructing and deconstructing in the sky over Merryland all afternoon long. Reverie interrupted by sounds of a zero-turning finishing-mower choking on rocks in a small paddock. Weekend help destroying the equipment.

"It's not a bush hog!" I holler over the tumult. Down from the clouds. I feel eyes say: Gone a week, comes back like Groucho.

Monday, July 25

Bull Lea. Bold Ruler. Northern Dancer. Mr. Prospector. Storm Cat. A.P. Indy.

What's the adage? A good stallion is half the stud farm, a bad stallion all of it? Fortunes of farms are tied to a moment they don't even realize. Is Babe Ruth in the stud barn?

Bull Lea bred bottom mares at Calumet to get started. Triple Crown winner Whirlaway drained off the top mares. Trainer Ben Jones told stubborn Warren Wright: If you insist on breeding to Whirlaway, send me more Bull Leas to pay expenses.

Bold Ruler early on was criticized for not getting distance horses. He sired Secretariat, football-field winner of the marathon Belmont Stakes. Northern Dancer didn't bring a $25,000 reserve, founded a dynasty in Maryland. Mr. Prospector started in Florida for $7,500. Storm Cat's knees scared off purists. Only A.P. Indy has been the most valuable horse of his generation every moment of his life.

What farm can look at a young stallion and say he's Babe Ruth? Not one. Malibu Moon had a champion in his second crop. Baby Ruth? Who knows? No one knows. I just think about it sometimes. Don't want to be like the Red Sox, all those years, that ghost.

Tuesday, July 26

Nominations for Eastern fall yearling sale just closed. We sent Chesapeake Moon to Dr. Riddle for survey exams. Not good enough to sell, but OK to race.

Sale repository demands perfection. Like new cars. Cover in vinyl wrap. No scratches please. Horses are not so easy to shield from X-ray vision. Malibu Moon's mom stepped on his left hind pastern when he was a foal, breaking it. He'll never race, was the word. He did, warranting a stud career. Pastern never bothered him. Chesapeake Moon looks just like Pops — shark eyes, whirl of white on face. History of hard play with field mates, confirmed by X-rays. Fine to race, not to sell. Whatever. All things for a reason. Who knows.

Wednesday, July 27

Notes into a tape recorder for farm meeting.

Old business. Cords for electric fans, hang out of reach of horse teeth. Order signs for road along training track: Please Drive Slowly, Riders on Young Horses. Fresh mineral blocks in all fields. Can Dietz' boom mower whack weeds on racetrack dike? Pick up trash along Bottom Road.

New business? Yes? Go ahead. Sure, we'll find a used bush hog to mow the smaller paddocks.

Thursday, July 28

Out of season, Belmont Park echoes. On the backstretch, stalls are thrown open, go unbedded, to dry out from constant use. The first-string is up at Saratoga. Untried 2-year-olds, unsound older horses, stay behind. Any day now, the main track closes to grade for the fall meet, Breeders' Cup coming to town. Only the training track open for business.

In a stall separated from the barn office by the gap midway in the barn, under close eye, stands an injured young equine athlete. Bandages are removed to let air breathe onto a surgery site, screws knitting a cannon bone. Chain over his gum, he is led out of his stall, taking his first ginger steps on the path to a new life.

Friday, July 29

Merryland Monroe and Alleged Moon both breezed in :39.4 for three furlongs, their longest timed work so far. Wahoo Moon in new shoes went a quarter in :25.8. Slow times certainly, but it's how easy they do it. Yeager can't keep up, worked an eighth in :12.4. Matriculation at Monmouth scuttled for community college Timonium. Such an advantage to clock the young horses, to peek at answers, before they are tested by finishing schools.

Saturday, July 30

"Now her other knee is bothering her," said Flint. "Sorry to be sending her home having missed breeding season."

On a stormy day a summer ago, Hookedonjoy burst from mid-pack in a maiden race at Delaware Park to win like any kind. Chipped her knee, though. Surgery. R&R at Merryland. Well, she's a sister to our best mare. A family known for big hearts, bad knees. So fast. So fragile. Speed supreme. Slow horses stay sound, but who looks forward to breeding them?

Sunday, July 31

Most valuable player this month? No question: JJ, poster child for Merryland graduates. Dirt to grass. Go figure. That move on the rail. Sweeping to the lead. Nice maiden special weight race. Hard to shake memory of that day. Powers us past disappointments of July.

Come August's shimmering heat, trumpets will sound from Del Mar to Saratoga, San Mateo to Timonium, post parades at splendid spas, at county fairs.

Back at the ranch, Merryland's new-old water truck splashes a path on the training track, tightening the cushion, securing the footing, stretching the skin of sand over the drum that beats a universal rhythm heard anywhere, everywhere hooves pound.

August

Monday, August 1

Most everyone in this game can name an experience in youth when the music started playing — a searching, yearning piano theme, a song of promise, lyrics calling down the road. Strong sense of secret invitation. Come along. Don't tell your parents. Or do?

Was it the smell of a pony on rides at the fair? Was it a grandfather's hug as he pulled you close to tell you about his horse? Was it a bicycle ride past the fence that separated shedrows from this outside world? Was it a book? Maybe *The Black Stallion*, read in one long sitting, afternoon light giving way to a lamp, a break to answer the dinner call, right back until the hardcover closed, legs aching from being curled underneath, unaware. Was it the gray Native Dancer on a black-and-white screen?

Adrenaline rushed at the thought of horses.

Tuesday, August 2

Summer reading, Red Smith: "Wherefore a small boy, if he is to be reared properly, must be taken to the track for the morning works."

Wednesday, August 3

Today we waited by the phone, absently, intently, to hear if a deal would be made for a new stallion. A meeting of the minds between Kentucky agents. Agreement in principle. A lot of marriages don't last as long as it takes to get a stallion's first crop to the races. In short order: blind date, courtship, proposal, pause.

Thursday, August 4

Filled out a marriage license of sorts today. A relief to have everything signed before Saratoga tempts other suitors.

Friday, August 5

"East Jet's off. Hasn't been quite right since the win. Probably a chip."

Iconic horseman John Gaines felt that we ask too much of young horses, fuel-

ing a sense that modern horses are more delicate than yesteryear's. Why? Because *everyone* pushes 2-year-olds. Gaines believed: If allowed to mature, horses would in fact be sounder than forebears.

But give up the thrill of 2-year-old racing? Pass up dough while training bills roll? Kind of like telling kids not to look into the sun. But Johnny, that's where the fun is!

Saturday, August 6

Two-year-old Merryland Monroe stepped down from a van this week at Delaware Park. Trainer took one look at her, said: "She's a star. I'll take my time with her."

Gaines' way.

Sunday, August 7

Confederate cavalryman Harry Gilmor was born near Merryland, at Loch Raven. He slipped across the Potomac when hostilities flared. In July of 1864, Colonel Gilmor returned to harass Baltimore, burning railroad bridges and cutting telegraph lines all the way to the Gunpowder River.

"At daylight we crossed the Bel Air and Harford Roads, but had not gone far when I heard a shot," Gilmor wrote. "When I reached the house of Ishmael Day, I found my ordnance sergeant, Fields, lying on the ground, his face and chest filled with buckshot. He was perfectly rational; told me he had ordered Day to pull down a large federal flag, which he refused to do; that he dismounted to do it himself, when Day seized a gun and shot him. Day's house was in flames. The men stood around us in violent gesticulation, swearing terribly."

I can't drive down Sunshine Avenue to Merryland without thinking a cavalryman died a horrible death here, while a neighbor lost his home, his barns. A roadside Civil War plaque won't let me.

Monday, August 8

It's one thing for Troy and Rachael to teach young horses to breeze, jogging up to a furlong pole with increasing speed until they break off in full gallop. It's quite another to break from a starting gate into a breeze — from 0-to-40 at the clang of a bell.

Though we have a gate at Merryland, gate cards require track personnel.

"If we had stalls at Pimlico," Rachael suggested today, "we could get gate cards from the starter, familiarize the babies with the sights and sounds of a mile track, and deliver ready-to-race 2-year-olds to trainers."

And so Christy orders blue stall webbings. Laurie paints colors onto tack boxes. Rachael negotiates with a groom named Butch to sign on. School is never out for me. The Education of Little Tree continues.

Tuesday, August 9

The County Hearing Examiner reviews plans for a 500-student private high school a half-mile down Old Joppa Road. Rural connector to become clogged

artery. We'll wind up stuck in our own driveway. Farming seems superfluous to municipal fathers — so delighted that someone other than the county might pay for a school, for road "improvements."

Resolve to fight made easier when farms are named Merryland, with its pony rides for grown-ups. Named Country Life, home to black stallions, soon a new bay. So we fight to keep a dream alive — Grandfather's idea, a suit or two he wore on trains to New York City still hanging in camphored closets, traded in decades ago for a life in the country. *A life in the country.*

Wednesday, August 10

For some, for many, the music fades. August is a month of evaluation, maybe followed by transition. Lucid moments in sleepless nights. What am I doing?

Employees recover, or don't, from breeding season. So physically demanding, farm work. Racetrack gypsy life weighed against options, like having a family and being a part of it.

Semester break in a hard school.

Thursday, August 11

In the summer of 1863, one month after Union victories at Gettysburg and Vicksburg signaled the end, gaiety reigned at Saratoga's inaugural meet. In 1865, the Saratoga Association for the Improvement of the Breed of Horses was incorporated. Parcels of land large and small were cobbled out of the old fairgrounds neighborhood to form today's grounds.

The New York Racing Association's license expires in 2007. Intrigue abounds as to who owns the land, reports today's *Saratoga Spotlight* paper. If NYRA's franchise is lost, title searches may reach back 144 years. Who owns Saratoga Race Course? NYRA, formed in 1955, has paid property taxes for 50 years. But New York says NYRA's title would go to the state's Capital Improvement Fund.

Rumors blow of a civil war in civil court.

Friday, August 12

Hall-of-Fame trainer Allen Jerkens sits atop his pony like an equestrian statue of a Gettysburg general. Grooms pedal bikes to detention barns, backpacks stuffed with bandages, brushes; haynets swing from handlebars. Flower baskets bloom in gracious green barns. Horses skim on a brown track, in relief against red-striped quarter-poles. Grooms drape flannel on lines behind barns. Horses — millions of dollars of horses — cross Nelson Avenue to parade down Crescent Street to reach barns in neighborhoods.

All around, the sound of shod feet echo on blacktop, or on the hard track — background music to lyrics of trainers rapping with owners, exercise riders singing.

A hundred years ago, Sherwood Anderson wrote of Saratoga: "If you've never been crazy about Thoroughbreds it's because you've never been around where they are much and don't know any better."

Saturday, August 13

When NYRA gives away 50,000 flimsy 100-percent polyester blankets made in China, it reports turnstile revolutions as the attendance figure. Total today: 70,000. Yet "spinners" number in the thousands. I saw a flip-flopped father headed home with a dozen blankets, each free with a $3 admission, each stenciled with the letters S-A-R-A-T-O-G-A, bearing a tiny image of a racehorse in 18th-century style; front

legs outstretched in the gap in the G, hind legs trailing in the preceding O, under an awning of Saratoga shaped like a badminton shuttlecock. Blankets to warm an NFL armchair come January.

If Secretariat paraded today, would 70,000 fans show up? But ... give away a Secretariat blanket? How can anyone come to the track, spin around, and leave without seeing any horses? It's a disconcerting disconnect at the heart of racing's attendance woes. *Horses* are an abstract. It'd give Sherwood Anderson the fantods.

Sunday, August 14

In zeal to comply with strict state oversight, NYRA officials sometimes put form over substance. In a sparse crowd before the fourth race, 11-year-old son August was escorted from the paddock under armed guard — for wearing shorts. He thus joined an august legion of horsemen to have run afoul of Saratoga's finest over the past century and a half — few at so tender an age, though, or for so slight an offense.

Monday, August 15

Tommy Voss doesn't say much, so I listen up: "The detention barn is a mess. High plywood walls. No windows. Stalls eight-by-eight. Horses holler and scream. Kicked walls sound like gunshots. Rowdy lost 100 pounds, time she walked into the paddock."

Terence Collier of Fasig-Tipton bolts breakfast while considering the Japanese solution: "The only vets allowed belong to the Japan Racing Association. Drugs are dispensed through the JRA only. Try doing that here and you'd have infringement lawsuits."

Dan Hayden of Sugar Maple Farm recalled last year's expensive sale yearling: "Buyer told me the colt bit into Christmas lights and electrocuted himself."

A 2-year-old race on today's card listed the babies' prices at auction: about $3 million total. Rainbows arc off the glacial plain of the Oklahoma training track.

Befuddling. Beautiful. Enlightening. Exhausting.

Saratoga.

Tuesday, August 16

"Don't you need a teaser? He'd be perfect."

First call at home is from Long Island businessman gettin' nothin' but bills for Nothin' But Heat. Perhaps a gelding with testosterone from a concealed source *would* make a nice teaser: no hardware for maiden mares to kick. Hmmm, he *is* well named. The morning teasing report come spring? "Nothin' but heat from the mares."

So, another mouth to feed, a utility infielder who bats .175 but sacrifices his body for the team.

Wednesday, August 17

The new fencing is weathering a tawny brown.

"I stuck my meter in it," said Nick of Buddy Bitt fencing. "It's still carrying 20 percent moisture. Oh, I measured the footage. It'll cost a bit to paint."

Fencing at Castleton Lyons, Malibu Moon's Kentucky home, is painted a unique color for the Bluegrass — not white nor black, but *taupe*, kind of yellow-brown. Our fence is pausing at taupe. But if black paint will extend it a generation? Before Buddy Bitt puts the bite on us, it'd help to win some races.

Thursday, August 18

Recruiting trip. Flight out to L.A., over arid Arizona. It's all so simple from the air, water on geology, as though a single giant wave had pounded in and rolled back out, bringing down mountains.

First thing I see at the hotel, headline in the Arcadia *News*: "Development plans for Santa Anita's surplus lands." This on the heels of Hollywood Park's sale. Who can stop the wave of development from bringing down racetracks?

Friday, August 19

Santa Anita when Del Mar is running is similar to Belmont when Saratoga is on. Trainers shuttle, stables split. Ron Ellis arrives at Santa Anita at five a.m., four hours after driving up from Del Mar. It's pitch black, save for diffuse light from the Santa Anita Mall's parking garage. Tricked by artificial light, a rooster crows. You could be at a farm, so complete is the illusion of Santa Anita's backstretch.

Ron's exercise rider appears, but he is dressed entirely in black. Ron shakes his head, makes a face. "He's gonna be hard to spot on Declan."

In the half-light of the walking ring waits the champion 2-year-old male of 2004, Declan's Moon, a black horse with four low white socks. Ron gives the rider a leg up, leads the undefeated champ down the raised path to the track. At the gap, Ron stands with Declan as horses gallop past, then he reaches down to hoof-pick packed dirt from Declan's feet. "I'm asking him to work. He needs traction." I think of horses in winter, balls of snow stuck in their feet. Declan disappears into the black.

Clockers catch the three-furlong work in :39 and change. Just right in his comeback from arthroscopic surgery in March. Back at the barn, I stand by his deep black shoulder and scratch his withers, in wonderment at what this one horse has meant to us. Who's responsible for whom? Us for him, or him for us?

Saturday, August 20

Scouting trip to Del Mar. During breaks to condition the chocolate-brown track, tractors stagger five wide, rubber tank-treads distributing weight on the cuppy mud after water trucks pass. A Munnings painting of anxious horses animates the chute. Riders circle on a living merry-go-round, like a huge walk-up start. Before the last tractor exits, a cavalry charge gallops down the freshly furrowed track. It's like

watching Custer's Last Stand, horses everywhere. If Sherwood Anderson were alive, he'd wax on about Del Mar, too.

Sunday, August 21

Surveillance guards are posted for 24 hours at stalls of entries in the $1-million Pacific Classic. "If it makes the fans more confident in racing, we'll do it," says Del Mar's brass.

Annabelle Stute tells about the peach-colored roses Del Mar presented when she won a race Thursday. Husband Mel says never mind, put these tickets in your purse for taxes. He says old-timers bet closers when the tide's up, the track turning heavy when sea water percolates underneath.

Trumpeters dressed like Zorro cruise the patios.

Where's Perfect Moon? I ask Mel, his former trainer.

Hess' barn.

Trevor Denman's voice drops an octave: *"and a-WAAAAY they go ...*

Monday, August 22

He's lost a step, certainly. His ankles are rounded, bone remodeling under the stress of hard California tracks. But this plain brown wrapper of a horse started the incredible journey to the taupe fences of the Bluegrass for Malibu Moon.

"If he ever takes a bad step and you want to retire him ..."

Bob Hess nods in understanding, but horses in claiming ranks are anybody's buy. As a $4,700 yearling (now a graded winner of $500,959), Perfect Moon was broken at Merryland the first year we had the farm. He'd make a perfect pony for J.R. Make a perfect ending to the fairy tale.

Tuesday, August 23

On descent across Virginia into Maryland, the Blue Ridge Mountains rise like a single fold in a vast carpet on the floor of the Shenandoah Valley. Farmland lies west of the fold; suburbs to the east, stretching unbroken beyond Baltimore. The plane overshoots northeast of the sprawling city, to turn back into the wind, the way geese land. The outline of Merryland's track appears below my tilted window, brown oval distinct against green fields.

All those *whereases* recited on the purchase agreement four years ago await me. *Now, therefore …*

Wednesday, August 24

Twenty-one horses in training come down to the track in sets of three, as Troy, Rachael, and Lauren instill a strong sense of routine to training hours. Back in the yearling barn, Loye lays tack on the first group of babies to be broken.

It's summer school for equine athletes. I can't resist this place. Wonder why I ever go away. Sort of like being president of a small college — the minuscule University of Merryland — away for fund-raising, recruitment, back at school enough to know the students. The best part.

Thursday, August 25

Block walls at soon-to-be-demolished Shenandoah got a head start from Jenkin Jones.

"I've wrapped his feet in flannel and duct tape, but he enjoys kicking the wall," said groom Mike Harvey. Shenandoah is third-world, held together by baling twine and dreams. Crude murals tell horse stories on plywood: ghetto graffiti. JJ shipped in yesterday from Penn National for tonight's allowance. Under lights for the first

time. The track announcer calls out as they turn for home: "Jenkin Jones will have something to say about it tonight."

JJ charges for the beam of yellow light that marks the wire at this night track, *just* runs out of ground. Chart-caller writes "second by a neck," but the reverse-angle shows a nose. Slots fuel second-place purses, too. A few more nights like this, JJ, and we'll get the fence painted.

Friday, August 26

En route to son August's soccer tourney in Gettysburg (dubbed the Battlefield Blast), my eye caught the unmistakable sweep of a racetrack turn, wooden railing, grass covering a once-dirt track. Brick entrance gates displayed the famous name of Bowling Brook Farm.

I had heard of Bowling Brook but never seen it. Googled it when I reached the motel. An odd reference popped up first, for antique "tall case clocks." Seems trainer Robert Wyndham Walden and wife moved to Maryland from New York in 1872, bringing a beautiful clock for the hallway of their home: cherry cabinet, 1810. Walden saddled five straight Preakness winners (1878-82), won seven Preaknesses in all. I could almost hear that clock ringing out over Bowling Brook's track on splendid spring mornings.

Several of Walden's fabulous barns have resisted neglect, have aged into a shade of taupe. They backdrop the grounds behind the manor house, now a country inn, a site for wedding receptions.

Online, I read further: "Top-heavy and unstable, tall case clocks went out of fashion."

Oh, my aching heart. The same may one day be said about horse farms in this intensely developing state.

SUMMER 2005

Saturday, August 27

At Charles Town last night, jockey Carlos Castro was launched headfirst at 40 mph onto the track when his mount snapped a leg, fell, broke its neck, never moved again. Castro crawled like a gunshot victim underneath the rail.

"Get the board! Get the board!" cried a woman to the ambulance crew half-a-mile across the track. In the suspense, she explained herself: "I'm a chiropractor. I visit the jocks' room every night an hour before the races. I know every ache on every jockey."

The ambulance crew lifted Castro to his feet as he clutched his shoulder. She winced in sympathetic pain, swore at the medics. Not 15 minutes later, Castro rode up out of the sunken paddock at Charles Town for the next race. I was shocked. Never seen anything in sports to rival it. Boom. Down. Forty-to-zero, from five feet high. Force enough to kill a horse. Back up for the next race? No way. But it was just another forgotten moment in a workingman's life. "Part of the game," clucked a valet as Castro rode up the hill. "Part of the game."

Poet John Hay described such risk:
The night comes down, the lights burn blue;
And at my door the Pale Horse stands,
To bear me forth to unknown lands.

Sunday, August 28

August's team won four in a row yesterday. Just skirmishes, really, in the Battlefield Blast. But they faced hardened veterans today. Zero for two by afternoon's end. August looked like one of Pickett's survivors, his coach glum as Longstreet.

"Dad, let's just go home."

Lee's troops limped away from here trailed by a 17-mile wagon train of wounded. I loaded bikes on the minivan, glad to have my boy back in one piece. He fell into his book and put the battle behind him. Bronze generals on horseback covered our retreat.

Monday, August 29

"I don't want any horses on the van, especially not a filly. He's 60 days off surgery. He's been in a stall the whole time. He could be full of himself. He could be studdish. Can you have an attendant? I'll meet you at Belmont at 11. You'll be bringing him home alone."

Tuesday, August 30

Scott the van man arrives at the chute. The van has been steam-cleaned, rubber floor black as new. Dividers set at a stall-and-a-half, so the colt can ride with his hindquarters against the cab, to brace for traffic. A closed-circuit camera in the cab. An attendant. Let's go.

The colt walks out of the barn in white shipping bandages. I snap a getaway photo of the trainer and the groom, one last shot with a favorite horse, then the doors close. Scott halts at the Stable Gate as the trainer signs out the horse, hands the Coggins and a health certificate up into the cab. The blue van turns right onto Hempstead Turnpike. Forty minutes later, cell phone rings. Scott's name. Heart skips. What's happened?

"Just lettin' you know we cleared New York. On the Jersey Turnpike now. Tell the farm we'll be there by three."

Wednesday, August 31

As a boy Tommy Albertrani, who trained Oratory, rode his bike up Elmont Road to hotwalk for his uncle the trainer. Ellen had a boy pony named Bonnie under cedar trees in her childhood yard. I read all *The Black Stallion* books. A partner's aunt married Exterminator's owner, trophies now heirlooms. Dad smiles when someone brags about how long they've been coming to Saratoga. "I was there *in utero*," he cracks.

You either hear the music or you don't. It's "Reverie" when the rooster crows the barn awake. It's "Garry Owen" when you win a race. It's "Taps" when you lose horses.

September

Thursday, September 1

It's reckless behavior to like horses. Four-legged creatures of infinite caprice, they inhabit a world all their own, where nothing is certain except a good story.

Mark Twain, on any horse: "My experience is that they never throw away an excuse to go lame, and that in all respects, they are well-meaning and unreliable animals."

A.J. Liebling, though, understood the sweet obsession, and wrote of J.R. Keene: "The triumphs of his horses were to him the most potent of tonics, accountable, according to his physicians, for his continued survival."

Friday, September 2

It's orientation day at Pimlico. Like parents of incoming freshmen, Rachael and Troy haul necessities into the Pimlico barn where Merrylanders Dancer in the Citi, Yeager's Jet, Flame in Moon, and Haldy arrive to begin college.

Ellen stenciled farm silks onto blue webbings: orange jacket, blue polka dots on sleeves. And a blue cap, tilted at the rakish angle of a confident jockey, sleeves cocked with invisible hand on hip. A jump-jockey pose. Awaiting riding instructions. As minimalist as Keeneland's wispy three-legged logo. Comfortably repeatable *ad infinitum*.

Dancer in the Citi leans out over her webbing, licks the logo loose, customizing her dorm room.

Saturday, September 3

These days, purse money for Maryland-bred stakes often is redirected to maintain daily purses. Solid populist thinking, but anathematic to breeders — this loss of easy black type.

When the Timonium Fair carded the restricted $50,000 Alma North Stakes today, every padded cell in the starting gate carried the hopes of delusional breeders. Farm silks on Mrs. Vanderbilt and Surf Light.

Haughty Mrs. V. considered lowly Timonium beneath her, ran last. Surf Light, though, ran fifth, just a neck and a head away from earning lower-case boldface type, from bolstering her chance to make the broodmare band instead of the mixed sale here at Timonium.

But *almost* only counts in horseshoes, and we filed on down the midway, past the Tunnel of Love, just another lonely heart.

Sunday, September 4

The 17-mile drive from la-la Merryland to hard-luck Pimlico carries you into the harsh world of the urban racetrack. East of the shedrows lie the killing fields of Baltimore, Reisterstown Road a shooting gallery for heroin and handguns. Looking west, over the starting gate for the Preakness, rise the handsome slate roofs of the

tony Mt. Washington neighborhood. Pimlico is the Berlin Wall separating East from West. Tacit understanding in debate over slots: If Pimlico falls, the haves of Mt. Washington will be overrun by the have-nots. Prejudice unspoken, fear palpable: for safety, perhaps equally so for real-estate values. There goes the neighborhood, the Mounties will cry.

Monday, September 5

At 7 o'clock yesterday morning, a red subcompact spun out on Bottom Road below the racetrack dike. It crashed through two pipe gates, three panels of board fencing. Slivers of oak lanced the windshield, ripped past the dome light. Four teenage boys climbed out, unscathed, but easily could've had a fence post between the eyes. They left a note, radioed a friend, and got the hell out of their Dodge before the fuzz arrived to breathalize.

In this fashion, an all-nighter ended violently in a breakfast wreck in Jersey Moon's paddock. Maurilio heard the whole thing, ran down to make sure the colt didn't escape out the yawning hole in the fence. Last week, the colt was withdrawn from a New Jersey-bred yearling show because we didn't want to risk holiday traffic. Instead, a car rockets into his field.

"Found a lot of drugs scattered about," Teddy told me this morning, his back sore from setting new posts in rock-hard drought ground, from tacking up boards. "Meth. Pot pipes. Stuff like that." Teddy loaded gnarled gates and splintered wood into the tractor bucket, hoisted it high to see underneath as he maneuvered back through the farm. Ellen took photos for insurance claims.

If God didn't look after drunks and children — *both* in this case — we could have had a quadruple vehicular homicide to remember this Labor Day.

Tuesday, September 6

Rachael recounts progress of Pimlico students as I stare over the infield and consider the nickname "Old Hilltop." When Alfred G. Vanderbilt owned the track in the 1930s, he ordered his workers to smooth out the gentle infield knoll that obstructed the view of apron patrons. He cared about the fan, and in 1938, so many thronged to see Seabiscuit duel War Admiral that Vanderbilt opened up the infield. One out of three Americans listened to the race on radio.

The Cohen brothers made parking spaces after the classic clubhouse burned in 1966. Google preakness.com — history, and up pops the Magna Web site, the iconic clubhouse its signature photo: wedding cake construction, cars with fins, men with hats. You can hear history any morning at Pimlico. Careful, though. It's not all as romantic as Clem McCarthy's call of the match race.

"And Seabiscuit's the winner! By four lengths! And you never saw such a wild crowd. Trying to drown this crowd out here. Seabiscuit's the winner!"

Wednesday, September 7

On a spectacular opening day at Laurel, in celebration of a new $30-million turf course, Magna dispatched its most recent executive spokesman, Paul Cellucci, the former Massachusetts governor who oversaw overspending on the "Big Dig" in Boston, to inform local horsemen that racing days in Maryland will be slashed in half: from 220 to 110 days. Just gonna run a little 18-day meet at Pimlico for the Preakness, then close until November. When asked to elaborate, sincerity was sliced thin as a cue card.

Nearly 70 years ago Vanderbilt knocked the hill out of Old Hilltop. Today, Magna knocked the wind out of her. The Big Dig at Maryland racing is all over the news tonight.

Thursday, September 8

You're talking about a track that opened on October 25, 1870. Two days later a colt named Preakness won the Dinner Party Stakes. Almost a *century and a half* of morning gallops. How many, though, on a day with the track's fate in such debate? Entire top page headline of the *Sun:* "A Sad Day for Horsemen."

With our superb sense of timing, the first group of Merryland graduates galloped over the historic Pimlico oval. Like being late to the freshman party, rocking the keg to see how much beer is left.

Friday, September 9

A groom from the next barn over called: "Hey, I used to work here with your brother, Andrew. Tell him I was asking for him!"

The track is a community like no other, friends for life.

Saturday, September 10

Brother Andrew apprenticed under Hall of Fame trainer Henry Clark when Delaware Park was summer home to fashionable stables, its tree-lined backstretch second in charm only to Saratoga. By the mid-1990s, though, $2,500 claimers were daily fare. Under threat of development, Delaware Park was on her knees when the legislature legalized slots.

Amnesia reigned today as Delaware handed out $900,000 in purses on Owner's Day. Nouveau-riche owners couldn't set down complimentary lunch plates fast enough to ask: "When are you guys in Maryland gonna get your act together?"

Afleet Alex paraded in the paddock. The reigning horse-of-the-moment would not be Delaware's hometown hero without slots. Cash is king at Delaware, where 2,500 whirring collection plates extract the daily purse subsidy.

In Henry Clark's era, backstretch help climbed into a boxing ring once a week, to the betting amusement of other grooms. As Maryland boxes her way through a 15-rounder, I turned a cauliflower ear to the din of Delaware owners. All this largesse didn't come from brown horses running, but from yellow lemons, red cherries aligning in atavistic impulse, machinery of the luck business sanctioned by Dover politicians.

Farm horses Merryland Monroe and New York Moon are in Tim Ritchey's Delaware barn. Our hearts in Maryland, we hedge our bets in this funny-money game.

Sunday, September 11

Racing caricaturist "Peb" paraded in the Delaware paddock today, in his role as founder of the Amateur Riders' Club of America. A posse of his riders posed for a group photo. Anxious mothers prayed for a clean trip, a safe return. I closed my eyes when green racehorses veered into the gap on the turf course that runs back up the chute. Riders fought with the zeal of amateur boxers, but luckily finished unbattered, unbruised.

Monday, September 12

First day of Keeneland's yearling sale, a 15-day marathon, the pavilion like a hot-air balloon rising for four select days, then beginning a gentle descent to land three Mondays from now. Brother Mike took the first two-day shift at the most important trade show in the game.

Tuesday, September 13

At 2 p.m. on TVG, I watch a Storm Cat colt sell for $9.7 million. You can push paper anytime. Something big's going on 600 miles away.

"Dad, you want to drive to Kentucky with me?"

"Let me ask your mother." He shuffles over the flagstones to the house.

"How long will you be gone?" she asks me over the phone.

"Three days."

"When are you leaving?"

"Fifteen minutes."

"He wants to go. Let me pack his clothes."

Five hours to slice through the thinnest, longest, hilliest part of Maryland, at one spot only two miles wide between Pennsylvania and West Virginia, the leaves green in the drought, no moisture in them to begin the autumn turn. Three hours down, out, and deep into West Virginia, over to Ashland, Kentucky, its netherworld of refinery fires like blazing portals to Oz.

"A hundred miles to go, Pop."

"Call your mother. Tell her we made it."

Wednesday, September 14

Someone else's father rides shotgun from Keeneland to Ironworks Pike.

"For me, the horse business is my life insurance," he turns to a newcomer in the back seat to explain the fascinating attraction of this perilous game. "Remember when you were a kid waiting in the classroom for recess? So excited that you stared at the clock — and it didn't move. *Time stood still.* That's what horses do for me. I look forward to it so much. They make time stand still. Look at all the old guys in this business. They're not waiting around to die. They've got 2-year-olds in the barn they're living for."

Thursday, September 15

A hundred years ago, horseman J. Calvin Milam bought 531 acres off Tates Creek Pike two miles from downtown Lexington, named the farm Merrick Place after the gelding Merrick, who made 205 starts. The "kindliest" of Kentucky's "older generation of horsemen," Milam cared for Merrick until the horse's death at 38 years old, a Guinness record at the time.

Milam practiced the art of selling young racehorses, such as Exterminator, to rich men to win the Kentucky Derby. If the sport of racing were a 10-story building, he made a smart living riding the elevator to the fifth floor. A pioneer pinhooker. An admirable horseman. Dust-to-dust now, though.

Tonight, at dinner at the Merrick Inn, in all that remains of Milam's career work, premonitions visited me. I don't want the back of a menu to ever read a similar story for Country Life, for Merryland.

Friday, September 16

Raise a Native is buried at Spendthrift Farm. Dad folds his arms across his belly. I know where he's going with this.

"Your grandfather bred Raise a Native's dam, Raise You, by Case Ace, by Teddy. Foaled at the farm in 1946. Sold her at Saratoga to Corty Wetherill. I guess he should have kept her, but he'd carried the farm through the war while John and Addie and I were away in the service. Raise You won the Colleen at Monmouth. She produced Raise a Native, who sired Mr. Prospector. I look at the gravestone there and I know we played a part."

We stopped at the farm J.R. Keene made famous as Castleton, said hello to Malibu Moon. Smiles all around. Limestone cliffs of Eastern Kentucky sailed past the car window on the ride home. We stopped at a Kentucky Fried Chicken for lunch, not ready, just yet, to let go of the promised land.

"Better take some home for Richard, for Monday Night Football," Dad said as he stared at choices, waited for me to figure it out. With authentic integrity, he carried a little bit of Kentucky back home with him. In just three days, the trees had turned ever so subtly toward fall as we lifted out of Mink Shoals, West By God Virginia, and made for Maryland.

Saturday, September 17

Brice Ridgely bull-horned his way around the equipment of a farm selling out to buyers of two-acre lots.

"See you brought the brains with you," Brice grumbled at me, winking at son Josh. I stared at a 15-year-old water truck that I thought might someday replace the 30-year-old one at Merryland, but didn't bid. After it sold cheap, I paused and stared: nonbuyer's remorse.

"Dad. It sold. OK? You had your chance. You can't buy it now. Keep moving."

You got to admire a kid who knows when to let go. The essence of auction success. There will always be more horses. There will always be more trucks.

Sunday, September 18

The 900-horse catalogue for Maryland's October yearling sale can occupy you right through a Sunday soccer game.

"Didn't you see that push?" screamed a father next to me.

"No. Did my son do it?"

"No, the *other* team did."

Driving away from athletic fields built on a landfill made famous on Saturdays a generation ago (Dad, guess what we found at the dump today?), I told August he could see Country Life from this mounded ground. A mile away, a row of pine trees stood sentinel in the lane. Oriented at an odd perspective. Somebody has to teach you where to look.

"Wow, I see it," he said, left-handed, left-footed, left-brained, so facile.

Monday, September 19

Teddy rises at five, first to arrive. He kicks over the ancient engine on the water truck and settles the 1,800-gallon tanker underneath a welded I-beam elbow suspended gallows-like 10 feet above ground. Teddy's track-maintenance routine is underway.

Two-inch plastic pipe crawls down the I-beam, runs buried to a pool in the bubbling brook that courses through the farm. A dam of locust logs, anchored by boulders, conceals a submersible pump that jets creek water at 60-gallons-per-minute up the 40-foot climb to the hanging nozzle. Twenty minutes for the water truck to fill.

During that time, Teddy backs the tractor up to a 10-foot-wide steel plate that he uses to compress the sandy cushion to a less porous consistency. Two quick circles of the track, and he's back at the water truck. He cuts the electric switch to the submersible, slides in the '75 International, punches into first gear, and lumbers through the double gates on the track's outside rail. In two loads, he spreads 3,600 gallons on a 3,000-foot oval 30-feet wide.

Then he opens the track back up with the Perfecta harrow, its curled teeth cutting furrows, a whirling set of blades like old manual lawn mowers bolted to the rear of the harrow, fluffing the sand into a soft landing.

Ninety minutes of maintenance. By the time Teddy grabs his Thermos cup from the tractor seat, riders' cars stream in the driveway.

Tuesday, September 20

You go with what works for you. Stalls of Merryland are full of the progeny of one sire. Mark Twain said keep all your eggs in one basket, *but watch that basket.*

Wednesday, September 21

Dad keeps a diary, a day-at-a-glance book, in the telephone room. He scratches the weather in it mostly, but terse racing news is archived as well.

New York Moon woke up today in a breeze at Delaware, I tell him. I'll see a scribbled "NYM, 5/8 good work" in the book he leaves open by the phone in the hall.

Thursday, September 22

Former star teaser Jazzman took up babysitting to earn his oats, teaching manners to orphaned foals. These days, arthritic beyond comprehension, Jazzy leans out

his yoke screen with the quiet dignity of an ancient warrior. Age undeterminable. Maybe 35? Maybe Merrick's age?

There's high ground up near Freedom Field in Merryland's woods, for horses whose day has come. I'll watch Jazzman be turned out for the night, dragging locked knees. When I think we're keeping him alive for our sakes not his, I'll take him up the hill. A broken-down teaser as a Gladiator? The line from the movie of that name, implying we'll all know the moment when it comes, won't be silenced in my head: "*Not yet.*"

Friday, September 23

Merryland's beguiling charm on display yesterday, as sister Alice hosted a retreat for nurses from the Johns Hopkins oncology ward. The theme, "Stepping Towards the Future," required the nurses to write of traumatic experiences. Journaling on perches throughout the farm — in haylofts, under trees, on hillsides — the nurses evoked the gentle inmates who escaped the nuthouse in the movie *King of Hearts*, taking over an abandoned French village in World War I. A fresh cast of characters seeking asylum at the old sanitarium.

Saturday, September 24

"You understand what a condyle is, don't you, son?" Dr. Stephen Selway began the lecture last month, the day we picked up the new stallion Oratory. Socrates in the open-air theater of the Belmont backstretch. He answered his own question. "Condyles are rounded protuberances of bone that articulate with other bones." He pressed a fisted hand upon the knuckles of the other. "The colt suffered a condylar

fracture at the base of his cannon in a workout. Momentum carried him before the rider could pull him up. When I put screws in, I cleaned out small fragments of broken bone.

"Bone takes time to grow. We are trying to minimize arthritic changes. Stall-rest for now. Take X-rays in 30 days, send 'em to me here at Belmont. I'll let you know when you can begin hand-walking him."

This afternoon, on Dr. Nick Meittinis' digital X-ray machine, instant images illustrated the Socratic lecture. Beautiful healing. Almost there. A matter of vigilance for now.

Sunday, September 25

In a room crowded with celebrants of sobriety, Andrew used his anniversary to impart a message to nephews and nieces. You may have a gene for this disease, but you also have a gene for recovery. The ventilator fan suddenly fell silent while he spoke of memories of Pimlico mornings, shifting sands in the luck game of a racing life. You could hear a one-day chip drop.

"I had to get out. At first, I couldn't find a sponsor. No wonder. I was looking for someone between Gandhi and Robin Williams."

Monday, September 26

John Steinbeck's story *The Red Pony* ends with buzzards circling.

A rich-chestnut colt arrived last month, was stabled in the broodmare barn awaiting breaking, when he extended his head outside and down on his stall door, grabbed the heavy drop latch, and made his nocturnal escape. Shanette heard a commotion as she turned off her lights, came up in her slippers to find the Red Pony scraped up near the fence, where he tried and failed to join other yearlings.

X-rays of his stifle were negative. Paint with DMSO.

His stall now has a safety chain on its latch. The barn now has two green boards on each end. They slide into sleeves. What one horse does to commit suicide, others will attempt. It's their nature. Read Steinbeck. They're all just death-bent ponies, buzzard-bait waiting to happen. If you understand that, you've arrived at healthy paranoia.

Last worker out, put up the boards.

Tuesday, September 27

At Pimlico again. Looking for 2-year-olds to show they carry the "run gene." Haldy, all 15 hands of him, swaggers back to the barn after his workout, ancestral senses awakening. I think: It's not the size of the dog in the fight. It's the size of the fight in the dog. His groom Butch never stops moving, a short-order cook, barn humming with his activity, quiet and quick-paced. He bends under a chain to duck into a stall, unmindful of exposure to a kick from a horse tied to the wall at the far end. The babies can't wait for Butch's hands on them. They love their groom. I could watch this interplay all day.

Wednesday, September 28

"Her barn name is Hussy Wench," Rachael explains about a filly next barn over, famous for dumping riders, for running loose midst the manure piles of Pimlico. "Be doing us all a favor if she kills herself before she kills a rider."

Thursday, September 29

Entries flood in to Fasig-Tipton for the December mixed sale, local breeders feeling the no-slots squeeze, scared of reduced racing days. Savvy Kentuckians search for venues outside the saturated Bluegrass. All of us ask: Who to keep? Who to sell? Who to simply *give* away?

Nobody wants used mares. Maryland's a weanling market. Unproven is better than unproductive. Sell the best. Cull the rest. Keep a filly.

Friday, September 30

Oh, it's such an uncertain future. Headlines of tracks in distress. It's like *A Day at the Races*, all of us in racing like Marx Brothers trying to save the sanitariums from the Mr. Morgans of this world, who wear suits like sharkskin.

But in this sport, all God's children got rhythm. There's just too many good people in this game. We'll get by with a little help from our friends.

FALL
2005

October

Saturday, October 1

On days when the old barn roof leaks, or the tax assessor ups the tithe, or the county approves another fast-food furnace nearby, or a mare dies, or Homeland Security screws up the Mexicans' paperwork, I think of Woody Allen's movie *Love and Death*, a send-up of *War and Peace*. Young Boris' idiot father cradles a piece of sod in his hands and exclaims, "Someday this land will be yours, my son!"

The look on Boris' face.

Sunday, October 2

Timonium's infield tents house half of the 900 sale yearlings. In the mist just after dawn, horses twice the weight of NFL linemen feel sod under their feet and bolt, dragging handlers away like stirrup-hung riders. Let go! Let go! Three years of planning for a crop of one, which in an instant runs loose with a Chifney bit in its mouth, tripping on its shank, heading for racetrack harrows in the corner. The crop lost faster than in a flood.

Explain risk? Draw a horse.

Monday, October 3

E-mail to distant partners sounds shrill sales week. On setting a reserve: "He walks like Charlie Chaplin. Got bad X-rays. Be 17 hands before he starts at three. It's $2,000 a month to get him to the races. First loss is best loss. Horse business a card game — success is how well you play your bad cards. No reserve."

Tuesday, October 4

From upstate New York comes the reply: "I'll be watching on the Internet. It's time to fold the hand."

Wednesday, October 5

That wired feeling you get when you come home from the sales, details swirling. Trading titles to horses like an auto auction. Best moment? Yesterday morning, nephew Philip idling in driveway with carload of high-schoolers. Josh, urgent: "I need a note why I missed school on Monday!"

How to explain playing hooky to help out at horse sales? August suggests "assistance required at family business gathering."

Well done, August. Almost Mafia-like. Let me sign it. Thanks for helping, Josh. Please thank Phil, too.

Thursday, October 6

Silver-tongued lawyers argue before the racing commission to obscure the binding effect of signatures. A deal's a deal, the commission answers. Pimlico's racing dates secure through the Belmont of '06.

Horsemen expected the town meeting from *Blazing Saddles*, comically rancorous. Instead, debate was confined to fellows paid by the hour, not by the horse.

Friday, October 7

"All these big shots in suits. No one wants to talk to a little guy like me."

The Maryland Million Gala is an oyster roast disguised as a fancy fund-raiser. I tell him: "You're wrong. It's *all* about guys like you, the Maryland Million. It's your

shot at The Big Apple. It's my shot, too. So what if your horse only cost $4,500 at Timonium? Ours only cost $3,000, and I had to bring in two partners. These swells dress like skippers at the yacht club, but they have clients with them, or they're schmoozing race sponsors. No, *you're* the reason for these races."

Saturday, October 8

Raining hard at dawn: No turf races today! Surf Light loves the mud, never won on grass! We've got a shot!

At 7 a.m., Michael's on the line.

"(Lou) Raffetto called. Parking lots at Laurel are underwater. Races postponed till next Saturday."

Farm office now a charity phone-a-thon to partners on the move already. Get the word out, by e-mail, Web site, cell phones. Stop the buses. Next: What to do with a hundred sandwiches?

Sunday, October 9

An "Autumn Day in the Country" party at Merryland was a rainout. Folks on the road arrived anyway. We had sandwiches. Suddenly, a caravan in the lane: The Russians are coming! The Russians are coming! Water so high in farm streams they *could* have come by submarine.

Comrades-in-horses just bought 50 yearlings at Timonium. Their leader, the Willie Shoemaker of Moscow, said:

"In Russia, not so much drink coffee ... but vodka?"

Come back next week.

Monday, October 10

Visas for Mexican brothers expire soon. Last project? Rubber stall mats for the training barn. Straw is outrageous. With mats down, we'll bed in pine shavings, delivered monthly in roll-off containers. Quicker to clean. Sweet smell of pine in the barn.

Stalls measure 14-by-14 feet; mats 4-by-6. Jesus drives a skid loader down the shedrow, bucketing stone dust for Maurilio to level floors; Gerardo, Fabian, and Benjamin trim mats on sawhorses. Heavy, back-wrenching work, but immediately labor-saving, dollar-saving. New recruits watch the industrious brothers, miss them already.

Tuesday, October 11

Rubber-topped test tubes at my desk contain souvenirs of chip surgeries, so routine that after-care instructions are mere fill-in-the-blank forms. Trainer Tim Ritchey on New York Moon: "Had some heat. Found some chips in his left knee."

I pull down a tube, examine such fragments of bone: rougher than peanut shells, *bigger* than peanuts. I wouldn't want them in *my* knee. I compose the latest e-mail of disappointment to partners. New goal: Saratoga next summer.

Wednesday, October 12

My name's Jonesy. When I pulled in the driveway this morning to deliver some stationery, ambulances were everywhere, motors running, lights flashing. Two in the front yard. One in the back. Red medic truck parked on the basketball court. Doors to the Big House open. Josh comes flying out of the house and runs into the office. When he comes back, he's carrying some papers. He had that look. My brother died in a fire when I was 11. I *know* that look.

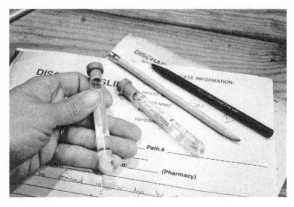

"Jonesy, Dad just had a heart attack. Mom slipped and broke her arm getting to the phone for help. Medics are pulling out all kinds of equipment. I got his living will right here. It says: 'No Heroics.' Oh, man!"

"What can I do?"

"I don't know, I don't know. Keep your phone on."

"Call me."

When I drove out, the horses were running. It was cloudy but the sun popped out for a second. I swear — it was like the gates to the Promised Land had opened. I knew Mr. Pons had died.

Thursday, October 13

It's 4 a.m.

All I can think about is his 15-year-old grandson, his namesake, a few hours ago in bed, fighting sleep, staring at photographs in his biography project, chapter on "My Grandfather" open in his lap.

"I never got to show him this," Josh cried, turning his head into my chest. "I miss him already. I'm never gonna make another cup of tea for him. Why did he have to die?"

Dreams came to me for a few hours, full of Dad's friends, good dreams of his great buddies — but not a night for sleep. In my study, a book of poems:

When your father dies, say the French,
you become your own father.
When your father dies, say the Russians,
he takes your childhood with him.

Too deep for me. Instead, I'm drawn to a dog-eared copy of *The History of Thoroughbred Racing in America*, by William H.P. Robertson. Dad's book. Familiar ground here.

An envelope falls out. Return address: Stoner Creek Stud, Paris, Kentucky. Postmark: JAN 4 1965. Inside, the lives of two friends, on the eve of a Notre Dame–Kentucky basketball game.

Country Life postcard, Dad's hand: "Bet: one Irish whiskey vs. one Kentucky bourbon on game tomorrow. Fee payable at time of foaling in lieu of vet certificate."

Stoner Creek return memo, Charlie Kenney's smile: "Joe. You are a *dog*. The one year we haven't the power to blow a bubble even, and you want to skin me!"

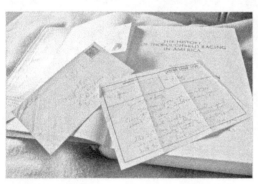

The give-and-take of life in two scraps of paper: horses and sports and booze and school and friends you love to tease. Dad was 42 when he scribbled that note. If he hadn't dropped the bourbon 15 years later, at 57, we might've been filling out that vet certificate. Over the next 25 years of clean living that ended yesterday at age 83, while laughing with Mom about a baseball score, he gave back more than he ever took.

When your father dies, say the Armenians,
your sun shifts forever,
And you walk in his light.

I watch dawn break over Winters Run, first day without a best friend.

Friday, October 14

A stallion named Lochinvar savaged Dad way back when. His left hand in the horse's teeth, Dad poked the stud in the eye and escaped, ring-finger dangling by the skin.

"Wedding ring saved my finger," he told Mom. The great metaphor on the hidden powers of marriage was born.

At the last rites (a little late) at the hospital on Wednesday, I stared at his hands, while Ellen noticed the hands of his watch turning. Time *doesn't* stand still. He wanted his body donated to science, a flip at funeral home expenses. Andrew thought his liver should go straight to the Smithsonian. Alice gently removed the out-of-round wedding ring, preserving a legendary heirloom for a grandson someday.

"What do we do now?"

"Just what he'd do. Everything."

At the Maryland Million crab feast tonight, my hands were too peppery to shake; folding chairs on carpet discouraged rising. Friends pulled my head to their stomachs, the way parents comfort children.

"How's your mother?" they all asked. She broke her arm, I answered, thankful for the shift in focus. I thought of Mom at home, arm in a sling, cousins on the porch, stories through the pain. August, pick enough to make a crab cake for Dodo.

Saturday, October 15

Hot sun banks through the magnifying glass of Laurel's grandstand. A reed-thin gentleman, atrophied hips and an aluminum cane, totters in the sweltering stairwell, a breath away from death by concrete.

An Allen's Prospect won the first race. A Citidancer has just won the second — a daily double for farm sires. Josh and I are en route to honor Dad's tradition of being in winner's circles for sires' offspring when we discover the doddering handicapper.

What would Dad do? Set the fellow down on a step, run to the winner's circle, come right back? No time. This guy's in crisis.

Josh takes his arm. I steady his waist. The three of us limp down steep steps, find a seat by the bar. The frail racetracker spins on heron legs and bounces onto the bench.

A compassionate waitress comps us a bottled water. The absurdity of this man think-ing he could negotiate a day at the track! Well, maybe the track *is* an assisted-living facility. Look around! No, no, none of this passes for common sense. He wears a polo shirt with the logo of the Goddard Space Flight Center. When he's not handicapping, he's sending men to the moon. We find a security guard who speaks only Spanish.

"Will char? Will char? Wha?"

"No, *wheelchair*! Wheelchair!"

The Gambler might not live to valet parking but he's tugging my sleeve, asking in a croaking voice:

"Who do you like today? Circle me a winner in the *Form*!" Dad's kind of guy.

Oh, what the hell — she's 15-1 and never won on grass and I'm about to tout her to a dying man. I think of the two winners already. *Something's* going on.

"Number eight in the fifth. Surf Light." I circle her name in his *Form*. Josh looks at me quizzically. He knows she's the longest of shots. My shrug says: What have we got to lose? What does *he* have to lose?

As we walk away, my arm around Josh, I say: "I guess we did what Poppa Jody would've done, don't you?"

Sunday, October 16

The Big House, quiet on a Sunday night. Lights from wraparound porches wash the yard. Inside, they're scrambling eggs, frying potatoes, having breakfast for din-ner. Mom needs food, fuel for tomorrow. Norah's high-school buddy Michael does the cooking; Alice's friend Elizabeth sets the table. Friends are like crutches now. Teddy, J.W., Jonesy. Family members respect family friends for coming, coping, cooking, laughing.

Until she married Dad 55 years ago, she was Mary Jo Ryan. A smiling battle cry circulates quietly among family, among friends, movie theme at work: Saving Mary Jo Ryan.

Monday, October 17

You just can't know, Dad, how much we missed you today. Everybody was here. All the people you loved. All the people you helped. Such a great gathering. No one had ever seen anything like it before. *You saved people's lives in AA.* Who can say they saved a person's life? Well, yes, I know, they saved yours, too — other guys that died ahead of you.

Mom shook hands for five hours, Dad. And Ellis, playing his guitar in the yard, said he wasn't stopping until she stopped. So he played for *five* hours. Nonstop songs in the air over the farm. You would have laughed: He finished with the Notre Dame fight song.

Ellen put a guest register under that black-and-white photo Skip Ball took at the sales, where you're napping, your head in your hand, next to a horse looking under its screen. Eva sent a note that arrived this morning, wrote what you taught her about life, some rules you lived by. Mom didn't want any kitschy funeral parlor card, so Christy put the rules in a frame under that photo. Here you go:

1. "Don't pass up free food."
2. "Always have a joke or quip on hand — a pun will do."
3. "Try to get into as many winner's circle pictures as possible — each one makes you a tiny bit immortal."
4. "Go to Saratoga every August."
5. "When you win, buy everyone a fried chicken dinner!"
6. "Treat everyone as an old friend."

If ashes come back from the anatomy board, Dad, I'm taking you to Winters Run, and you can hear the stream like you always liked to do. Oh, I miss you so much. I know, I know you had to leave us sometime, and you made a great deal with the powers that be, but I can't see beyond my fingers and I can't stop myself right now. This diary has outlived you and it will outlive me and I just need the kids to know I couldn't let go of you easy as I tried.

Tuesday, October 18

So quiet at the farm this afternoon.

Cheryl's off with her dad. Christy left early to pick up her kids. Mom's at the hospital with Alice and Norah. Rig pinned to her arm, she'll probably spend the night. Andrew and Marva went to see Marva's sister. Mike and Lisa went to Liz's field hockey game.

Alone in the yard I stand, where yesterday they massed on the porch, filed down the stairs, lined up on the driveway — all sad and gay at the same time.

We'll all get through this lonesome day.

Wednesday, October 19

Flint Stites jumped in the van at Penn National at 4 a.m. By the time Mom got home from the hospital this morning — external fixation gizmo screwed in four places into her arm, a "wristjack" — Flint was in the receiving barn at Belmont Park with P. J. Indy. Fresh off a third-place finish at Charles Town, at 4½ furlongs. The *Form* handicapper scoffed: "Trainer Stites trying big leagues today with Charles Town shipper."

Sunlight breathed life into Mom's bedroom as she adjusted pillows under her broken arm. We talked for hours, and she fell asleep. When I returned, she was watching TVG, as P. J. galloped across the finish line. Mike on the phone from Belmont: "How 'bout them apples, Mom!"

Surf Light on Saturday scored the biggest win in farm history — at the moment we needed it most. Now P. J. today — first time our silks ever won at Belmont.

Ombeleevobul.

Thursday, October 20

The crew at Merryland is one farm removed from the recent high drama of Country Life, but their contributions are immense. Last Sunday, they produced a brilliantly seamless "Autumn Day in the Country." Set-after-set of yearlings paraded down from the training barn under Rachael and Lauren and Troy. J.R. posed stable pony Tim with children for refrigerator photos. Troy side-reined Jackie Wilson steady as a walk-behind mower.

On the dining-room table rested Waterford vases won by Surf Light, filled with peppermint patties in memory of Dad's ubiquitous sugar fix. Cream-of-crab soup ran out early, but fresh sandwiches held out until riders joined the crowd.

Merryland, so well named. Country Life, even better. How he loved these two old farms.

Friday, October 21

Tape of new stallion's races arrive from Belmont. We gather to see what we could barely discern in choppy digital images on RaceReplay.com. All we hoped for.

Hey, where's Surf Light's tape? Replay of the most emotional race on the 20th anniversary of the Maryland Million. Mike's comforting quip to shaken track handicapper Frank Carulli during interview, as Surfie exits the winner's circle: "Do you believe in miracles? *I do!*"

Saturday, October 22

Rain again, all hosses in stalls. A fine, quiet Saturday for us to catch our breath after such a week — such a historic week.

Sunday, October 23

Confident enough to question authority, he wouldn't salute a statue when ordered to do so. A nameless colonel busted him to buck-private, shipped him off to some remount fort, where farm experience landed him in equine taxidermy, stuffing Gen. Pershing's dead horse. Meanwhile, the colonel's green troops perished in the Battle of the Bulge.

"Those poor city boys were cannon fodder," Dad said. "Didn't even have time to train 'em. Officers were too busy making them salute statues."

He told this story with great empathy for those city boys. The lesson, though, should not be lost: Have the courage to question authority. It might save your life, or better still for others, *perhaps* make authorities question themselves.

Monday, October 24

Monday Night Football. Richard's little house. *Sports Center.* Ice cream on hot apple pie. Dad's chair, the "mean chair," home to cryptic comment, armchair quarterbacking raised to a comedic art form. Empty this night, out of respect, or inadequacy. We tried taking turns filling the void. Josh called me "Captain Obvious," since all I could muster was the apparent.

And so to Rich fell the task of providing veteran insult, in his gentle way: "Testaverde hasn't gotten any faster."

Back into the rain we ran, to get kids home on a school night, our respects paid to Dad; to Richard, for continuity in this temporal farm life.

Tuesday, October 25

Richard nurses the broodmare Like Yesterday back from near-fatal laminitis. So painful was the fire in her feet last week that Dr. Russ Jacobson clipped the deep flexor tendons to relieve pressure on coffin bones. Today, she whinnied to Rich.

Naturally, the worst-off is one of our best. Her half sister is Meadow Flyer, dam of Breeders' Cup Juvenile entrant Henny Hughes. Such monumental pedigree updates are usually reserved for Paris Pike titans, not tiny Route 1 farms. Take good care of her, Richard. Saturday could be a big day.

Wednesday, October 26

He visits my dreams. Last night I was back in the seventh grade, spinning Dad's poker-chip holder from his card-playing days with The Jolly Boys, seven openings for chips; in each opening, the face of a friend. Duffy Rathbun in one, reassuring me, pointing to a piece of paper in his hand, the certificate for his first stallion share, in Seven Corners. It's gonna be OK.

If I could stay asleep instead of waking up with tears in my eyes twice a night, I'd dream of his good nature so hard it would become mine, unerasable, as much a part of me as the shape of my head, which mirrored his, an odd thing I noticed in a photo from some paddock, as we stood superimposed on each other.

Grief's the damnedest thing, so tied to the subconscious, to memories of youth.

Thursday, October 27

On the Circle Line cruise around Manhattan, a gifted historian on a wireless microphone recited Gotham mythology. On origins of "The Big Apple," he professed the phrase originated at Belmont Park in the 1920s, when the prize to the winning jockey included his choice of apples from bushel baskets filled with the state fruit of New York.

Surrounded by blank faces of weary tourists, I took notes, and seemed, like racing itself, to be an island of interest in a sea of indifference.

Friday, October 28

On Belmont's backstretch, I stared at a dormitory where I lived in 1970, at 15 years old, working for Jim Maloney the season Dewan won the Brooklyn; Dutiful, the Adirondack; Loud, the Travers. First lesson in quirky justice of racing gods. An exercise rider killed. Ducked his head riding into a stall, but the horse spooked. Broken neck on door lintel. Black cloud. Half the Claiborne foal crop and Maloney didn't win a race the entire Belmont meet. Over to Aqueduct? Stakes money stacked up. Saratoga? Streak continued.

Fast-forward to Surf Light, P. J. Indy, that monkey Jenkin Jones at Laurel two days ago. Even Alden's Malibu a good second. Three wins and a second since Dad died. A friend with a sardonic sense of humor suggested we stand by the volcano and throw in another family member to keep the streak alive.

Saturday, October 29

Belmont swallows 50,000 fans like no other track. Red lights on trains lined up for the ride back to Penn Station. It might have *been* 1970: pre-OTB, pre-TVs in

every simulcast parlor, preplanned obsolescence of large crowds. I hope the racing gods are kind to Belmont, the mother of American racetracks.

Sunday, October 30

The World War II generation is passing fast. Farewells are short; sincerity is not. There's just more living to do. I'd asked him about a departed friend.

"Funeral's at 11. Post time's not until one. J.B.'s got a horse in the first race."

Monday, October 31

Upset at pirated charts, Equibase upgraded, so we downloaded. Clicking "yes" inadvertently grabbed Ellen's digital photo albums. In fear for my life should the computer "lock up," I watched as a thousand images flashed before my eyes: Stallions and sunsets, cookouts and construction, mares and foals, grandparents and kids. In seven minutes, a lifetime. Could have locked up on any moment, on any photo, like life itself.

The morning of the celebration of the life of Joe P., while brooms swept porches, I glanced over the top of the house, thought I saw a hawk.

"That's no hawk," Kentucky Ted exclaimed. "Watch the sun catch his tail. That's an eagle. That's a bald eagle!"

It seemed as though even the howitzers of nearby Aberdeen Proving Ground had ceased their dull daily thunder, pausing for a morning of silence, soldiers sending us one of their nesting eagles as a symbol of peace in the valley. A hundred feet above the house, such an easy leap to a belief in an afterlife.

Of a thousand images to choose from in this wild month gone by, the one I'll never forget:

That rare bird, banking against the blue October sky, watching over us.

November

Tuesday, November 1

Lost cultures.

Susquehannock Native Americans paddled the rivers of this region: the Little and Big Gunpowders, Bush River, Winters Run. Granite cliffs where the Susquehannocks carved images of animals now lie impounded by dams on the Susquehanna, by dams near Merryland under the Loch Raven reservoir.

Type an address on Google Earth. Satellite zooms down on local farms, green against the gray computer-chip flood of development. Look *very* closely: horses a still-life petroglyph, carved into photographs from space, brown backs inlaid into the green.

Development seems unstoppable in this region. It takes good horses to keep the high ground.

Wednesday, November 2

At Laurel last week — watching the thrilling replay of that monkey Jenkin Jones, moments after his win. Eyes flash to the track, where a loose horse defiantly breezes one lap around, two laps. Then a riderless pony gallops past, outrider pulled from his saddle by the obstreperous horse. Track announcer Dave Rodman: "Fire Monkey has been scratched by the stewards." The polar swings of racing, two runners by the same farm sire, in back-to-back races. Parable for a New Owner's seminar.

There's more: TV today flashed footage of a barn fire at the Fair Hill Training Center. Twenty-four horses down in smoke. Helicopter view of a black hole. Fire Monkey's barn! Her name a fatal omen! *No!*

"No. She's Pennsylvania-bred. I sent her to Philadelphia Park two days ago."

Thursday, November 3

Fasig-Tipton produced short movies on fancy fillies selling Sunday at the Newtown Paddocks. Like NFL films: stirring battle scenes, omniscient narration. For Brice Ridgely's mare Vee Vee Star, Hip No. 111, carrying a full sibling to champion Declan's Moon, the movie opens with a black-and-white photo of a youthful Brice on the reins of workhorses, leaning into their collars, intricate leather harness.

In 18th-century England, in the pre-machine age, a loose union known as the Society of Horsemen rose through the working ranks, an agrarian aristocracy of labor. Watch all the other Fasig films. No one so steeped in the Society of Horsemen as A. Brice Ridgely.

Friday, November 4

Philip and Josh arrive home from school to bring in sales mares for blanketed nights. Josh stands in the grass by the gate. I say: I'm heading to Kentucky tomorrow.

"But I don't have school Thursday! You said we'd drive down together!"

Tell a kid something, they never forget. His grandfather's voice in my mind, Yoda-like: *"Take the boy. Take the boy."*

What classes do you have on Monday?

"I won't miss anything. I'll make it up."

Kentucky is powerful juju, a can't-wait-to-get-there-place, at 50, at 15.

Saturday, November 5

On approach to Louisville: "Dad, how did the horse business get so big in Kentucky?"

Well, geology, and a war. Four-hundred-million years ago, shallow oceans came and went as the continent heaved. Skeletons of marine animals settled as sedimentary rock, as calcium-rich limestone. The oceans were far away from mountains and didn't silt in with erosion. Ice Age glaciers stalled out above Cincinnati. No rocky deposits here, just a thin layer of topsoil above the limestone that builds strong bones in animals.

Buffalo grazed on this great savannah, broken only by bur oaks — thick bark, resistant to grass fires, standing alone through fearsome lightning storms.

Easterners were migrating through the Cumberland Gap, or down the Ohio River. Dr. Elisha Warfield, father of the Kentucky Turf, was a Maryland-bred. He foaled the great stallion named Lexington, who survived the Civil War safely while many fine Thoroughbreds in the East perished as cavalry mounts. And where there's stallions, there's breeders.

That's how.

Sunday, November 6

Allaire du Pont and Kelso. The Taylor-Hill team and Seattle Slew. W. T. Young and Storm Cat. Jack Price and Carry Back. Brice Ridgely and Vee Vee Star.

"Any man can own a horse," said Samuel D. Riddle, "but only one man can own Man o' War."

It would take King Solomon to explain why it's not all about money, your best horse. You can't explain "reserve not attained" unless the baby is yours.

Monday, November 7

Tommy Roach grabbed me by the arm.

"My dad fell right before the Keeneland yearling sale. For the next two weeks,

the sales were like a wake while he was still alive. Then he died. I was worn out."

Alice Chandler honored a Keeneland dinner with a story about her dad, that last day, when he worked sets of horses, scurrying up honeysuckle banks to the track. He ducked out of the tack room. Somehow the lock clicked. When he collapsed in the barn, she couldn't get out of the tack room. "I loved him. He loved me. He's always there."

Josh slept from Lexington to the Louisville airport. In three days he learned a great deal about the Bluegrass, her fine characters, about shared losses. He missed school but not an education.

Tuesday, November 8

Dancer in the Citi danced in distress.

"I think she has colic," Rachael said from Pimlico.

The Marion duPont Scott Equine Medical Center in Leesburg, Virginia: "Looked like colic, but it's ulcers. We started her on GastroGard."

E-mail to partners: "The good news is no surgery. The bad news is she won't race this year. Vets say half the horses in training suffer from ulcers."

Same ratio for owners.

Wednesday, November 9

Colic. The bane of our last 24 hours. With no commercial haulers handy when Timmy the pony went down, J.R.'s wife Laurie loaded her best friend on the trailer for Leesburg. They opened up his belly and untwisted his intestines.

"He's my wings," she thanked the surgeons.

Proximity to fabulous equine hospitals, New Bolton an hour north, Leesburg two hours south, is not taken for granted. They can't save 'em all, but they sure try with a passion.

Thursday, November 10

P.J. Indy breezed fastest of 15 at Penn this morning, came back favoring his left hind. Flint: "Best get him to Dr. Riddle's for some tests."

Fresh off a five-length Belmont score, the 17-hand center is now on the disabled list. Handicappers had him favored for Saturday. A rich New York-bred pot slipped away today.

Friday, November 11

Horse sales at Timonium next month. In warm stalls, retired racemares transition to broodmare prospects. Weanlings wear pajamas, preserving summer coats for winter sales.

Two thousand years ago Hittite kings consulted the first sales catalogue, compiled by Kikkulis, master of the horse. When King Solomon bought warhorses from the Hittites, he paid commissions to such horse masters — the infancy of agency. Solomon accumulated 16,000 horses, as prizes of war, as tribute, as collateral for pledges, as gifts from other rulers. The solution to the growing stable, then as now: sales.

Saturday, November 12

Childhood included Saturday trips to the Bone Mill, the animal rendering plant halfway between Country Life and Merryland. We knew the ride home meant lunch at the Blue Bell: shuffleboard, crab cakes, Cokes, football on TV in the bar, colorful cast of locals. Never mind you rode in the pickup with a metal bucket fomenting a week's worth of afterbirths, or the sleeping form of a dead foal under blowing burlap bags.

Dad spoke the unspeakable in the air of the unbreathable: "I'll never forget the time *my* father brought me here the week the circus was in Baltimore."

The Bone Mill was an environmental bull's-eye — toxic disinfectants leeching under bridges of the Little Gunpowder. These days, Valley Proteins of Winchester, Virginia, collects the carcasses. Mad cow disease threatens this vital service. The FDA says "uninspected cattle" are high-risk for bovine spongiform encephalopathy (BSE).

Farms aren't in the country anymore. Bury a dead horse? A sentimental favorite perhaps, but not the annual attrition. Aquifer effect? Suburbs crowd old farms; ground water oblivious to tenure. So today, I lobbied on a form letter sent by Valley Proteins:

"We strongly urge the FDA not to adopt the new rule."

Sunday, November 13

Scrawled in a slanting hand on Oct. 12 in his diary was the reminder: "Maryland Million entries." Standing where he tersely chronicled farm life and farm weather, I back-filled the last month.

Oct. 12: Cloudy. Dad died.

Oct. 15: Sunny. Surf Light wins.

Oct. 17: Warm. Celebration of Joe P. at farm.

Oct. 19: Beautiful. P.J. wins at Belmont.

November 13: Cool. Michael's birthday.

On shelves behind the telephone, I noticed a row of thin red journals. From childhood through this moment, in hours of borrowing books from this eclectic library of family hand-me-downs, I had never seen Grandfather's diaries. *His* dad.

Oct. 12, 1939: Rainy. All horses in.

Petroglyphs on cliffs. Horse paintings in French caves. Journal entries in telephone rooms. Same impulse. Validate life. Evidence the day. Preserve for posterity. Lost cultures.

Clear today.

Monday, November 14

Under the narcotic Dormosedan, 17-hand P.J. Indy rested his head in my arms like a great gray dog.

Dr. Riddle. Digital X-rays.

"Rough spot on cartilage of his stifle joint," Doc said. He injected it with hyaluronic acid. "Stall rest two days. Hand walk two days. Then jog him easy at Merryland. In three weeks, he can go back to Flint."

A Dodge minivan pulled into the parking lot. A man carried in his arms what appeared to be a small brown dog. Then the dog whinnied. P.J. awoke from his trance to stare at the smallest horse any of us had ever seen: a dwarf miniature, a circus freak, the head of a horse on a 45-pound frame. Not as tall as P.J.'s knees.

A bystander shook his head: "You mate the smallest miniatures, and you're surprised you get a dwarf, with feet so small he falls over sideways without special shoes. People just go to extremes in animal breeding."

I looked at P.J., so rangy he barely fits into the trailer. But that move at Belmont, one long stride equal to two of his opponents, Shaquille O'Neal against NBA guards. Dr. Riddle smacked P.J. on the rump: "Don't work him much. Just run him."

Without going to extremes.

Tuesday, November 15

Merryland graduates receive a periodic report card, wins and losses detailed on the track sheet, comments in code from the Maryland Thoroughbred Purse Account.

Mrs. Vanderbilt 9/3/05: NM $50 (nominate to Alma North Stakes); EN $350 (entry fee); ST $350 (starting fee); GF $15 (gate fee); JF $75 (jockey fee). It cost us $840 to run last in a stakes.

Cape Cosmo 10/7/05: PU $7,980 (purse transaction). CL $15,000 (claimed). A $22,980 sale of a racehorse through the claim box.

Surf Light 10/15/05: NM $750 (to Maryland Million Ladies); EN $750. ST $1,500. It cost $3,000 to enter the gate at 15-1. What if she tanked the exam?

Up the hill from Merryland is the Hickey School, for juvenile delinquents, Dad's favorite kids. He wanted a bumper sticker that read: My Child's an Honor Student at the Hickey School.

Truant Surf Light, a frequent delinquent in racing class, aced the exam. On bumpers: Our Child's an Honor Student at the University of Merryland.

Wednesday, November 16

Last of the yellow leaves loose in the air, as tornadoes flash on news.

Client on the phone: "My 2-year-old is at the clinic with an infected hock. They're worried about laminitis in the good leg."

Fatal premonition in his voice. Owner will die too when he sees the pharmacy bill for a dead horse. I want to say: Save your money. Shoot him now.

Tough talk. Been reading Hemingway. *Esquire*, June 1935:

"A bullet there from a .22 caliber pistol will kill him instantly and without pain and all of him will race all the rest of him to the ground and he will never move except to stiffen his legs out so he falls like a tree."

Instead, I say: Is there anything I can do?

As he answers no, I watch leaves float to the ground, feel winter touch down. I know instinctively that the clinic bill will amount to 10 grand, and the racehorse, should he survive, will amount to nothing.

Thursday, November 17

Each morning at Merryland, when J.R. opens the gates, the unpredictable awaits.

"Yesterday, Michael brought a busload of government visitors from China," he said. "I'd seen on the news that President Bush was in Mongolia. Well, we almost

made the news here. The interpreter said one man wanted to ride Tarsky, my lead pony while Timmy recovers. This fella scampers up into the saddle, my stirrups twice as long as his legs. He slaps the reins and gallops away on Tarsky, who is 22 years old. Now, remember, Tarsky was an excellent timber horse. He won the Maryland Grand National. I'm thinking he's either gonna jump the rail or die trying. So I'm yelling Spanish to the Chinese to stand back!

"Turns out that fella was a jockey in China. He breezes Tarsky around the whole track, pulls up at the finish. Still, I could see the headlines: 'International Incident as China Man Dies in Fall from Russian Horse at American Farm.' "

Friday, November 18

Murderer's Row: the 10 courtyard stalls, layups like cars at the bodyshop.
Stall 1: Ancient Jazzman, no cinch to see Christmas.
Stalls 2 & 3: Beds held for Leesburg patients Timmy and Dancer.
Stall 4: Mrs. Vanderbilt, condyles flattened from pounding.
Stall 5: Rasta Dancer, fractured sesamoid.
Stall 6: Hookedonjoy, knee chip.
Stall 7: Passionate yearling, eye surgery.
Stall 8: New York Moon, knee chips.
Stall 9: P.J. Indy, injured All-American.
Stall 10: North of the Moon, double-bowed.
Dreams of the "Big Horse"? Check 'em at the door.

Saturday, November 19

She had a brilliant photographer's eye, did Neena Ewing, before a fatal brain aneurysm took her at 45, in 1996. Merryland fascinated Neena, whose photos often guide us in renovation.

In Neena's day, the infield spread like a green sea between the sandy track. An intervening owner threw in three large paddocks, indispensable now. But paddocks wear at gates; erosion follows; cribbers gnaw. To bring Merryland back, we've painted cupolas, installed new oak planks on bridges, rehabbed the old starting gate. The original infield, a lake effect, lives only through Neena's lens.

Sunday, November 20

The Golden Rule: Them that's got the gold, rule.

Bill Rickman struck slots gold for his Delaware Park in 1995, enriching horse owners in the process. With spare change, he bought worn-out Merryland Farm from Baltimore County in 1999. First thing he did was pour a 18-by-36-foot helicopter pad. Rotor blades sliced the Long Green Valley. He was not popular with many locals.

"Hey! You know what's happening in Kentucky?" he screamed into the phone in the spring of 2001, as Bluegrass mares aborted by the hundreds.

"A fungus?" I answered.

"Hell, *nobody* knows what's going on in Kentucky," he shouted back. "And nobody's goin' back there until they figure it out. *Now*, you need to buy my farm and board all those mares that'll be staying home next spring."

Mr. Rickman once blacklisted certain horsemen from his backstretch. Recent obits about him were sterile reading. I bounce a basketball on his helicopter pad and give gratitude to the tough old developer: He didn't shop Merryland to them that's got the gold, and he knew good ground when he saw it.

Monday, November 21

Like brushing into a former sweetheart in a stairwell:

"How've you been?" I ask Cape Cosmo when she pops up in e-mail entries.

"Splendid, thank you. My new owner runs me in allowances."

She was Dad's last Winner's Circle photo. Laurel's Jumbo-Tron flashed a tribute to him on Maryland Million Day, a cut-and-paste from the Cape Cosmo photo.

When she runs, I cheer for her, but not wholeheartedly. I don't want to invite second-guessing should she win an allowance. People see 20/20 when they look back. Still, I'm sentimental.

"Good to see you, Cosmo. Stay well."

Tuesday, November 22

Merryland sits at the end of Baltimore County; Country Life, at the bottom of Harford County. Eight miles apart. Farmers in these two counties fear the fate of the Susquehannocks. Lands threatened by impoundments under car lots, house lots, parking lots, Big Lots. Wal-Mart is breaking ground a mile from home. Farmers, even on high ground, soon to drown in a sea of traffic.

Wednesday, November 23

"Jazzman's not right," J.R. phoned. "Hasn't passed manure. I think he's shut down. How *old* is he?"

"Maybe 35."

"Dr. Russ is on his way."

"I'm on I-95, headed to Virginia for Thanksgiving."

"Warfield's backhoe is here this week. We could bury him on the hill next to Popeye."

"Yes, please. Sorry to ask you to do that."

By the time I arrive in Virginia, Christy has uploaded a photo of Jazzman onto the Web site. The reason horses evaded extinction is because they let us come into their herds. Did we become part of their family, or they ours?

Thursday, November 24

Fun of a family football game interrupted when brothers-in-law collide and fall on each other.

"Just trying out my spin move," I heard from above.

Glasses bent, but no headache until after dinner, phone call from a trainer deputized to claim a warrior from the depths of racing's hell.

"I couldn't do it. He was so sore when he came into the paddock. He's got a suspensory, or a knee, or something about to go. I thought his leg might fly off on the turn. You don't want him."

It's a long story, I answered.

"He won on heart," he said.

I don't feel like giving thanks to anyone right now.

Friday, November 25

Cell phone voicemails:

"Did you see he won? Why didn't you claim him?"

It's a long story. I press seven and delete the messages, but they play all day anyway.

Saturday, November 26

The drive home up Route 301. A roadside marker. The tale of John Wilkes Booth, who fled the theater, floated across the Potomac, and ended up shot to death in a barn right here, 150 years ago. Booth and his older brother, Edwin, were famous actors of their day. They rode horses past Merryland en route to Baltimore theaters. The Booth family lived six miles from Country Life.

There's a line running through the universe. Find it, and long holiday drives seem shorter. The kids sleep through my ruminations.

Sunday, November 27

Empty chair at Thanksgiving.

In quiet moments — the transition at dusk in particular — I find myself vulnerable, memory a rapid-access file that pops open like a broken lock. This mood affects what I select to write. It's all black and white. It's a reality show I can't turn off.

A big winner would help. When the legendary oracle of the Nez Perce Indians, Chief Joseph, was near his end, he was asked for a final wish.

Bring me a horse, he said, bring me a horse.

Monday, November 28

With rain moving in, Merryland is Busy Town.

Chesapeake Moon, Jersey Moon, and Jackie Wilson ship out for 90 days in Delaware. Down to the track come Mel Stute's California-bound yearlings. When Mel sees snow on the nightly news, he'll phone from Pomona.

New yearlings spin under saddles in spacious stalls, riders ready to flop on their backs, then onto the shedrow, circling the barn before heading down to the track.

Bay Citi Girl breezes three-eighths in :38. Runs soon. A win puts her over $100,000, an illusion to her, but a plus to her broodmare value. A post-pounder hammers like cannon fire, as Buddy Bit Fencing drives 12-footers for new round pens. A nail gun fires short staccato bursts. Tesio, on horses during wartime: They'll get used to anything.

Teddy bolts boards on the refurbished bridge. Bobby the blacksmith bangs shoes on fresh arrivals. Dr. Meittinis drives in, injects an ankle, feels a shin, prescribes remedies, rolls out. Loye empties a wheelbarrow of evening feed. By dusk, lights pour from the broodmare barn, where repro exams for mares in weekend sales are certified.

Suddenly, everyone hops in pickups for home: the world for which we work.

Tuesday, November 29

Plans for a "Maryland Horse Park" prompt halcyon visions of the old Havre de Grace Race Track, preserved in the movie *The Sting*, when bookmakers adopt a convincing French accent on tickertape results from "*Hava de Graw.*"

The selection committee opted instead for a dairy farm near Annapolis. How colorful is that? Had "The Graw" survived the mugging in 1950, she might today be the Saratoga of the South. Instead, she's a retrofitted clubhouse for the National Guard, a gal with a past, mahogany inside, plywood outside.

The Horse Park passed on the idea. What a shame. What a Runyonesque narrative could have welcomed thousands.

Wednesday, November 30

Best feeling of the month? Closing the barn up for the night, listening as young racehorses settle, the warmth of a barnful of lucky, happy horses.

For other souls? Tough month for folks at Fair Hill, or for the horse with the hock who didn't come home, or for Jazzman, or for a claimer in New Mexico. Like reading the prayer for the sick in church: Sometimes the list is longer than the sermon.

This is one tough business, and you can't be romantic about it. That's what I learned before Saturday lunches at the Blue Bell. You can love it, but you can't be romantic about it.

December

Thursday, December 1

Dreamily cinematic, this old horse farm grew from thoughtful placement.

Rule One: Build barns near water.

Rule Two: Build houses near barns.

Rule Three: Build to last.

On banks of the farm creek, an Amish farmer could dip buckets on the coldest of December days. Ancient decision lingers in the air: Josef, build the barn here. In basements, brown porridge falls away to reveal perfectly stacked stones. A ghost taps a masonry trowel clean of mortar. Floor joists of poplar still carry bark. Hair from tails of workhorses insulates basement from kitchen above.

Outside, horseshoes clap on blacktop, down and back to the track, three and four yearlings in a set, eight or nine sets these busy breaking days. All day long, a training farm. Diesels growl on vans shipping to sales. Two-way radios chirp as equine commerce moves.

In the bustle of Merryland, the fellows who built the farm, the barns, the houses, the track, they remind me: It's fine work to be a horse farmer.

Friday, December 2

"Thank God it's Friday," the crew sighs.

J.R. and Rachael drive into the heart of a Friday night, bound for Charles Town to saddle Bay Citi Girl.

Lauren apologizes: "The reason I didn't speak is because the filly I was riding had a hump in her back. I didn't want you to say to your clients: 'Pay no attention to that rider on the ground.' "

My cousin Rick is checking in from afar: "Doin' anything this weekend?"

"There's a lot cookin'."

Saturday, December 3

"What happened with the first two pregnancies?"

When the wind slices through Timonium, it bounces off crooked blacktop straight up your pant legs.

"First one miscarried. Second one was early fetal death. Not bred back that year. Now she's in foal on one cover. She's the best mare in the sale, no question. Still, it'd be smart to carry some pro-foal."

Prospective foal insurance can cover half the value of an auction mare, stiff premium in the range of 18 percent. Consider it sales tax. Recall the foal from a Keeneland mare, delivered from a hoist at Hagyard vet clinic. No pro-foal when they put him down in the OR, contracted tendons. In one long night, no foal, torn-up mare, sudden vet bill. Cold wind of the horse business. You understand: It's not such a fine trade sometimes.

Sunday, December 4

Median price for 200 mares was $3,700.

An agent says: Why even own a mare?

Some mares, young mares, worth more to sell. Like young racehorses in training, young mares are undefeated. But three just ordinary foals and they're out.

Wonderful client, elderly man, the owner of the sales-topping mare, disperses his two-mare broodmare band for all the money. Less is more. He thanks Mike for the teamwork of the sales crew. The top mare's name a prophecy: Your Out.

Self-centered me, thinking end of big board account: No, *we're* out.

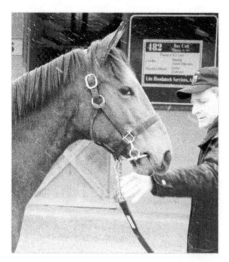

Monday, December 5

A weanling filly with *his* hip, *his* eye. Three trips to her sales barn to make sure. I don't ask if she has any vices. She vets clean.

Thunder in your heart. She's the one.

Later, amid irresistible announcements from the auction stand, a binding beware: "This filly is a cribber."

My blind date is a smoker.

Fences be damned. She's the one.

Tuesday, December 6

Merryland in the snow. The drive over. Four inches, melting fast. Through the woods meander railbeds of the Ma and Pa. At the farm, wood grain of wet fenceboards recall the miller's saw.

She's the one, in the back barn. Telltale exhale, white eye guilty as she backs away, kickwall damp from her mouth. Bad girl. Scarlet leather thonged around her neck. Cribbing strap on a weanling. Bad girl.

Another dream horse, vices and all, has checked into the hotel.

Wednesday, December 7

Mild case of the fantods today as track snow-removal shortcutted by discing dampness into the cushion, not whisking it into the infield. Track'll be slick as a ski slope if it freezes. Why bother buying a snow blower last year?

Confucious say, the essence of equipment is, having it, using it!

Thursday, December 8

December catalogue won't leave my desk, awaiting decoding of scribbled messages. The procrastination is exhilarating. Surf Light was chosen as cover girl — battleship-gray filly in orange silks, orange blinkers, racing to victory on Maryland Million Day.

Perfect Moon, catalogue cover boy for the October sale, was a $4,700 Timonium yearling. Surf Light a $3,000 Timonium weanling. The run gene, unknowable until the starting gate opens, pumps in the hearts of the unlikely. Without this great unfactorable aspect, there would be no layers in the horse business, no little guys, just tycoons, monopolies, predictability.

Friday, December 9

Baltimore Gas and Electric is preparing a contract to run service underground, to bury the overhead wires now braced to barns. So much safer, this electrical upgrade. No frayed insulation. No exposure to weather. To eliminate shock, I stand away from the minutiae of details. Lou, our electrician, plugs me in to the costs. What little hair I have stands on end.

Saturday, December 10

Yearlings work in winter coats. Morning gallops soak them. Quick baths add moisture. The solution? Body clips, trace clips. Falling asleep in the barber chair is tranquilizer induced. Still, the humming of clippers is a foreign sound even through Ace. Yearlings resist, fidget, duck, startle, spook. Mohawk racing stripes pattern out in the first few passes of the blade. An hour later, coats are velvet.

Sunday, December 11

Mom runs the nonprofit Radio Reading Network of Maryland. Folks who can't see to read may order transmitters for their homes. Mom and her volunteers read newspapers and novels over the airwaves. Last Wednesday, I substituted for Dad, driving Miss Daisy to town. In the control room, Mom's blind assistant Robert turned to me, Stevie Wonder-like, and said: "Anything good in today?"

To get a horse started at stud, you'll breed any mare with a pulse, including a blind mare.

"Momma's Eyes in the seventh," I tipped Robert on the resulting foal.

Monday, December 12

In the mailbox arrives the weekly newspaper *Lancaster Farming*, front page ablaze with barn arson photos, courtesy of a psychotic on a Thanksgiving spree.

In discussion for Merryland are dry hydrants, in place already on the pond at Country Life, where fire hoses could access the farm stream. It's winter. All horses in barns. Lights on. Outlets full. It's a season for worry. Let's get the hydrant idea out of committee.

Tuesday, December 13

Letters for Pop find my pigeonhole in the farm mailbox.

Blue Cross Blue Shield Patient: Pons, Joseph. *Relationship to Subscriber:* Self. *Provider:* Bel Air Volunteer Fire C. *Service:* Ambulance. *Billed charges:* $600.

Let's see … Was this the ambulance that pulled into the horse-van entrance? Or the one that turned around at the manure pit? Or the one that bounced Mom, broken arm and all, on the roundabout near the hospital?

Oh, the confusion of emergency vehicle drivers. I ask Stan to tack numbers to the driveway sign, street addresses of farm homes. Academic two months ago, in broad daylight, after the fact. But an emergency at night? They can't help you if they can't find you. In an elegy to his father, poet Wendell Berry wrote: "He's hidden among all that is, and cannot be lost."

Spirit of Chief Joseph smiles, chides: "Do it while you're thinking of it, sonny boy."

Wednesday, December 14

Legendary horseman John Madden liked to name horses after acquaintances, finding it a useful selling aid. We tweaked that tactic with Merryland Monroe. Betty Miller, mistress of Merryland for five decades, bought a piece.

"How's the filly?" Betty sings into the phone. I want to say Merryland Monroe is our Oaks filly, but if Betty hears "oats" instead, well, clarification could run us into the Christmas holiday.

"Trainer likes her," I answer. "He took her to Oaklawn with him."

Trainers moving gypsy-like across the land, just as Madden did 100 years ago, are performance-driven. At the moment, Merryland Monroe is just another unraced 2-year-old. She may be an Oaks filly at three. Who knows? Unlikely. Success of any kind is unlikely in this game. It's enough to say, for today: "Trainer likes her."

Thursday, December 15

Fund-raising letter from Marion duPont Scott Equine Medical Center: "Our faculty played a key role in the development of Marquis, the first FDA-approved treatment for equine protozoal myeloencephalitis (EPM)."

The letter jogs me to phone the owner of a filly with EPM. Marquis treatments have not made her faster. She runs like two men in a horse costume. Her workout times are glacial. The February sale closes this week. I implore her owner: Please turn the tap off.

Hope springs eternal. So do obstacles. So do losses. A fine mess a horse can get you into.

Friday, December 16

Today's headline: Declan's Moon Needs More Time.

Two years ago, Malibu Moonbeam made an impressive first start. For a workout days later, her trainer sent her out after the harrow break. Empty track. Deep into her workout, she was headed straight for a riderless filly out of nowhere. They swerved at full speed. New Bolton put three screws in Malibu Moonbeam's hind cannon bone after the work. She is back at Pimlico, firing bullets — just a quick two-year layoff.

Madden was the way he was because of the business he was in: training horses. It'll make the Pope cuss.

Saturday, December 17

In Richmond today. How to get away to the Broad Street OTB? Merryland grads on display. Starleena in a Laurel stakes. Perfect Moon hoping to limp home at Sunland Park.

The very first yearling we broke at Merryland, Perfect Moon has run nonstop for three years, beginning the spring of his 2-year-old season at Santa Anita. Winless in a trio of two-furlongs sprints. Kentucky Ted appraised his late-closing efforts: "I think he wants to go three."

Starleena runs second. Perfect Moon, who won for $5,000 on Thanksgiving Day (too crippled to claim, said the man), steps up to $15,000 company. Tired legs don't fire. Like watching a champion boxer's descent to pro wrestling.

Miles from nowhere, not a soul in sight — old song plays lonely in my heart as I drive out.

"How'd he run?" Ellen asks at Granny's birthday dinner.

"He came home on all four."

That claiming game ... that's a hard part of this business.

Sunday, December 18

Blackbirds by the thousands lit on the steep hillside, rose in great waves, spun in frenetic perfection, never touched wings. They shook the winter air like a great curtain pulled. In a blanket of motion, they dropped into a field of yearlings that, feeling no threat, returned with mild annoyance to grazing.

"A biological storm, a chain reaction, a feathered tempest in a traveling blast of life." Aldo Leopold on passenger pigeons, extinct a century ago.

The blackbirds lifted off with furious intensity, climbed to a uniform altitude in the white sky, then poured away as liquid as the tail on a kite. We stood, disoriented, overcome by silence, as though headphones were taken from our ears. Sights and sounds on a farm can overwhelm the senses. A fine day. A day to remember.

Monday, December 19

Virtually color-blind, horses shy at unfamiliar objects. To have night vision, they sacrificed day vision. So why didn't the yearlings spook at yesterday's birds? Did they recall in ancestral memory banks the lost sights of great flocks, black in white winters echoing down the ages?

In the woods today, we dug a hole for a favorite dog, Woody, lost in the Woodlawn section of Baltimore 10 years ago, found days later by Ellen at the hound pound. Kentucky Ted on the phone: "Odds are, when you fall for horses or dogs, you'll outlive most of those loves."

Geese chevroned up in salute, blackened the sky. Leopold: "We are fellow voyagers with other creatures in this odyssey."

Tuesday, December 20

Dr. Jacobson snipped tendons six weeks ago on Like Yesterday. She now baby-sits two bouncy weanlings in a large paddock. Her coffin bone no longer knifes through the sole of her foot.

On a bronze statue at Gettysburg, General Meade is posed on a majestic stallion. The horse stands with all four feet on the granite base, a clue to the general's fate in battle. He lived. Reach up to touch the bronze horse's ankle: The artist sculpted the digital vein. Like Yesterday's pulse to her feet is almost that quiet now. Radical last

resort in a battle to save her. Today, she stands like Meade's horse, as weanlings look up to her.

Wednesday, December 21

Tomorrow is payday. Christmas bonuses, such potential rifts. What's fair? What's fair?

Prepare testimony for tonight's hearing examiner, to oppose school that would add hundreds of cars a day to Old Joppa Road.

Farm crew pauses to gaze at TV mounted sports-bar style from office ceiling. Jenkin Jones in Laurel feature, flat mile, second finish line, *long* stretch. Henny Youngman joke as JJ hopelessly trails the field: *The horse I bet on was so slow, the jockey kept a diary of the trip.*

"Get him outside!" In the final stride, JJ switches leads like Gene Kelly leaping onto a curb. Bonus worries eased. An hour later, with the win at our backs, we plead with the hearing examiner: "Please keep that parcel zoned ag! You put that many cars on us, we'll never get a horse van in."

FALL 2005

Thursday, December 22

Peppermint-loving Mrs. Vanderbilt didn't make the broodmare team, was sold for $4,000 at Timonium. It's a cold coach who can cut players without thoughtful pause. The filly lucked into a fine life after the track because her half sister is Sagamoon, the Ruffian of our yearling crop. Sagamoon is serving 90 days in Delaware, at the farm owned by the friend who bought Mrs. Vanderbilt. So pleased, as former coaches, to have suggested: Watch Sagamoon rise. You could own a sister to a star.

Friday, December 23

A scientist in New Jersey is soliciting umbilical cords from mares' afterbirths this spring, storing stem cells for the day when the foal races, tears a tendon, wobbles, develops EPM, ulcers. Archives arrive in the horse business.

Saturday, December 24

Morning sounds bounce out of the bowl. A tractor shifts through the farm, thumps across the bridge, idles at the manure pit. A newly arrived yearling cries out as he runs an unfamiliar fenceline. Doors slam on pickups.

Yearling colts are *almost* 2-year-olds. They require separate fields, play too rough, mount fillies. For such boys, three new round pens are christened, fresh sand settling with each rain.

Christmas wreaths hang on stone posts flanking the farm entrance. Away from malls, away from the maddening world, this farm, any farm, is a mesmerizing workplace.

Sunday, December 25

Urge is to simply parlay stalls, shake fresh straw, have an early day. But the Christmas crew is also tomorrow's crew. And pride goes into the mundane making of a clean stall each day.

Rain falls lightly by lunch. Horses are hustled in before the coming storm. By 5 o'clock, roads are rivers. You pass through barns and listen to the rain on shingled roofs, on metal roofs, on slate roofs, horses nestled away.

"An inch of rain equals 10 inches of snow," someone says at dinner. The kids moan: how close is the snow. I retreat to watch from steps as they unwrap presents. Spirit of Christmas past sitting next to me. Teacup steaming.

Monday, December 26

For a handful of newcomers, an honest little gelding named Alden's Malibu is their first horse. They patiently waited for him to recover from a cracked cannon bone. Today, the endearing fellow gave everyone an excuse to go to the races. Warmth of the

glassed-in grandstand. New shirts, new sweaters. "Honey, I'm just gonna run out and return a few presents!" They found the track, not the mall.

Alden can't win for $15,000. I prep them: May have to drop him to $7,500. Could lose him.

A partner says: "I was just a handicapper. Now I'm an owner. This game was easier when you didn't personally know the horse you bet on."

Tuesday, December 27

With butch-cut body clips, the five yearlings bound for California could be equine marines. In their bunks at night, they wear blankets. In their shaved faces, they no longer wear the look of children. They are mere months away from flying around Santa Anita in two-furlong races, the way Perfect Moon started. Young horses live such a condensed life, not pausing long at one stage before racing to another.

Wednesday, December 28

In the mail today came The Jockey Club release for the name New York Citi, freed up 10 years after a horse with an identical sound (Citi with a "y") proved forgettable.

Like an Ellis Island arrival, New York Citi wanted into the country. With door propped open, she snuck past the man with the fork, ran from the barn. She cantered over to the new round pens, luckily was caught uninjured. It might've been otherwise. When the old fence was ripped out, every empty posthole was filled with stone dust. If there's a hole, a horse will find it, sooner than later.

Thursday, December 29

Stalls in the training barn are 14-by-14 feet. Huge. Stalls at tracks are often 10-by-10. So how do Merryland horses still get cast? Back-scratching. Boredom.

When a yearling rocked the walls this morning, cast tight as a wedge, J.R. calmly walked up the shedrow and returned with a long cotton shank. He approached the momentarily resigned colt, and carefully dropped the center of the shank over the colt's two hind ankles. With one end of the shank in each hand, J.R. positioned himself near the colt's withers, just out of striking range of flailing feet. He bent low for leverage and steadily pulled the shank taut. Hobbled, the colt's hind legs folded into his belly like a kitten cradled in the palm of your hand. J.R. pulled. The colt's center of gravity moved to his back when his legs were in the air. He finished rolling away from the wall on his own, scampered to his feet.

J.R. executed the cast-horse technique coolly as roping a calf back home in Nebraska. He concluded the seminar: "Fellow told me, 'One day you have livestock, next day you have dead stock.' These horses are always trying to commit suicide."

Friday, December 30

A year ago, Prospective Joy was opened up to relieve a twisted uterine artery. It almost killed her. Two months later she foaled Malibu Miracle, who in 24 hours will be the biggest, best yearling in the barn. He is a half brother to Hookedonthefeelin, just another Timonium sales grad until she won the La Brea Stakes, a grade I

event. Hookedonthefeelin's first foal is Pussycat Doll, on the cover of tomorrow's advance *Form*, longshot in this year's La Brea. The *Sports Illustrated* cover jinx runs through my mind as I rub the blaze-face of the miracle colt.

Saturday, December 31

Running a farm is fine work if you can get it. It can also be punishing, no escape. Part of the deal when you live where you work.

Some days, though, are too good to be true. Today, for example — reaping the harvest of crops planted in earlier years. All from in front of TV's racing channels.

At Santa Anita, Pussycat Doll runs like a cat on fire to win a grade I. Her mother's half brother, the miracle colt at Merryland, will now head to a select yearling sale this summer with a huge update. Her mother's blessed mother, full of grace, is bedded deep in the foaling barn, dam and now granddam of star performers.

At Calder, a filly by a farm sire almost falls down, recovers, runs from last-to-first in a rich stakes. The announcers in awe: "Sometimes all you can say is *Wow!*" At Laurel, a filly broken and trained at Merryland goes wire to wire at 35-1 to break her maiden. Wow!

You can't show the tape of all three races to other family members fast enough. Midnight is coming. Fireworks on a horse farm are a nonstarter. You spend New Year's Eve with rockets in your eyes from the day's excitement, farm spirits whispering: It's fine work. Keep it going.

WINTER
2006

January

Sunday, January 1

From the high top fields at Merryland, Bottom Road winds away like the River Kwai through a jungle of mid-Atlantic hardwood. The "upback" is a remote region. Access is by steep gravel road. Only a few old geldings and a few little foxes have wintered here in the four years of our ownership, sheltered in a spacious loafing shed. As New Year's Day becomes night, white-tailed deer startle and careen downstream like gazelle, into woods near the training barn where a herd of Thoroughbred adolescents celebrate their second birthday.

In the film *The Bridge on the River Kwai*, British prisoners-of-war whistle the "Colonel Bogey March." "Be happy in your work," the Japanese colonel commands.

Earlier today at Laurel, Alden's Malibu sent infantry boogeying down to the winner's circle, whistling a happy tune. He won *and* wasn't claimed. Whew!

Fire and fall back. Reload. Better ammo this year. Crop of 2-year-olds strong as lifeguards. Walk back down the hill. Whistle past the training barn. Drive out of the farm recharged, rededicated.

Half hour in the upback will do that. So will a win. *Any* win.

Monday, January 2

Breeders reporting early January foals may get a house call from The Jockey Club. Hiding a Christmas baby until New Year's carries risk of discovery. Sorry, your week-old foal is a yearling. A discouragement to breeding sheds that open on Groundhog Day instead of Valentine's Day.

Bred March 14 of last year, Tangier Sound bagged up before the bowl games, but is still holding her pregnancy. Val's memo to mare owner today:

"Ultrasound shows no apparent placental separation. Started mare on antibiotics and doubled her Regu-Mate dose."

Not out of the woods, but at least into the New Year.

Tuesday, January 3

The *Washington Post* stuck a dagger into the New Year's Eve edition. Memo to readers: Surveys rank racing at bottom of sports, so no more entries or charts from Laurel.

Before expanded gambling, before the Internet, racing and newspapers were inseparable allies. Monopolies no more, the two now seem insufferable in each other's company.

Wednesday, January 4

Unplaced for a $15,000 tag Dec. 26, Alden's Malibu one week later won for a $7,500 price. Mortality insurance is weighted automatically to lowest claiming price. If Alden runs for 15 again, we'll need to secure a fresh vet certificate, or sign a declaration of health, then petition to reinstate the higher value. All between entry and starting.

What if he runs in a starter allowance, that ambiguous nether world where claimers can't be claimed? Run cheap once, get a year of no-claim starter-allowance protection. What's he worth, slow, with no clear-cut value?

Alden's insured value when we started this partnership was $45,000. Then he ran unplaced in the field of dreams — save for a timely win here and there in modest company, to earn his oats and our regard, which is measurable by insurance companies.

Thursday, January 5

Under the desert sky of New Mexico, fading star Perfect Moon awaits his next race. Unplaced for $15,000 last out. Unclaimed winner for $5,000 before that. Likely they'll drop him back down. I watch Stable Mail for news of this gladiator on the skids.

WINTER 2006

Friday, January 6

J.R. slaps his cell phone shut.

"Pimlico's got five horses in isolation, and the state vet put a quarantine on Barn 5."

Dr. Russ Jacobson: "Don't take this lightly. They put a horse down at Pimlico on Monday. It was neurologic. Equine herpesvirus is suspected. There is no treatment for that strain of EHV-1."

Deadly disease on the move. Last summer at Churchill. Last month at Turfway. Today at Pimlico.

Saturday, January 7

Faster than a telegram, a trainer's imagination:

High fever. Sometimes not even that. Stop.

Any cough. Every cough. Sunlight catches droplets of moisture sailing 20 feet. Stop.

What if we've run behind a positive horse in a morning breeze, or a race, breathing in fire? What about the starting gate? Disinfected between races?

Fearshot words. *Ataxia. Encephalitis.* Loss of muscle coordination. Inflammation of the brain. Stop.

"He can't stand. What's wrong with him? Now he's sitting like a dog. Can't he get better? Some do! Won't he? No? Then we'd better stop this."

Pink needle. Stopped.

Sunday, January 8

The starting gate at Laurel thunders under low winter sky. The break, heard first from the mile-chute, then the crashing sound carrying over the infield lake.

During the race, a horse throws its jock, runs wild. Riders steer clear. Outrider makes circus catch. On the ramp down from the track after the race, losing jockeys blame the loose horse. Trainers acquiesce. A reprieve from the same old excuses.

Tear up the tickets. Bet the next.

Malibu Moonbeam wins by nearly 10 — *after a two-year layoff!* Owner herds family for the photo, finds no room to stand, ducks down under the mare's neck, like he's a crazy parachuter about to jump for joy.

Every picture tells a story. Three screws. Nuclear scan: Not yet. Second scan: All clear. Good as new, just like New Bolton said. Still, a 5-year-old maiden until 10 minutes ago. What a risk! *Would I have done that?* Not and been a sport about it.

Click. A photo worth the wait.

Monday, January 9

Waking from the narcotic spell of Rompum, the colt with the condylar fracture who waited *so* patiently in a stall for six months — X-ray after digital X-ray until the wedge closed up — today found himself in a small paddock. Loose. Unfettered

and alive. What an exuberant moment it is when a stall-bound horse is returned to freedom. Such celebration, such fireworks in the joyful rediscovery of play. Only a foal's first breath is equal.

Oratory. Feet off the ground, jackrabbit glee. Eloquent name. Ebullient action.

Tuesday, January 10

Twenty-seven times Perfect Moon has answered the call to the post. Career earnings: $511,017. Won a grade III, a grade II, led in the grade I Malibu Stakes at the sixteenth pole, lost by a half-length. But he *made* Malibu Moon.

Today, $7,500 platers at Sunland watched Perfect Moon skim the rail, steal the lead. But *he* didn't see the closer, way outside. Lost by a head. They went in 1:10 and change. New trainer took him back to his farm tonight, turned him out in a sand pen.

Never in our wildest dreams have so many owed so much to one horse.

Catch your breath. Won't need much of a winter coat. You're coming home.

Wednesday, January 11

Last night Michael hung around Keeneland long after the dinner bell. Pavilion almost empty. Third-to-last hip. Perseverance paid off.

"He's a little sickle-hocked, but he's a rugged rascal. Good bone. He's also a Kentucky-bred, and if KEEP keeps on going, he could run for state-bred bonuses at any of the four Kentucky tracks. Could be fun."

Kentucky Equine Education Project. Raising awareness of Bluegrass-breds. Pumping life into the Kentucky Thoroughbred Development Fund.

Another state subsidy program enters the market's mind in, of all places, the Big Place.

Thursday, January 12

At Ames United Methodist Church today.

"Sister Hester was not *dee*-manding," the preacher recalled. "She was *com*-manding."

Hester's oldest daughters wept over her open casket. They were born in a house on Country Life in the 1950s. Born on a farm. Not in a hospital.

In the mid-1960s, as Hester's husband, Gene, led the white teaser from his paddock, the black stallion Big Brave was led into the barn for breeding. In a blink, attack. White horse on black horse. That fast. Troubled times had come to my home farm. Dad coped, phoned Bull Hancock, told him the young stallion had been cut up in a fight. Things happen on a horse farm, they both knew. I imagine they both had a drink that night.

In the years since, discuss a stallion-fight in company, and eyes look down. It's that scary. The best horse usually gets the worst of it. A recurring truth in all matters pertaining to the Thoroughbred.

Hester, say hey to Gene. Remember when he lifted me from a snowdrift and set me on the porch step? Hester, say hey to Pops. Hester, put in a good word for us.

Friday, January 13

Jack Keene studied stone work in Europe, became enamored with a pattern that gave order to the chaos of stacked stones. Standing in the rain on a January day admiring Keene's stone work, we set a goal to win a race at Keeneland — someday.

Don't underestimate, though. There are a lot of rocks in that path. You need to know Jack Keene's history. Born out of his broken dreams was Keeneland Race Course.

Saturday, January 14

Flint left Penn National with P. J. Indy at 3 a.m., bound for Aqueduct, favored for the New York-bred "one other than." Cell phone message recorded at 7 a.m.: "Raining pretty good here in North Jersey. Call me."

At 8 a.m., I check my messages. Damn, he's been driving in the rain waiting to speak with me. I know what he didn't say. He thinks we should scratch. He's concerned about P. J.'s stifles in the mud. He's worried partners might be en route.

First rule: Try always to *do what's right for the horse*. The people part will work out. He turns the rig around. Still has time to pick up Penn filly for Laurel race. Learns on arrival in Maryland that if she runs, she can't return to Penn. Second scratch. Turns the rig around, again.

All the road running not in vain. Still has two healthy horses.

Sunday, January 15

Flat Stanley (the popular literary device for grade-schoolers to learn storytelling) wrote to me about his Christmas visit here with his grandparents:

"We drove to the training center where they teach young horses to race. Grammie's and Gramps' new weanling Klondike Moon was teaching other fillies to chew on the fence. Everyone kept telling me to watch where I walked and pretty soon I found out the reason. We had crab cakes for lunch. Gramps said if I ate any more I'd be Fat Stanley, not Flat Stanley."

Ask an older person how they got started with horses. They begin, "Oh, when I was a kid, my ..."

Monday, January 16

At Laurel today, all they could talk about was Pimlico. Weekend press release: Friday morning, Barn 6. Second Horse Euthanized. Previously healthy. Unable to rise even with assistance.

Friends outside the circle: "Wow, like you guys need more good news!"

Drive me out of this movie. Mail me away like Flat Stanley.

Tuesday, January 17

Radio on. Driving to horse farm in southern Pennsylvania. This road is taking Marylanders across state lines to drop foals, buy land. This road moves Kentucky stallions. *This is the road to riches.*

Not so fast: *Battles rage.* D.J. reads news, "Crossroads Gaming Resort and Spa at Gettysburg very controversial."

Consider: 50,000 casualties at Gettysburg in 1863.

Listen: Pennsylvania wants 60,000 slot machines.

Hear: Casino at Gettysburg is asking for 3,000; would like to have 5,000. In Connecticut, the nation's largest casino has 6,000.

Think: Twice about visiting Gettysburg again.

Wednesday, January 18

Horses of all ages hop vans for regional demands.

Today, 2-year-olds Sagamoon and Spectacular Malibu returned from 90 days in the Delaware Certified Program.

New Jersey's new deal: *No matter in what state you foal*, if that foal is by a registered New Jersey-stallion, it's eligible for the New Jersey Restricted Race Program and the Breeder Awards Program.

Pregnant mares shuttle to Pennsylvania to reside 90 days.

New York-breds are born into money. A friend owns Jump Judy, winner *once* in 18 starts. Career earnings: $85,273.

Hereafter for Kentucky-breds: mare *must* reside, from date of first cover until foaling. Breeder of a Kentucky-bred Derby or Oaks winner gets a $100,000 bonus. Breeders of maiden special, allowance, or stakes winners get a bonus equal to 25 percent of the winning purse, capped at $10,000. No 20 percent off the top to trainer/jockey combo. All yours. Suddenly, regional mares vanning to Kentucky may be breed-and-stays, instead of breed-and-returns to familiar farms of home.

Horses move with fluidness of kids in weekend tournaments. Races in different towns, school-bus germs in every sneeze. Horses under stress, in transportation. You did disinfect this van, didn't you? Time is money?

Is it any wonder EHV-1 is suddenly so opportunistic? Track in Canada says they got it from track in Michigan. It's a moving picture.

Thursday, January 19

Third barn at Pimlico isolated. Maryland Department of Agriculture posts a Web site timeline of EHV-1 cases.

The neurological form taking down racehorses is one strain. The strain that causes abortion storms in broodmares is another. On one farm we train racehorses. On another we breed mares. Stop!

Professors use the term "parade of horribles." Don't wanna walk in that parade. Do all you can. Watch your horses. Take temperatures. Update vaccinations, but don't overdo. Careful of pregnant mares. Limit traffic. Quarantine.

Beyond that, it's Russian roulette. If your number's up, your horse is down.

Friday, January 20

Save $50 by naming 2-year-olds before the first of February. A cost we can control!

For a West Virginia-bred filly: Harper's Fairy, hinting at state program.

Sorry, taken. Sounds like Harper's Ferry.

Marx Brothers had this game right. *A Day at the Races* stereotyped perfectly. All right, then. How 'bout *Harpo's Fairy*?

No direct match to the famous idiot, I announce idiotically, then click *Submit*.

Cheryl and Christy were afraid of that.

Saturday, January 21

In arenas, barns, and pavilions the size of football fields, Horse Expo should be a place to lose yourself in a fantasy of rainbow blankets and saddle pads, of round pens and fence displays, of new ideas how to escape into some horse utopia. But you bump into a Pennsylvania breeder.

"Vet says there's a case at Penn. Horse ran at Laurel three weeks back."

Sunday, January 22

"They're closing Penn National to outside horses at midnight. Who knows how long this quarantine will last? Haldy's a Pennsylvania-bred. I'll sign him in. Can you have him here by dark?"

Shin-bucked Haldy is in light work at Merryland. He's not quite ready to breeze, but what if we get locked out indefinitely?

Cindy wakes him from his Sunday afternoon nap, throws red shipping bandages on him. An hour later on I-83, I glance over to see the York Barbell logo, a muscle man posed on the factory roof. He has just jerked the weights over his head in triumph. Symbol of something? What?

We cross the great divide at Harrisburg. Lights on the river, lights on arched bridges. Half-hour later, guard waves us through the Penn gate. It's dusk. Trailers and vans idling everywhere, running lights on. Feels like an army base inside the perimeter, bugging out, or in. We drop and go, lift off into the gloaming like a helicopter.

Barbell man winks as we fly silently by.

Sunday night in Susquehanna land. Life in the time of cholera.

Monday, January 23

All day long, a Monday.

Worrisome conversation with maintenance man. Workers' comp issues; previous injuries compounded here. Bad backs, bad moods. Helicopter rides for Merryland riders haunting our rates for all employees.

On the wall, a 1930s photo of the coal-tipple in Jenkinjones, West Virginia. Three open stairwells reach down to the landing where coal cars load for the train ride out. Flint on the phone. "If Jenkin Jones leaves Penn to run at Laurel, he can't come back to Penn. New York won't let in Penn shippers, so P. J. Indy's gonna have to run at Laurel, too. Maryland gave me stalls at Bowie. It's a 2½-hour drive from Penn. I'll take JJ and P. J. to Bowie next week. OK?"

Vans, like coal trains, loading up for the ride out.

A Monday, all day, all 'round.

Tuesday, January 24

Seventy years ago: Uncle Johnny's diary. January 24, 1936. Rain. Vanned by trailer Green Flowers to Hughes. Paid check for whitewashing. Stallions exercised. Paid Lutz for installation of lights.

Today: Rain. Paid check for fencing. All stallions out. Mares playing in mud. Paid Lou for installation of lights. Traci Hughes called. Perfect Moon laying over at Spendthrift. Trailer here week of February sales.

Wednesday, January 25

The stallion barn at Merryland is a steep-roofed, two-stall barn, very French-looking, very pretty. In the barn lobby, stall doors oppose each other; one to the right, one to the left. Each stall also has a back door, for free access to paddock. Like a run-in shed for one. Modeled after old-fashioned Kentucky stallion boxes. Labor-saving. Groom-saving, especially with hard-to-handle stallions.

But what if a stud man leads a stallion to the breeding shed and, on return, puts the horse in the wrong stall? And what if the second stallion can't be seen? He's grazing in his field, back door open? Disaster awaits.

In an earlier age, that happened here at Merryland. Of course, the champion sire was killed. Not the forgettable one.

Only a matter of time before human failings repeat. Today, we killed the run-in shed design. We fenced the stallion paddock away from the barn. The stall's back door now opens into a fenced aisle that leads to the paddock. If another horse is already in the paddock, a groom can clearly see him.

Thursday, January 26

Somebody half-a-century ago paid good money for construction of this big daddy of a training barn. Plans included a modern septic tank and drain field. Only problem, no map of buried utilities. With no old system in sight and no maps, we paid good money to install a new tank and drain field. Such mundane matters matter greatly.

Yesterday, while fencing the stallion fields, we found the old tank, buried under two feet of topsoil, invisible until the post-pounder crashed through the concrete lid.

It's five-feet wide, eight-feet deep. Mercifully empty. We filled it with No. 2 stone so a horse never finds it, and covered it back over.

New meaning to money pit.

Friday, January 27

The win photo arrived from Malibu Moonbeam's romp earlier this month. Stuffed in the same plastic sleeve was the New Bolton X-ray. Three screws in hind cannon. This afternoon, she won by $6\frac{1}{2}$. Champion Personal Ensign won the 1988 Breeders' Cup Distaff with *five* screws in a hind leg. What a precedent.

Seven brothers stepped off a bus from Mexico today, tired as Pony Express riders, legs stoved up like stallions on alfalfa. U.S. Customs quizzed them at every stop. H2-A cleared the way. The cavalry has arrived. Bad backs get a rest.

Saturday, January 28

Dead horse at Laurel. Pelvic injury, perhaps. Couldn't get up. Fifth horse euthanized this month. Farm in Kent County downstate is under a Hold Order. Suspected case of EHV-1, clear link to Pimlico, the track now under complete quarantine, in or out.

Whistling past the graveyard. Be happy in your work.

That is all we have at this time.

Sunday, January 29

Very rainy — a cold, dreary, stay-at-home, straighten-a-study-kind-of-Sunday, because breeding season is coming, and it will be six months before you think of anything again. That exuberant, consuming, devouring odyssey called breeding season. That love-hate thing.

Monday, January 30

Steam rising from hillsides. Horses rising from steam. Huge foal by Malibu Moon born this morning at five. Everyone loves it. Two foals on the ground now. Thirty more on the way. Happy prisoners-of-war we are, whistling the Colonel Bogey March.

Late afternoon. Merryland. Up in the woods. Deer with white tails the size of college pennants. Very warm. Sixty degrees. Beautiful.

Still, wouldn't a good cold-snap knock the virus out?

Flint called. Moved JJ and P. J. down to Bowie.

Pimlico trainers locked in, locked out. Be careful. Tempers short. It's a minefield. Watch where you step, Flat Stanley.

Tuesday, January 31

This day is full of rumors that become fact. The Laurel filly tested positive. On the news at noon. More details at six. Story in every paper, of course, and on every channel.

That is all we have, at this time.

February

Wednesday, February 1

Merryland, in winters during the 1940s, was a resting site for trainers and horses home from seasonal runs to New Jersey, New York, and New England.

In the 1950s, winter racing arrived at Bowie. Maryland became a year-round circuit. Trainers looked at their cars: "Hey, I don't have to live in this anymore!" They quit the nomad life, bought small farms. With the Maryland Fund in the 1960s, trainers kept fast fillies as broodmares, their foals running in races restricted to state-breds. Such a stimulus to the local scene! Nothing like it in America!

Maryland's racing and breeding industry intertwined, intermarried. Roots took hold. Kentucky farm owners, in search of hybrid vigor for managers, were frustrated trying to import fine Maryland horsemen. Couldn't get them to leave home.

That's why this herpesvirus thing has everybody on edge. The overlap between track and home, the traffic back and forth. Vets say it's mostly horses in nose-to-nose contact. But remote barns are infected. How? Until we know …

Boots walk, dip into bleach tubs at barn entrances here, there. Everyone trying not to step on a snake.

Thursday, February 2

Sick horse at Bowie today. Quarantined immediately.

In a rocky gorge of the Gunpowder River downstream from Merryland, a National Guard Armory blasts away on rifle ranges. A muffled cannonade thuds through dead  winter air. Sounds like an approaching army. You feel like Aunt Pittypat in *Gone With the Wind*. Thunder of artillery. The Yankees are coming! The virus is coming!

Eyes fall on an empty run-in shed, 70-feet long, up on the hill. With double-fencing added, stalls framed in, electric and water run, it would make a fine quarantine facility.

Merryland has 100 stalls in three big barns. Built before our time. We're about to add five stalls, all by their lonesome. If the state vet ever pays a house call, he'll see a bona fide attempt at quarantine.

Friday, February 3

Web site banner: Perfect Moon Heading Home To Merryland.

What's he look like?

Well, he's probably all wrung out from hard racing. He's not big. Maybe 15.3. Plain bay. Balanced. Handsome head. Kind eye. A nice horse. When we broke him at Merryland, Jake used to ride him right into the tack room. Said the horse would do anything you asked.

The crew has seen only framed photos of him. Dramatic close-ups of graded stakes. California sun on a perfect Moon.

I will call him Little Big Man. He will be a pony for my tribe. My heart will soar like an eagle when I see him.

Saturday, February 4

Pounding rain at Laurel. Detour sign on Whiskey Bottom Road. Street name a portent of clouded decisions.

Grandstand sirens shriek. "Fire in the kitchen!" a waiter hollers. Flashing lights on clubhouse walls. No one cares. Nagging thought becomes full born. P. J. Indy could get hurt in this mud. *Do what's right for the horse. Scratch!*

But we're stuck. He's tearing his stall down. It's been raining since Christmas. It's muddy everywhere. Besides, nowhere else to run. New York's off-limits to "herpes states." No end to the ban in sight.

P. J. banks his 17-hand Mack-truck-of-a-body into the turn for home as the 7-2 favorite. Far ahead, a horse snaps a cannon, falls gunshot to the track. The crippled horse attempts to rise, rump-first, like a camel. "Nowhere-else-to-run P. J." rams into that poor horse like a truck hitting a deer. He ricochets into a third horse. Three jockeys down in the mud now, crawling on hands and knees. P. J. staggers away from Whiskey Bottom Road, stirrups flopping.

The official chart will read DNF for three horses. One horse *literally* did not finish. The other two will live to run another day. Oh, the things we ask jockeys to do, horses to do. Partners' heads down. A deadly bargain played out in every race. I could read the deal in every face.

Sunday, February 5

Baby face. Leans out over his yoke screen in the courtyard.

Traci and husband, Scooter, drove through driving rain for 12 hours from Lexington to bring Perfect Moon home. He ate carrots out of her hand while he peered over familiar land.

Safe and sound, back where he started. Oh what a happy day for us all.

Monday, February 6

Half the catalogue scratched from today's mixed sale at Timonium. Grounded on home farms. Fear of flying into the face of the EHV-1 storm.

The sales company did a superb job of moving horses through this crisis. Their A-team posted in force. Paperwork punched at every turn. But we're a week away from breeding season. What if we buy a yearling, or RNA an offered mare, and the flu follows us home on the van?

Neither a buyer nor a seller be. We sit on our hands at the sale.

Tuesday, February 7

Weather coming. Let it get cold. Knock this virus out. Yesterday, a second horse was euthanized on an Eastern Shore farm. Today, though, the state vet lifted "Hold" orders on Barns 5 and 8 at Pimlico after horses tested negative. Twelve Pimlico-based runners are entered for Laurel races tomorrow.

Come on, Winter. Hurry up. Get cold. Let's plow through this mess.

Wednesday, February 8

A well-intentioned friend asked, "This herpes stuff affecting you guys?"

Let's see. We ran a New York-bred in Maryland. He wasn't sick but he almost died. We hoped to sell mares at Monday's sale but kept them home, expenses running. Next mixed sale is in December, *10 months away.* Owners aren't shipping mares in for breeding season. And I'll betcha we'll hit rock trenching a water line to a new quarantine barn. Frost line is 32 inches.

The good news? Virus only lives a few weeks. No new cases reported at the tracks.

Thursday, February 9

Merryland Monroe hops a van back from Oaklawn.

She bowed.

Euphemistically, a "tendon tear." Ultrasound defines what the eye sees. The prescription is a few months on the exercise machine, then a return to training. But a core lesion in a tendon is bad news.

Said the late Hall of Fame trainer Woody Stephens, "The only person who ever got lucky with a bow was William Tell."

Friday, February 10

Perfect Moon makes me perfectly happy. It's hard to describe. I think it's because he has no clue, and I have *all* the clues. Galloping around in his sand pen, cribbing strap like a collar on a big, friendly dog.

He reminds me of my best friends when we were all teenagers. Come on! Let's just horse around today!

Saturday, February 11

For nine months every year, our men from Mexico live separated from their children back home in Michoacán. I am at home with my children every day. I feel guilty shooting baskets with my boys when the men walk by. What a sacrifice they make.

Sunday, February 12

Standing in the courtyard in 18 inches of snow under a full moon. So still. So quiet. Tree branches touch against each other soft as a caress. Like conversation overheard.

The foaling barn's steep roof is outfitted with fan-shaped metal snow catchers. Holding back an avalanche. Hung up on keepers, last night's snow melted at a rak-

ish angle today, then froze up tonight. Light pours from barn windows. Tonight makes the list of exquisite farm moments.

Monday, February 13

Gleeful horses revel in the snow, roll away winter coats shedding out in the lengthening days. Kids fly over snow jumps, then gather 'round a makeshift fireplace in a grove of trees. You can feel it lifting, the cloud we've been under for six weeks, the threat of the virus. We know we're only as good as the last van that dropped a horse off. But after a while, human nature and Mother Nature tire of worrying each other. The snow is a white flag of truce.

Tuesday, February 14

Old-time trainers sent tired-legged racehorses to the mountains in winters past. Stood them in snow for a few months. Brought them back with fresh legs for hard summer campaigns.

I'd like to turn all the racehorses out in the snow, but they've got shoes on now, and they'd grab themselves, and cut their legs up, and my good intentions would backfire. I can't even watch yearling colts in adolescent play — wrestling each other to the ground — without thinking of separating them into individual paddocks, lest they suffer tiny insults to X-rayable joints.

I'm ashamed sometimes to stare at a 1950s photo in the Merryland kitchen, of 19 yearlings galloping headlong down a steep hill. Racehorses at heart, at play. It was the cover photo on the Sunday *Sun* 60 years ago. These days, we hothouse raise 'em and wonder why they break down so easily.

Wednesday, February 15

Brice Ridgely's cell phone plays "When the Saints Go Marching In" as he John Waynes his way into the Cracked Claw OTB in rural Urbana, Md.

Mutuel clerks take smoke breaks under awnings frayed since the joint hosted all the local proms, before it failed as a restaurant. Brice waves for them to get back inside. "Can't take my money standin' out here," he calls to them by first names. The buzz spreads. That colt Brice raised, named for his son Randy, makes his first start at Santa Anita today.

Mel Stute bought Randy's Moon at Timonium even though vets said he'd never run on those sesamoids. Randy's Moon rocks the crabhouse to its feet with a last-to-first burst that sends us screaming to the TV screen. There is no volume. The whole place watching this one race, and nobody in charge will turn up the sound. Brice shrugs that racetracker's shrug. What the hell? He won, didn't he?

Randy's Moon was raised just like champion Declan's Moon at Brice's home-style farm in Howard County. Broken at Merryland for Mel. On the ride home, Old Man Brown, a Baltimore band, plays an Allman Brothers-kind of slide guitar road song called "For That Someone." Nothing like a winner, especially for these someones.

Thursday, February 16

Merryland Monroe leaps off the van into the snow like nothing's wrong. I give her a hug, then stare poker-faced at the profile of her superficial flexor tendon.

Think of the *Mad* magazine strip "The Lighter Side." A boss stoically manages various job challenges. Then he closes the office door, falls to the floor, no one looking as he cries, "Mama! *Mama!*"

Friday, February 17

Big red tractor on the fritz. Needs a clutch, hydraulic work. Get it hauled out of here. Fix hayloft door at training barn. Snow blows in. Floor stays wet, rots out. Workers' comp claim waiting to happen.

Why do we leave stall lights on at lunch? Utility bill is exponential, huge rate increase on the way. How many buildings waste electricity on these two farms? Forty?

Water bucket is empty for horse in sand pen. Not smart in cold weather. More colic in the cold. Driveway gate still open after quitting time. How come?

In fits and starts, some days mostly fits, a farm is managed.

Saturday, February 18

Oh, we should have gelded Moon Drive when he first started acting like an idiot. Old-time horsemen cut almost all colts. Made them better racehorses.

Moon Drive on the training track spun sideways like a snake. Silly colt had an ankle next morning. X-rays showed a fracture. And so another 2-year-old bites the dust.

"Mama, it's only February!"

Sunday, February 19

Fair Hill Training Center 20 miles away is concerned that someone might try sneaking Sally through the alley to race at Laurel, perhaps returning with the herpes bug. They've hired armed security to man the gates.

A friend on the phone. Had a colt on his farm with a fever of 106. *That's smoking.* But probably not herpes. Probably just strangles. How about that? He'll be relieved if the culture comes back for just strangles.

All this stuff's been around forever. John Steinbeck's *The Red Pony* died of strangles, and he wrote that book in the 1930s. Meanwhile, we keep working on the quarantine barn.

Monday, February 20

M.C. Escher was a graphic artist who drew trick images. Black geese in perfect V formation flying to the right, becoming white geese in a perfect V flying to the left.

We're buying metal stalls for the quarantine barn from a farm sold to become a school. We attend zoning hearings to prevent a nearby farm from *becoming* a school.

Snow melts fast. Half the land white, other half black. Overhead, a flock of swans whoops its way across the sky. Which direction are they flying? Question what you see.

Today's *Sun* says Maryland is about to spend millions on farm preservation. That's certainly good news, but it didn't say the state has taken millions away the last four years. Escher demonstrates the picture isn't just what it appears.

Tuesday, February 21

Kentucky vets, fresh from Turfway's experience with the virus, provided Marylanders with impressions at a Fair Hill forum tonight.

After age one, 80 percent of horses are clinically infected with EHV-1. Neurological strain has been with us for many years. Testing is by nasal swab or whole blood, and neurological herpes shows at a much higher level in the blood.

No current vaccine is labeled *just* for neuro.

Transmitted through respiratory secretions. Incubates 3 to 7 days. Sheds from noses for 8 days. Virus will run for 21 days: length of quarantine.

Management practices: Take temps once a day. Twice is better. Virus survives in water, so don't drop end of hose in buckets. Don't use common lip chains or bits. Disinfect equipment and wear fresh gloves between horses.

It's not going away. We'll constantly see herpesvirus, year after year.

Wednesday, February 22

Bruce, a finished carpenter, was almost finished for good before a mutual friend lifted him out of the ditch. Now he lives in a loft at Merryland. Hanging a pocket door in Mom's living room, off its rocker since all of us kids had the measles in '57, Bruce discovered a toy soldier. Bruce left the soldier and this note on my desk:

"Another M.I.A. found at C.L.F. The War Dept. has been notified."

Like an Escher drawing, the note says two things. Has a double meaning. That's how Dad would have seen it through AA eyes. He loved finding lost soldiers. There were two of them in the living room.

Thursday, February 23

Median price at our mixed sale was $2,000, down from $4,000 a year ago; 24 of the 56 horses listed as "not sold" failed to draw minimum bid of $1,000. What do you do with a horse that isn't worth $1,000? Costs that much *a month* for feed and care.

Unwanted Thoroughbreds. An increasing problem, at farms and tracks.

I needed information. Googled the subject. Mad cow disease is killing horses. High demand for meat other than beef in Belgium, France, Italy, Japan. Congress attempted to starve out export meat plants in DeKalb, Illinois, and in Kaufman and Fort Worth, Texas, by withdrawing USDA funding for horse-meat inspection.

No problem. These three plants simply offered to pay the USDA to continue the inspections. You should Google. You'll see graphic photos of handsome horses in crowded pens, or crouched on low-slung, double-deck trailers. Photos of the retractable killing bolt to the brain. Bloody photos of Horse Hell. You *won't* Google the sites twice.

What if Perfect Moon had ended up there? He ran in bottom claiming company in New Mexico, a short haul to discard heaps in Texas if his knee had gone in a race. My eyes have been closed. Perfect Moon, the way his story might have ended, is opening them.

Friday, February 24

Obstreperous Pagan Moon came to us at Merryland two years ago. Our riders wanted no part of his devilish antics. He'd drop you quick. We demurred, sent him away. He wound up in the Laurel barn of trainer Jann Anderson. She's been on his back about his behavior. From the gate in morning workouts, he'd lurch to the inside rail, Jann hanging on somehow. Sometimes he'd spin round and run back toward the gate. You can't put a jockey on a horse who might do that in a race. She stuck a whip in his face, got his attention.

"Not yet," Jann answered owners, work after work. "Not yet."

Pagan Moon's conversion was complete today. He broke clean, ran true, won his first start in style. Pagan Moon. Baptism by fire. Jann, a missionary sent to save his soul.

Saturday, February 25

Pagan Moon is a West Virginia-bred. But he's locked out of Charles Town because he trains at a "virus track." Same ban applies to Laurel-based Yeager's Jet, who seems well suited for $4^1/_2$-furlong sprints at Charles Town.

So Yeager plies his trade in six-furlong Laurel claimers, but the five-furlong Merryland training track of his youth is indelible in his thick head. He leads until the five-eighths pole, thinks he's done a furlong from the finish. And he is.

Another hidden cost of the virus. Lost opportunities elsewhere.

Sunday, February 26

No one unloads a horse here without history of inoculations. Precedent is on our side. On my desk is a fabulous compilation of old-time stallion advertisements titled the *Harford County Stud Book*, by Henry C. Peden Jr. A broadside for Archduke is condescendingly pitched. "A glance at his pedigree is sufficient for the intelligent horseman, while to all others it is Greek."

Name of the 1890s Harford County establishment where Archduke stood? Maryland Vaccine and Stock Farm.

Monday, February 27

The swelling in Moon Drive's ankle has subsided. In his 12-by-12 prison cell, serving a long sentence for bad behavior, he's stir-crazy. He hangs over his yoke screen, white blaze, white eyes flashing. I search for some humor in the age-old battle of patience and perseverance with injured horses. Find it in a passage from A.J. Leibling's *The Honest Rainmaker: The Life and Times of Colonel John R. Stingo*, when Colonel Stingo visits the skeleton of the great racehorse Sysonby, on display at the American Museum of Natural History.

"He looks so small when he is divested of his outward integument," the Colonel said. "I remember him as a big horse. It is easy to see why 2-year-olds go so frequently askew. They are of surprisingly fragile construction."

Tuesday, February 28

Boats against the current, borne back ceaselessly into the past. Nothing new in the sport of horse racing. Her history a great sea of perspective. Sysonby lost only one race, to the filly Artful in the Futurity — for 2-year-olds, of course. But Escher taught: Read backward. Sysonby was doped. A groom confessed. Two sides to every story.

Horses have always been prone to disease, misfortune. Sysonby died in his stall at Sheepshead Bay in 1906, victim of a mysterious skin disease. "Septic poisoning," the official cause of death. Septic just means infected. With what? Like wondering what the X stands for in colitis-X. It's a mystery. Vets at Fair Hill said, "Neurological herpes has been with us a long time, misdiagnosed often in the past."

It's a life-saving technique, to know what came before. Colonel Stingo would call history a "labyrinthian digression." Still, a little history steadies the boat against the current.

March

Wednesday, March 1

Perfect Moon in the brick aisle.
Swollen left knee.
Wedge-shaped fracture on digital X-ray.
Stakes horse on the slide.
Face of carpal bones chipped away.
At the bottom. In the desert.
Now home again, safe and sound, well, sound enough for turnout.

The incredible journey, over now. How he did not break down in a race feels providential. Kettle drums boom in my head in celebration as I watch Perfect Moon perfectly at home, running in a field with a friend today.

Thursday, March 2

Yesterday. Strange circular feel at Merryland. X-raying biologic half brothers; a yearling headed out into the world, Perfect Moon just back.

Dr. Nick Meittinis surveyed the yearling's joints from 30 angles, looking for flaws fixable in time for select sales. X-ray plates the size of textbooks up under the colt's hind legs. Stifle shots. He kicked through the tranquilizer. Nick centered an imaginary line to the lead plate, pulled the trigger. Bloodless computer voice. Hal in *2001: A Space Odyssey.* *"Acquisition Completed."*

Nick taps the laptop keyboard, adjusts contrast. "No OCDs."

Next, the hock.

"Tiny chip, away from the joint. Never bother him racing, but it will put off pinhookers. Ought to take it out."

"How much?"

"Fifteen hundred. And a van ride."

Silly ass-backwards game. Cosmetic surgery on a soldier. So many other factors make a racehorse. Like heart. Or lack of.

Achilles' heel in the statement: OK to race, but not to sell.

Friday, March 3

Sounds on a farm. Swans above, crane calls swallowed up by the *tat-tat-tat-tat* of hydraulic jackhammers chipping away at outcrops. Erratic rock from an ice age. Ankle breakers in new paddocks.

Tank treads on a loader *click-click-click-click* right out of a war movie. Hooves pound the dry track. Suddenly, absolute quiet during an ultrasound scan. Merryland Monroe. Rest or retire?

"Did she ever show any signs of lameness?" Nick asks. "The ones who bow but don't go lame sometimes make it back. Never lame? Then I'd try to bring her back."

Saturday, March 4

King T. Leatherbury is not just trainer but also breeder and owner of today's stakes winner, Ah Day. Though he's trained 6,000 winners, and bet on most of them, Leatherbury appeared stunned in the winner's circle interview.

"Did you handicap it this way?" *No.* "Did you think you had a shot against the favorite?" *No.*

There are Hall of Fame trainers who couldn't carry Leatherbury's condition books. He's uncertified by serious critics because his winners are mostly claimers. Because he trains from behind his windshield. Because he's a bettor. Because he never left Maryland for The Big Apple.

But seriously ... *six thousand winners!*

Sunday, March 5

Drive into Laurel past the stable gate. An abandoned railroad platform just feet from the clubhouse. In our time, the train has left the station. This joint pulsed hardest in the days of the Washington, D.C., International, at the dawn of jet travel for racehorses.

Overhead on the vast brick edifice, three immense snow-white art-deco horses take flight toward the heavens. A three-horse entry from the 1950s.

A privacy fence can't hide the red cross on an ambulance. Keep the engine running. You're in heart-attack country for aging patrons. Twenty years ago this end of the grandstand was the avant-garde "Sports Palace." It's been down-themed to "the Carriage Room." Sounds like a retirement-home closet for storing wheelchairs. Outside, signs for handicapped parking abound. Subtle or not, demographics apparent.

Monday, March 6

Quittin' time!

Just a phrase at the end of a long day. Sometimes, it really *is* quitting time.

He didn't appreciate being questioned on the depth of a water line. "Come on! We're in global warming!" he pitched. He'd hit rock. In his life. In the trench.

Next morning, his cell phone in his pickup, parked at the shop. No note. Just the sound in the distance of the other shoe about to fall. Certain to come, workers' comp complaint. Today's solution to backbreaking work.

Tuesday, March 7

Horse farms. Assets to any state. Yet here, no help from Annapolis. Across the Pennsylvania border, farms expand, fueled by pro-slots legislation. We're like a dry county next to a wet one. Even a one-time purse-enhancement bill languishes in a desk drawer in our state capitol.

Oh, well. The heck with Annapolis. Know the advantage of a training center, of a Merryland? Doesn't matter where the horse *foaled*. He's gotta *train* somewhere.

Wednesday, March 8

"Last Hold Orders Due to Virus Lifted in Maryland."

Headline on press release today from Department of Agriculture. Racetrack head Lou Raffetto: "It has been a two-month process. We learned a great deal about this virus. This knowledge will help us in the future."

Put fear of paralytic herpes second only to barn fires. We've become Gestapo guards. Cold hands to arriving vans: "Your papers, please."

Thursday, March 9

Cell-phone reception fades out across the Gunpowder River to Merryland. Up out of the cool woodlands. Stopped at the light behind an Imperatore van, slope-backed shape distinctive as Secretariat's hip. Staring at van warning in plain block letters: CAUTION HORSES.

Message ring. Missed call. What now? I'm upset in my mind. Today, I need to let someone go. It's a task I've put off. I proceed with caution, to dismiss a loose-horse of an employee before he lets another horse loose.

Today, I need to let someone go. It's a task I've put off. I proceed with caution, to dismiss a loose horse before another horse gets loose.

Friday, March 10

Back from Merryland. Climb out of the Gunpowder Valley to the highest point in Harford County, Mountain Road. Instead of a scenic overlook, you stare down into the Valley of the Cars, where dealerships bulldoze all things green. Trees incompatible with new-car finishes.

Nearer to home, surveyors move furtively in the oak-lined lane of Mt. Soma Farm, our abandoned Route 1 neighbor. Silently under siege. Surveyors are like birds knowing an earthquake is imminent. They fly off and soon the land shakes with grading equipment. Oak trees in the path of progress.

Pleasing travelers, mares and foals spread out over the hillside above Route 1. Like an urban zoo glimpsed from windows of a commuter train.

Saturday, March 11

Dungeon stalls of the old bank barn. Dark and narrow and long. High walled. Impenetrable to the eye. Light bulbs behind bars. Hannibal Lecter cages.

Time for a once-a-century freshening. Mindful of weight-bearing beams, Buddy Bitt's crew gut the ground-floor stalls. Crowbars rip and tear. Power drills scream in pain as bits hang in the petrified wood. Sounds of barn renovation reach the ears of horses and riders. Moans from the crypt. Eyes of the 2-year-olds grow wide. "I'll be good," they seem to say. "Just don't put me in that barn!"

There was a moment 100 years ago as the barn was being built, the floor was open. Just beams holding up a hayloft. In our own good time, we'll be back in that moment.

Sunday, March 12

A gentleman named William V. Elder owned the farm in the 1930s. He added a wing onto the house, but his wife died before they could move in. Broken-hearted, Elder visited the farm only to bring payroll.

You have to know this stuff. This isn't a vacuum. Something came before. Something is coming after. *You're* just a moment.

Monday, March 13

Ah Day's next start: the Private Terms Stakes 12 days from now. Leatherbury is a serious bettor. So is everyone in this business; wagering every time a check is written for board, or a mare booked, or a foal born, or a Breeders' Cup fee mailed away. Van bill. Vet bill. Feed bill. Two-fisted bettors. Little Leatherburys. Sums in private terms. Revealed to accountants at tax time.

Leatherbury's best mare was Dronette, dam of both graded stakes winner Thirty Eight Go Go and a full sister, Endette, who went winless in 14 tries and earned $12,220.

"That's OK," said Leatherbury. "I'll bet you throw me a runner someday."

And Endette threw him Ah Day.

Now *that's* betting on horses.

Tuesday, March 14

Corn husks, dry as parchment, blow onto the track from fields across Bottom Road. J.R. says: "Hope they plant wheat this year."

A husk blows up underneath Sagamoon's belly as she heads to the track. She arches like a cat. When her feet touch the soft sand of the track, she bolts off. Rider's head thrust back from the sudden acceleration.

Excuse to spook No. 730.

Wednesday, March 15

Trainer's caustic assessment of any horse of modest ability: "He won't die a maiden." How perfect! Just enough faith to find a winner's circle — at whatever level. Mike and partners drove two hours for the eighth race tonight at Penn. An ill wind blew the card off after the fourth. Jockeys wary of the ides of March.

Pennsylvania-bred Haldy *still* a maiden. Long ride home.

Thursday, March 16

A dropped ceiling of bead board was attractive 75 years ago in the first renovation of Merryland's bank barn — a soaring Amish treasure of mortise and tenon construction. Built when chestnut meant a plentiful tree, not just a red horse. But I'd like to know what's up, up there. Out of sight is not out of mind. Ceiling may be hiding rotten timbers. Floor above holds great weight. Hay trucks have unloaded on the second floor for decades. Wide gaps in floorboards sifted chaff, now trapped atop the dropped ceiling.

Summon the barn cats. Mickey Mouse's house is slated for demolition. Get crowbars, dust masks. A nasty job is about to come down on our heads.

Friday, March 17

When Traci dropped off Perfect Moon a week before Valentine's Day, she asked: "What's with all the neon hearts in your neighbor's windows? We don't have those in Kentucky!"

In a flat yard before the plunge to Route 1's car dealerships, one man decorates his road frontage in the holiday of the moment. Tonight, inflatable leprechauns rollick on his lawn. Tacky?

Essayist E.B. White lived off a neon stretch of Route 1 in Maine: "Probably a man's destination colors the highway. Steering a car toward home is an emotional direction. Familiarity is the thing, the sense of belonging. It grants exemption from all shabbiness."

Life in the not-so-country. Leprechauns today. Bunnies in April. Uncle Sam on Independence Day. Balloons tethered to new-car lots. We live here. Home is where the neon heart is.

Saturday, March 18

Cooling out Jenkin Jones after his fifth in the Laurel stakes today, Flint suggested: "Let's take him to the farm. Need to geld him. One testicle is much smaller than the other, and could be painful when he runs."

The "Gelding Report" at The Jockey Club interactive registration site asks for date of alteration: mm/dd/yyyy.

"Whywhywhywhy JJ, it's for your own good," I stammer as he rolls his white eye in resignation.

Sunday, March 19

Friday letter from the Anatomy Board: Joseph's ashes are ready for pickup.

Luck of the Irish, Notre Dame alum returns to Country Life on St. Patrick's Day. Rests on the table next to his diary until this morning, St. Joseph's Day. No saint, yet two feast days make up his final exacta. Perfect whimsy. Ironic smiles when Mom notes the symmetry.

Kids and grandkids gather on the basketball court at 11 o'clock. Up the long soft hill to the top of the mares-and-foals field. Dry ground dust coats leather shoes.

No bagpipes. No eulogies. Just the 14 of us, one by one, taking a dash of ash and throwing it up into the strong North wind. Watching it sail like chimney smoke in a wide arc over the dry hills. Dust-*on*-to-dust. A liberating motion, the throw itself.

Mares and foals move over the spot where we stood. Reclaim it as theirs. No drama. Just cycle of life blowing in the wind.

Monday, March 20

Slew Sunny Slew threw herself against the wall when the shock of losing blood from her ruptured uterine artery sent her out of her mind. Then she lay still, barely breathing, hardly making a sound. I thought of Hemingway's childbirth story "Indian Camp" from *In Our Time.*

Richard and the Mexican men, surrogate uncles, carried the colt in the pickup bed down to the lower barn. Val placed him in the stall with 24-year-old Cruella, barren but carrying an udder of milk. Irresistible surge of seasonal hormones. She had just been bred. At *24*, still cycling life.

That was Saturday night. Today, Cruella's irritated kicks warned the hungry youngster not to tug on Momma's scanty milk machine, but the unlikely adoption has taken.

Tuesday, March 21

Mass e-mailings to partners in 2-year-olds Jackie Wilson, Jersey Moon, Chesapeake Moon, Moon Drive, Mr. Guggenheim:

"These modest-bred colts are not likely to become stallions. About the same chance of a junior-high basketball player making the NBA. It's a good time to geld them; before serious training, before they put on weight, before flies hatch out. When their racing careers are over, they can be somebody's riding horses."

Google Jackie Wilson the singer. His bio mentions many offspring. Not to be the case for four-legged Jackie, singing in the choir with his buddies.

Wednesday, March 22

The Fresh Air Camp. Right next to Country Life. Names out of fairy tales.

City kids spent summers at the camp; 40 acres of ballfields, cabins, swimming pools, basketball courts. At dawn, camp loudspeakers played "Reveille." At dusk, "Taps" poured mournfully across summer fields. Bugle notes like an opera to young ears at Country Life, freezing us in our sneakers.

Now a religious school is emptying the collection plate into wallets of hired guns. Praying, paying, for rezoning of the old camp. Not quite a done deal. Hearing Examiner is reviewing it. But let's be real! Someone *other* than the county is volunteering to build a school.

The school could add 600 cars a day to Old Joppa. We'll live trapped near the Bad Air Camp, on the last horse farm near Bel Air — a town named for clean sky. A grim fairy tale if it's "taps" for the Fresh Air Camp.

Thursday, March 23

Alden's Malibu has improved from running in $7,500 claiming company on New Year's Day to an allowance race today. Still, he couldn't outrun his biologic half brother Hello Jerry, winner today by almost 10.

Names of stallions' offspring become embedded. Hello Jerry is pronounced with a snarl, the way Newman greeted Jerry on TV's *Seinfeld* show. But good horses get hurt. Careers canceled fast as TV shows. Sidelined by injury, Hello Jerry was almost Goodbye Mr. Chips.

Friday, March 24

J.R.'s eyes sweep ahead as he harrows Merryland's track each morning. Scanning the beachy sand for bottles hurled from cars on Bottom Road.

On Old Joppa Road at Country Life, so close to Bel Air, America's obsession with packaging is evident in an endless insult of litter. Early spring the worst, no weeds yet to conceal winter's crop. I can't even send my sons out with empty feed bags; local traffic brakes for no one. The pony-farm lady at the other end of Old Joppa got blown off her feet fetching litter. Broke her arm.

Whywhywhywhy? *Why* do people throw trash out of cars?

Saturday, March 25

Ah Day seizes the lead in the stakes. Leatherbury headed to the windows. But, *Ah!* Look out! Here comes A.R. "Rosie" Napravnik on a 70-1 shot. Centered in a circle

of balance over the withers of the eight horse. At the wire, Ah Day behind the Eight Ball.

Out of Maryland have come Mc-Carron, Desormeaux, Prado. Another Maryland phenom is on the way.

Sunday, March 26

It's all a circle. John Eisenberg's book on Native Dancer tells how Harry Guggenheim's Dark Star hung the only loss on the gray champion. Breeder Warner Jones' wife said: "Harry came by the yearling sales barn, 'picked out' a brown yearling, but 'picked up' a different brown yearling in the ring." She's saying Guggenheim won the Kentucky Derby with a horse he bought by mistake.

From 1962 to 1986, Merryland was owned by Guggenheim's niece Barbara Obre. Her steeplechasing son Michael Wettach recruited owners, and Betty Miller managed the farm. Betty owns a piece of Alden's Malibu. On race days we throw her sporty wheelchair over the seat and drive back to her day. The gilded age of Merryland. Stories more colorful than merely winning the Derby with the wrong horse.

Monday, March 27

Notes from a workers' comp office worker: "You would not believe how cynical we become here. We see it all. *'Everybody owes us something'* is the mindset of every injured employee who files a claim. Well, some are legit, some aren't. That's our adjuster's job. Where labor-type jobs are involved — for horse farms, for trainers — be sure to do background checks for pre-existing injuries or conditions when folks apply."

Tuesday, March 28

Driest March in history. Tonight, a rain fell so lightly you could only hear it under the roofs of run-in sheds. Not hard enough to dissolve the fertilizer. But just this faint dampness caused the thirsty ground to reach up. The smell of damp dust. The smell of spring. The ground not wanting to let the secret out. Shush. It's raining.

But the roofs, which care not for moisture, began to tell everyone. Then the rain stopped. Roofs fell quiet. The event ended.

Wednesday, March 29

Yearling inspectors here today from Kentucky.
"He's too straight in the pastern."

"You did check ligament surgery as a foal? That needs to be in the repository."
"This colt needs to grow. Save him for the fall sales."
"You took the chip out? Good. Now he'll make the preferred sale."
"How do we get to the next farm?"
Like the auction itself. Two minutes is all they need. All you get.

Thursday, March 30

Chuck Lucier does boutique shoeing on the sales yearlings. He apprenticed under Harvey Powell, brought to Merryland by Mrs. Obre. Powell hammered straight pieces of bar steel into racing plates on the hand-cranked coal forge in the blacksmith shop built for him by Mrs. Obre. Chuck wants to retrofit the old shop with a gas burner. I hesitate. The coal forge melted steel at 2,000 degrees. That seems mighty hot for the old wooden barn. I see rows of cool shoes, ready to wear, stacked in racks on blacksmith trucks. Times change.

Friday, March 31

Racing is *still* the greatest spectator sport. Just watch the life of racehorses, in all phases, unfold all day, every day. Why, look! Here comes Perfect Moon, ex-jock, arthritic knees cooling out as he swaggers to the fence to acknowledge his fans. He was a star! The best 2-year-old in California the summer of '03. No paunch yet, but at least weight over his ribs since retirement.

Here come vans rumbling past, faces of 2-year-olds from the Delaware program peering out windows. This year's stars.

Geldings hobbyhorse down the brown stretch ahead of trick rider Troy, sitting long stirruped on a bucking bronc — new arrival, $800 3-year-old from the Virginia Tech booster auction. Humblest pedigree. Toughest temperament. Best boned. A lesson in hybrid vigor?

There goes Merryland Monroe, coming in off the walker, determined to make the Olympics, rehabbing her torn tendon.

Watching it unfold, the farm carries you forward in time like the "people mover" at the airport. It's all happening faster than you can blink.

These moments. In our time.

SPRING
2006

April

Saturday, April 1

The things they carry.

Troy carries a stick. Rubber handle. Plastic core. Wrapped in leather. His heels anchored in the irons, his hands quiet on necks of recalcitrant 2-year-olds, Troy merely flicks the whip on babies' shoulders to maintain attention. A nun's ruler.

Troy's wife, Rachael, carries 11 pins and a plate in the bones of her right arm. Injured in falls. Once in a timber race. Her father, J.R., carries a grudge that wealthy horse owners do not always carry insurance for riders in jumping races. Nevertheless, on Saturdays in April, Merryland's riders travel in packs to such races in Virginia, in Maryland, a most un-genteel game carried on their fragile, uninsured backs.

To tack up 2-year-olds, sweet Myranda carries her heart on her sleeve, a treeless saddle on her arm, a race bridle on her shoulder. Cindy carries her grooming expertise quietly. In her days as a pony girl at Pimlico, she carried 1993 Kentucky Derby winner Sea Hero to the starting gate for the Preakness.

Three Serbian riders carry a loose handle on the English language and memories of a country unimaginable.

Young horses-in-training carry deep-seated ancestral fear. Let it go, implore the riders they carry.

Sunday, April 2

A modest Hall of Fame goes unnoticed in the Pimlico clubhouse. Inadequate for Preakness legends. War Admiral in a can. Alliteratively dubbed "Hoofbeats Through History."

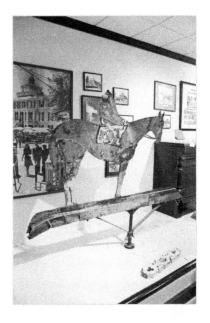

Yet in spite of its size, it succeeds. You can *hear* hoofbeats.

And smell smoke. The original clubhouse burned in 1966. Charred weathervane of horse-and-rider all that remains. Focal point of the exhibit. The cross in a shrine. The weathervane fell three stories when the famous cupola collapsed. Just another jockey at risk. This one decapitated. Forevermore riding headless, on a loose rein, aboard a ghost-eyed horse. A powerful image of our enduring trust in horses: You take care of me. I'll take care of you.

Monday, April 3

In her 24-year-old uterus, Cruella carries a 15-day-old vesicle. A fertilized egg. A half sibling to her grade I-winning colt Diazo. You can carry a farm on the sale of such embryos as yearlings.

Meanwhile, Cruella's adopted foal drinks 25 hand-fed bottles of milk each day. High maintenance. Obstinate. Refusing a self-serve bucket. A matter of time. He sniffs at pelleted baby food. For now, though, both foal and Momma seem happy; and if Momma ain't happy, ain't nobody happy.

Coaxing one more precious conception out of a grand old producer. A 340-day gestation. One day at a time. And so, bottle after bottle, you carry on.

Tuesday, April 4

To ship a horse *anywhere* these days, carry a health certificate drawn in the past 48 hours; proof of vaccination within 7 to 90 days for equine influenza and rhinopneumonitis; and a current Coggins.

State police are carding horse carriers. Legacy of the herpes plague.

But vets can't complete a health cert without a current Coggins. In urgent cases, J.R. runs a test tube of blood to the lab at Laurel for expedited processing. Or blood is FedExed to Cornell in upstate New York for next-day clearance.

To move horses, you must first move paper.

Wednesday, April 5

Vet bills from the racetrack arrive separately from trainers' board bills. Lessens the blow. Trainers under the radar with only the day-rate. But vet bills cause the radar to bleep in itemized confusion. Potassium Estrone. Depo-Medrol. ACTH. Quest. B-1. Amicar. Amino Plus. RVI. Staminade. Methacarbonal. Lasix. Legend. Dantrium.

Often between $500 and $1,000 a month in vet bills. The modern racehorse is a magnet for pharmaceuticals, for elixirs, for the expensive things they carry in vet trucks.

Thursday, April 6

Christy entered the vet charges into the billing program. Tina's Prospect. Maturity Digital Radiograph: $135.

"Shouldn't that be $35? The others were $35," she called out into the farm office, floor-plan like an old-time newsroom, where reporters accessed colleagues' knowledge simply by shouting.

Yes, just $35. A two-second procedure using a $100,000 portable digital X-ray machine costs $35.

"Christy, were her knees closed?"

Friday, April 7

Pensioned three years ago, Carnivalay walked boldly onto a van today at Country Life. Merryland is eight miles away. A refurbished stallion barn and a rested paddock awaited. Salad years in deep clover. Still, I worried plenty about stress on the old boy, leaving Country Life for the only time since his arrival 20 years ago. In his new stall

at Merryland, he stared out the window at fields of green.

"I've died and gone to grass heaven," I heard him think.

Saturday, April 8

Sloppy track for today's Primonetta Stakes at Laurel.

"Malibu Moonbeam has been pulled up. And Sun Sapphire has also been eased."

Two fillies, each on three legs at the quarter pole. Malibu Moonbeam. Chestnut flash. Three wins in three starts this year. Owned by a friend. Just trying to get black type.

On the backstretch:

"What happened?" I asked the driver of the ambulance that follows jockeys.

"They carried off two horses. Put one down first."

"The chestnut?"

"I think it was the red one. Is red chestnut?"

Fenced-off morgue. A form under the blue tarp in a roofless pen. The dead pen at Laurel, back by the machine shop. So insensitive, inappropriate. Exposed to the weather. Exposed to a prying camera, a PETA photo perhaps. Not a proper cold box like a major track should have. I didn't care if racetrack security chased me away. *Was it the red filly or not?* I pulled hard on the drop latch. It swung free. I lifted the end of the tarp. Red face head-first. Thin blaze. Bared teeth. Death stare. Blood showed on a hind ankle through the white run-down bandage. Catastrophic injury. Broken skin. Broken bone. Back there with the broken equipment.

Spirit of a horse gone. With the wind racing in her ears. Carried off. Purely borne.

Sunday, April 9

On the wall in "Hoofbeats Through History." From the days of bookmakers at Pimlico.

Betting Rules.

Rule One.

In all bets, there must be a possibility to win when the bet is made. "You cannot win where you cannot lose."

Monday, April 10

Dr. Nick Meittinis' assistant, Jay, bets me that the knees on the 2-year-old walking toward us have not "closed."

"I'll bet you all the money I have on me." Pulling his pockets inside out. Smiling: "Nothing here but rabbit ears."

Twist on Rule One. I'm also holding rabbit ears.

Nick clicks the trigger on the X-ray gun. A thin black line appears above the knee. Cells encased in synovial fluid. "Knees close from 24 to 26 months of age. She's an April foal two years ago. Not closed yet."

A closed knee on X-ray resembles a welded seam. No black line. Graded A, B, and C. Only three A's out of 18 babies.

"How many 2-year-olds at sales this spring had closed knees?" I ask Nick.

"I don't like to work 2-year-old sales," he answers.

Tuesday, April 11

Sagamoon's knees were A's. Today was her first day at Belmont Park.

From day one, this filly has been special. Best foal. Best yearling. Best 2-year-old prospect. She's a New York-bred. I won her mother on a coin toss at Alfred Vanderbilt's dispersal at Timonium. I had bought her for a client who knew I wanted her for the farm. He said, "Let's flip for her." Her sire gets 2-year-olds, but don't be in a hurry.

I stanched my enthusiasm, recalling John Nerud's retort to a breeder: "Don't tell me who they're by. Tell me who they can *run* by."

Breeding farms are filled with underachieving broodmares that received embarrassing sendoffs as 2-year-olds.

Wednesday, April 12

J.R.'s unauthorized Merryland Diary:

6:30 a.m. I telephone trucking company bringing sand to replenish the track surface. Tell him we need screened "flume sand." Same sand ordered by Pimlico's track super Jamie Richardson.

7:30 Driver arrives: "Got a load of that there 'cone sand.' They didn't have no 'flume sand.' Better take a look before I spread it. Think it has loam or clay mixed with it. Not like that mason sand you usually get."

8:00 I call Jamie. He says: "That cone sand might work better anyway. It's screened. That flume sand could turn to grease if you got too much rain. Get your tractors buried out there."

8:30 I phone Paula at the quarry. She says: "Hey, why is everybody calling me? Pimlico. The trucker. Now you. That flume sand is full of clay clods and you're better off with the cone sand, which is what I already sent you!"

In such nightly e-mails to me, J.R. uses punctuation marks to censor offensive language he hears that day. He screens his prose, presents a surface smooth as racetrack sand. And just as illusory.

Thursday, April 13

Farm worker with bipolar history discharged from hospital today. With strict orders to *stay* on his medicine. A doctor pulled me aside: "*Do not* get sucked into his orbit. It's all in his head. The mind is the most powerful instrument on Earth."

I sat in the parking lot waiting for his wheelchair. Thought back to a visit to Tartan Farms to interview Nerud. Apologies from a worker who'd fallen off the wagon — again. Nerud reined in his disappointment. Said an encouraging word. Drove on. A long moment passed. He turned and said: "Got to leave a man his dignity. Always leave a man his dignity."

Friday, April 14

Forty horses in training at Merryland. Ten sets of four. Steady horsebacking. Meanwhile, at Country Life, farm crew staying late tonight, finishing up breeding. Twelve-hour days now the norm.

Phone call from New York: dead foal.

Phone call from New Bolton: suspected peritonitis.

Soft sunset. Light rain moved out. Beautiful evening. Cool night air settling down on the creek. Ellen and the boys in Virginia for Easter. Must find a way to get away.

Saturday, April 15

A farm spins in details so encompassing that you sometimes feel suffocated. Windows down on drive to Virginia, stereo blasting.

In the driveway in Richmond, cell phone messages carry you back home: "Hi, this is Dr. Short from the New Bolton Center, calling about your foal."

Sunday, April 16

Easter morning message: "Hello, there. Dr. Short again. Update. The foal has diarrhea. We're moving him to a different barn, where there is no visiting. Hope to hear from you. Hope you're having a nice day."

Diarrhea calls for biosecurity measures. You'll receive a fax that reads: "Certain stress factors include transportation, hospitalization, relocation." Check. Check. Check.

I think: Extraordinary measures. Extraordinary bills. Check.

Bullets fly in the horse business. Don't worry about the ones that miss you. Look out for the ones coming at you.

And have a nice day.

Monday, April 17

A happy camper is Carnivalay at Merryland. Comic piebald face greeting visitors.

Brass plaque on empty stall at Country Life: *Maryland Stallion of the Year 1990*. The year daughter Valay Maid ran third in the Breeders' Cup Distaff, after sister Go for Wand fell so horribly. Such promise that day. Such an awful memory. For a moment there, he was the next Danzig. Kentucky quit calling, though, after his skittish foals discouraged breeders, unnerved trainers, dropped riders. Still, he sired 37 stakes winners.

Brass nameplate on empty stall: Carnivalay. Bay. 1981. By Northern Dancer out of Obeah, by Cyane.

Take all this brass to Merryland. Visitors, newcomers, need to know his name, his history, his famous pedigree.

Tuesday, April 18

Sixteen years ago, the horse who was to become racing's all-time leading earner was carried *in utero* from Kentucky. Solar Slew delivered her precious cargo into the gentle arms of farm strongman Richard Harris at 5:45 a.m. on this date in 1990.

Ellen hangs a banner on the Route 1 farm sign every year: "Happy Birthday Cigar!"

Gas station attendants. Barbers. Fed-Ex drivers. School teachers.

"Hey, we saw the Cigar sign today! Tell him 'Happy Birthday' for us!"

A decade after his last race, Cigar still the champ.

Wednesday, April 19

Reflected Gold was uncomfortable at 11 a.m. Within an hour, she became violent. Owner notified. Sedatives and analgesics no help. Insurance company fine with any decision. She crawled onto a van, and up the road to New Bolton she went at 1:30 p.m. Surgery. Phone calls. Updates.

Not optimistic tonight. I wish I'd taken a gun to her misery, but I don't have a gun. In the old days, a horse or two were shot here. This is an old farm.

Thursday, April 20

The women grooms carry themselves with poise and dignity. They move with graceful confidence around the young horses. Always touching the babies, rubbing  their noses, pushing hindquarters, lifting feet, pulling manes. The horses are complicated, often dangerous, especially unbroken new arrivals. Each horse is different; but they are different the same way every day, and the women grooms teach them to trust. Today I saw a bruise on a groom's face. Worried she might have been kicked. It is not from a horse, I learn.

Friday, April 21

The intensely religious Mexican brothers appreciate the Friday night pizza tradition. At quitting time the past six weeks, I've phoned in orders for veggie pizzas.

"Maybe pepperoni tonight. Maybe sausage," they tell me tonight.

"Not veggie?"

"No. Hey Zeus has risen. Hey Zeus has risen." They point to the sky. I am confused. Jesus is one of their brothers. Why has Jesus risen at five in the afternoon? Has he been night-watching?

Then it comes to me. Lent has ended. No more abstinence. Easter passed over us last Sunday.

Saturday, April 22

Cell phone message. 9:58 a.m.

"Dr. Nutt calling from New Bolton. Distension in mare's abdomen. Understandable, the stress she's been through. Passed a trocar tube to relieve gas. She has loose feces. Primary concern is her gut."

My gut says she's cooked. Instead of a gun crack like the old days, we'll hear the gravel crack under the UPS tires. Please don't send her halter back. Please just throw the damned $30 thing away up there.

Sunday, April 23

Yesterday at Pimlico was Pat Day Day. Hall of Fame jockey at a fund-raiser for the Race Track Chaplaincy of America.

Earlier, atheist Pagan Moon runs like the devil to win a sprint stakes. Ah Day takes the Tesio. Two stakes for a home sire in an hour. Ah, we needed a day like today.

Monday, April 24

Before New York Moon left for Aqueduct, I pulled his file to check his Coggins. Taped to his folder was the test tube of chips scraped out of his knee last October. I shook them like the glass snowball in the last scene of *Citizen Kane*, as Orson Welles whispered in a mysterious voice: "Rosebud. Rosebud."

Time heals all wounds. The horse Old Rosebud won the 1914 Kentucky Derby, broke down in the Withers Stakes. Spent the next three years turned out on the Texas prairie. Came back as a 6-year-old to win 15 races. It was an axiom in the old days that injured racehorses never came back. Old Rosebud proved them wrong. Do you follow, New York Moon? These are the good old days; you're our Old Rosebud, Bud.

Tuesday, April 25

Right below conscious thought, van drivers carry nightmares of every freakish episode hauling horses. The yearling filly that wouldn't come off at Timonium. Backed her down the ramp. But, no, she lunged uphill, back into the van. Didn't leap far enough. Coco mat gathered in her scramble, exposing the gap between the ramp and van floor. Her hind legs found that narrow opening. A 1,000-1 shot. Tendons ripping in struggle.

Drivers in a hurry carry a chute board. J.R. says: "No way. Take a minute to yank out the long ramp." Some drivers carry a sign on their rig: Not For Hire. Eluding commercial insurance rates, but hiring out anyway.

Every van that survives the clogged beltways and tunnel backups carries the dream: the next 2-year-old stakes winner, the next Broodmare of the Year, the next Cigar.

Wednesday, April 26

When MRLS hit Kentucky in spring of 2001, every van with four good tires carried a mass evacuation from the Bluegrass. Dunkirk on wheels. Carrying evacuees from abortion storms, foal blindness, heart attacks. Testing the adage that mares needed to be in foal at 45 days before shipping home. Mares were shipped 600 miles for breed-and-returns. Checked in foal two weeks later.

So we thought there was little risk in bringing home a mare from Kentucky at 32 days in foal last week. Had a van coming this way. Checked her today at 40 days. Empty. Turned the van around.

It's been that kind of month. Embarrassing phone call to mare owner. He reasoned. "A board bill in Maryland is the same as a board bill in Kentucky to me. Why did you bring her home?"

My position was weak. MRLS was a crisis. We're back to 45 days.

Thursday, April 27

The racetrack is an addiction. When they say it gets in your blood, they're wrong. It gets in your brain. It's dopamine. It's adrenaline. Hooks you when you're young. Ask folks when they first became infatuated with horses. A grandfather, an uncle, took them to the track when they were kids. Next thing you know, you don't know anything else. You play the ponies, or invest in them, or work with them.

I met a trainer this month whose alarm goes off at 2:30 every morning. He leaves the house at 3. Gets to Laurel at 4. Some nights he doesn't get home until 7. His wife makes dinner. He takes a shower and goes to bed.

And that's his day, every day. He has the exhausted look of a coal miner.

"My life is over," he said to me. His brain, the most powerful instrument on Earth, hooked on racing.

Friday, April 28

P. J. Indy, running scared since he poleaxed a downed runner at Laurel in February, found his courage again today. Bulled through horses. Tired at the 16th pole. Finished 5th at Pimlico. But as good as a victory to those around him.

Jenkin Jones, though, stood stiff-kneed in his stall a day after running last on the hard turf course. X-rays were negative, but JJ was missing his mojo. I wondered if gelding had taken his heart.

Saturday, April 29

At Churchill Downs to meet with partners at lunch.

"He is not eligible to the Preakness, but he ran a '2' in the Tesio, after a '2' in an allowance race. We need to do our homework. Think what it could do for the stallion. We have until entries close on Wednesday, May 17, to nominate him. If he has to scratch before post-time for the Preakness that Saturday — *for any reason* — we don't get the fee back. That's 72 hours of exposure, before he even runs good or bad. The fee covers the Preakness *and* the Belmont. The trainer is the owner. We'd split any purses."

Thomas Edison said that many inventors get 75 percent through an idea, then get discouraged. "That is not the time to give up," counseled Edison. We are 25 percent of this idea. It's neither good nor bad yet. Just gathering facts. And looking for a guy named Consensus: "Let's see who comes out of the Derby next week. Let's handicap the Preakness before we decide."

At dinner: Back already? How'd it go?

Sunday, April 30

A yearling ran into the fence today. Vet at Leesburg: "Extensive abdominal lacerations. We need to put him under general anesthetic. Sew him back up."

It's not my horse. Owner unavailable on a Sunday. But by now, I know the drill. Five grand to get him back. There are no options. You are hooked. "Go ahead."

Is there some fantastic equation at work that says the highs are higher than the lows are low?

For weeks, I've been inspired by stories on my night table: Tim O'Brien's book *The Things They Carried*. Tonight, I collapse in laughter at bedtime, thinking back to the horse breeders' banquet last week. They presented the Federico Tesio award to two horsemen who died. Dad wiggled some magic wand in the skybox and made the presenter pronounce it "post-humorous" instead of "posthumous." It's a favorite phrase I carry now.

Post humorously. After laughter. An amusing amulet to wear in a game in which the first rule is all risk: "You cannot win where there is nothing to lose."

May

Monday, May 1

These spring evenings. After dinner. *Gotta* go for a walk. *Gotta* see the horses. *Gotta* see that red sky. In the glow of buttercups. On a bed of apple blossoms.

Why such compulsion? This need to be out. This need to walk the track after a rain, reaching down for small stones sifted up by the weight of water. This need to push fence boards. Posts all good? Nails wiggle out of wood. Tap 'em back with a fisted rock. This need to reach down into a spring pasture. Slide thumb up stalks of bluegrass going to seed. This obsession with all things small.

Compulsion surrounds you. Opens the door to May in Maryland. A month of transition, in a state of contrast. A force of nature. Irresistible.

Tuesday, May 2

Fireproof lock box holds The Jockey Club registration certificates. Papers colored and textured. Like new money. Like old money. Papers on all the yearlings. Papers on all the broodmares. But not for all the 2-year-olds — some already at tracks. Racing secretaries have a few of those papers.

The papers for Merryland fieldmates Perfect Moon and Mosby's Raider are in the lock box. The former's are heavy with ink from California racing secretaries recording Saturday stakes wins. The latter's couldn't even reflect a weekday claiming win. Mosby's Raider's papers? Confederate currency. Impossible to redeem.

When papers first arrive on newly registered babies, the question begs: Saturday star? Or Tuesday hayburner? They go in alphabetical order, and no one knows from Adam.

Wednesday, May 3

Named a Kentucky-bred yearling colt Daniel Moon to remind us that he might some day run in the Bluegrass State. For juicy purses in the nascent Kentucky-bred enhancement program. In the meantime, Daniel Moon is headed to Delaware. To serve 90 days in the First State. To be eligible for bonuses of 30 percent. Hedge funds. In case the hedge at Keeneland is too high for Daniel to blaze his trail.

Thursday, May 4

Working alone, Troy tacks up the broncs at Merryland, the unbroken new arrivals.

In between the training barns, Troy walks behind a green 2-year-old filly like he's plowing a field with a workhorse. He's already spent days longe-lining her in the shedrow. Block walls his assistant.

Fundamentals are imparted in the lengths of these side reins. A gentle mouth. Stop. Turn. Walk. Back up. From the safety of the ground. When the time comes to be ridden, Troy is first on her back. The day comes when J.R. announces her name at the gap. "First time on the track for Princess Malibu."

To get the filly around the sandy oval the first few days, Troy will coax and urge and encourage and scold, without actually saying much. It's all in his hands, his legs, his seat on the horse. There's nothing like it. It's like a whirl of wind being sucked into a bottle. A captured twister. A tamed bronc. Nature's instincts harnessed. A week later, railbirds ask: "Who's that filly? She's going good."

A magic show in all small things at Merryland.

Friday, May 5

In 1970, gonzo journalist Hunter S. Thompson wrote "The Kentucky Derby is Decadent and Depraved." Required reading. Casting himself as an inept loser, Thompson bet on favorite Silent Screen. This sport loops back on itself. Silent Screen is Merryland's most famous yearling graduate. Champion in 1969 for colorful sports impresario Sonny Werblin. No matter. The Derby winner, Dust Commander, was a better story:

"A dapper little man named Lehmann said he had just flown into Louisville that morning from Nepal, where he'd 'bagged a record tiger.' He had just won $127,000 with a horse that cost him $6,500 two years ago. His occupation, he said, was 'retired contractor.' And then he added, with a big grin, 'I just retired.' "

A good tip on the Derby is Thompson's piece, in full, every year on Derby eve.

Saturday, May 6

In Mel Brooks' movie *Spaceballs*, he parodies *Star Wars*' evil-father/good-son theme. Says Dark Helmet to Lone Starr: "I am your father's brother's nephew's cousin's former roommate."

Which suggests itself to describe the pedigree link between Hookedonjoy and grade I winner Hookedonthefeelin, mother of today's Humana Distaff Handicap winner on the Derby undercard.

"Hookedonjoy is a full sister to the dam of the dam of Pussycat Doll."

At the moment, Hookedonjoy is incapable of carrying on the family theme. She is zero for three in covers this spring to a Kentucky sire. Frustration seeks a reason. Stallion incompatibility? (Certain mares reject certain stallions.) Thyroid issues? (A frequent obstacle to conception.) Today's pedigree update is buoyant news. Maybe she needs a different boy.

Sunday, May 7

The Ah Day idea.

The owners of the sire contemplate putting up the Preakness nomination fee for the owner of the horse. To elevate the stallion by having a contender in the classic. A gamble consistent with the changing landscape of stallion promotion. Stallion owners now promise Dodge trucks, or Hummers, or Land Rovers. In California, a $500,000 bonus awaits the breeder of a grade I winner by a young stallion.

For now: Wait to see who comes out of the Derby. Wait for the Thoro-Graph numbers. Wait until the last minute at entry time the Wednesday before the Preakness.

Monday, May 8

To capture a loose horse, legendary trainer John Madden (reported the New York *Herald* of July 18, 1907) "threw his arm around the animal's neck, and brought the horse to a standstill, using the well-known method of squeezing the horse's nostrils so that he could not breathe."

Today, yearling colt Malibu Minister blew his mind after a procaine penicillin reaction. Neurons misfiring like flashbulbs in his brain. He crashed through his stall door, ran down the dike of the racetrack, out the back gate, and awoke waist deep in the neighbor's vast hayfield.

Fifteen erstwhile John Maddens closed in on him. I felt like someone was squeezing my air off. His insurance value shot through my mind. His sales future. His racing future. His partners' future. I watched as Virginia Jim turned the colt away from Beechers Brook. The colt sensibly gave up the chase, was led back to the barn. And the day resumed where it had left off, like a merry-go-round after a break.

Tuesday, May 9

Two-year-old Tina's Prospect has been away at college in Saratoga. The Spa is a popular training center for stall-starved Long Island conditioners. Tina is returning home after bucking shins. There are worse offenses in racing's school of hard knocks.

Wednesday, May 10

Two-year-old New York Citi is turned out in a grassy paddock at Merryland, too immature to bang baby bones on hard track surfaces. Her half brother, Iosilver, won a stakes as a 4-year-old. She is not the lone ranger in her family to be late developing.

Thursday, May 11

A quick thunder-shower rode in this afternoon, then as quickly rode out. Red sun peeked out from under a brim of purple clouds. Mares and foals, suddenly refreshed, danced across the field in exuberant displays of health and strength. For the first time in their  young lives, foals practiced rearing and landing, rearing and landing. They circled in long laps at great distances from their moms. Managing muscles hard-wired in ancestral circuitry, awakened by a spring rain.

Wildness in the herd this evening. An African savannah at dusk.

SPRING 2006

Friday, May 12

With Pimlico a carnival of activity before the Preakness, we sent a trio of 2-year-olds on a school trip from Merryland to Old Hilltop. A van ride down and back. For advanced gate work. For desensitization. For exposure to the tents and trucks and traffic, before the arrival of the Preakness runners next week.

Spectacular Malibu, Jersey Moon, Jackie Wilson.

How'd they do, J.R.?

The merry-go-round never stopped.

Saturday, May 13

Sense of taste ignites a memory. A fruit drink. I'm 12 again. Brothers dragging bales of straw across yellow ground for trailing wagons. Tractors driven by Dad, Uncle Johnny. On farm across the county. We ride home atop the tottering load.

Down Lake Fanny Hill on Route 1, the load shifts. Blows out. Explodes. Bales fly. Kids on top fly. Caught in the avalanche of straw. Rubber kids bumped around. Dug out. Still in one piece. Sodas from Sherman's Store still in hand. How'd you like a nice Hawaiian Punch?

Mom to Dad: Whose idea was *that?*

Hasn't it always been a little bit about the danger of farm life? The decisions. The threat and bluff. The unspoken challenge. The quickening pulse.

Sunday, May 14

Val carries a penknife. Handy to unscrew panels on the electric gate when wires laced into the roadbed short out in rain. She also carries the dream of a farm in New Mexico, where winters won't cause her arthritis to creak.

Kate carries a pulling comb to barber-up the wild manes that arrive.

Mom carries Dad's friendly ghost around, so light on routine days, so terribly heavy on days special.

On Wednesdays, Laurie and Ellen carry artist's palettes and canvases to corners of the farm. At dinnertime, you see a painting: an angle and a beauty to the farm you had never noticed.

Troy carries his Uncle Charlie's quiet way with a horse. The horses carry memories of who taught them how to load. Sometimes they carry a white egret on their withers, same as you've seen on cattle. Memory of a white bird on a horse's back is something you carry around in your head.

Monday, May 15

Beyer Speed Figures are discussed in the book *Beyer on Speed*, a title suggestive of all-night exam cramming. Ah Day ran a 102 Beyer in the Tesio. Barbaro's best Beyer before the Derby was a 103. They are not a mere one point apart. What am I missing?

Two days ago Ah Day worked five furlongs in :59 flat, the fastest of 25 works at that distance at Laurel. In my dreams, Ah Day wins the Preakness. King Leatherbury, his breeder, owner, and trainer, flies into the Hall of Fame. The sire is stratospheric. It's a Frank Capra movie. Then the alarm goes off.

Tuesday, May 16

Leatherbury is a disciple of the "numbers." The Thoro-Graph Sheets are delivered to him every day. They come in a binder that reminds me of a summer-school makeup course. I study the syllabus' opening lines.

The two most important questions in assessing a race are:
How fast has each horse run in the past?
How fast is it going to run today?

Time of the race. Beaten lengths. Ground lost or saved on the turns. Weight carried. Wind effects. Boiled down to one number. The lower the number, the better the race. Ah Day has just run two 2's.

"We could be fourth, maybe better," Leatherbury said after studying the numbers. I am a lifetime C student in handicapping. But this test is pass/fail. In real dollars. For real partners. This is why you went to school. To understand how to weigh decisions.

Wednesday, May 17

At his barn this sunny spring morning, Ah Day knew nothing of the wager at hand. He galloped on the track. Returned for an inspection. Trotted on the tarmac. Jogged in the shedrow.

With an 11 a.m. entry time looming, with racing secretaries on the phone, with money on the line, with veterinarians on hand, with due diligence completed, Rule One remained uppermost: In all bets, there must be a possibility to win when the bet is made.

The decision: no bet. In the final analysis, it was no more than a Zen-thing. A feeling after all the information. An athletic impulse not to make a certain move against a more gifted athlete. Instead, into the Sir Barton, on the Preakness undercard, went the name Ah Day.

Thursday, May 18

Sun in. Sun out. Rain on. Rain off.

Fire trucks and ambulances lined up in a parade at Merryland this afternoon. Lights flashing. Traffic blocked on Bottom Road. Helicopter disappearing over the hills.

The colt Onward and Upward went sideways and downward through the inner rail. The PVC pipe broke away a second before exercise rider Mark O'Dwyer fell face first onto the infield grass. When he came to, he asked incredulously, in his hard

Irish accent: "*Who da hell was I ridin'?*" The medics flew him off. In the old days, he'd have sat out the afternoon. Rested up to ride tomorrow.

Hours later, the annual Preakness Party ended when Ellis Woodward propped his guitar up against the stand. Sweet echo of music over the farm as I snuffed out lamps, flicked the breaker back on for the driveway gate. Lay awake in bed thinking how fast the days go by. How slow the nights.

Friday, May 19

Last foal of the year born at 10 a.m. Sunshine in Paris sneaking in a daylight delivery but caught in the act by Ellen. A flock of South Korean horseplayers photographed the scene. Someone said it was a filly. Born on Black-Eyed Susan Day. Let's name her Malibu Susan. First, double-check under the hood. Corrected: "Better wait on that name. She's a he."

"That's a 40 percent appreciation of a sales prospect in 10 minutes," said Kentucky Ted. "Market pays more for colts than for fillies."

And so a boy named Sue is the last one picked for the team.

Saturday, May 20

Exit out the far end of the oldest part of the Pimlico grandstand. Ancient. How many Preaknesses has this wooden grandstand seen? Not many like today.

Ambulances lined up by the dozen to triage wasted infield revelers. Sirens piercing the air. Unnerving.

Hunter Thompson's story redone. Guy on a cooler, clutching crutches. Decadent. Guy on a stretcher with I.V.s in his arm. Depraved.

A motorcade parts the sea of drunken humanity for the horse ambulance carrying Barbaro to New Bolton Center. Pennsylvania license plates on trailing vehicles. An urge to shout them a warning: Watch out for crazy infielders driving on the Jones Falls! Watch out on I-95!

Ellen's camera under the seat. Photos of a day we'd like to forget.

Sunday, May 21

Article in the *Sun* the morning of the race: The Lost Preaknesses.

Survivor won the first Preakness in 1873. In 1890, the Preakness was held at Morris Park. No track hosted a Preakness from 1891 through 1893. Gravesend Race

Track in Brooklyn resurrected the Preakness in 1894, and ran it for 15 years before it returned to Pimlico for the 1909 running.

Yesterday, a Lost Preakness of a much different sort. But for the moment, like the first Barbaro a survivor.

Monday, May 22

If Barbaro had broken down on the backstretch instead of the homestretch, it might be a different story today. He was pulled up by Maryland favorite Edgar Prado right in front of his groom, right in front of Pimlico vets. Dr. Nick Meittinis' digital X-ray machine revealed the fractures immediately. It was a job well done, a moment anticipated by visionary vets. Expensive equipment worth every penny. Enabling decisive handling.

Still, the casual public feels uneasy about what it saw on Saturday. Like we've asked them: Well, other than that, Mrs. Lincoln, how did you like the play?

Tuesday, May 23

Fireworks throughout the two-day Fasig-Tipton 2-year-old sale at Timonium. Baby racehorses for half-a-million dollars. Routinely, horses for six figures. What's fueling this demand? Racing is the riskiest part of this business. But wearing a hip number is also a risk. Although 370 2-year-olds were listed as sold, another 138 went unsold. Next stop for the unsolds? The racetrack, at thousands a month in training bills. The dark side of pinhooking.

A few purchases shipped to Merryland to let down briefly. Trainers' first instruction: "Turn these babies out for a few weeks. Let them get over the sale."

We'll throw polo bandages and boots on them. Ease them into a round pen. And their minds will slowly return.

Wednesday, May 24

The breeding season has peaked. Calendar on the easel in the Country Life office is cryptic. Initial letters in code: A for Arrival. B for Booked. D for Depart. F for Foaled.

More Ds these days than Bs. No more Fs. Some A's at Merryland from the 2-year-old sale. For R & R.

All breeding seasons are long. And by the end of May, all days are told in shorthand.

Thursday, May 25

J.R.'s doctor says: "How much time do you spend in the sun?"

"Let's see. I'm in the sun when it comes up. I get out of the sun when it goes down."

Armando's right eye tears up frequently. The eye doctor owns the dam of Spectacular Malibu. She does not want to operate on Armando, who does not want to wear dark glasses. So he moonlights on nightwatch.

Riders breeze at Old Hilltop every morning. Wind effect 40 miles an hour. For how many works a day? Grab a sandwich, ride at Merryland all afternoon. Six, seven hours of riding. In whatever weather. Every day. Think of Johnny Longden's wizened face. It's coming.

High noons at loading chutes. Pink sunsets. It's weather that causes weathered faces. In the magnificent month of May, no one cares. No one ages in fantasy horse camp.

Friday, May 26

Friend just sold his farm.

"Price of farmland's gone crazy. Bought a house in town. She's fixin' it up."

Like a lifetime sailor, coming off the water. He thinks for good. In my mind, though, a screen door slams. His wife calls to him: "Where you goin'?"

He's just going for a walk. Driven by imaginary breezes, ancestral stirrings.

Saturday, May 27

The modest racing stable of older horses is in a drought. Surf Light in previous seasons had won five races; now she's out of conditions. Yeager's Jet has been banished to Charles Town claimers, incognizant of the speed-demon test pilot for whom he was named. Jenkin Jones, named for a coal-mining town, is low on fuel. P. J. Indy is a mere two initials away from A.P. Indy. Recall Mark Twain's jest on the one-word difference between lightning bug and lightning.

So the mind searches for fireflies among the untested 2-year-olds. Sagamoon at Saratoga this summer.

Sunday, May 28

Falling behind mowing the pastures. J.R.'s former employer had minions who produced spreadsheets on the cost of Bat-Winging the fields. Add to that calculation our recurring cost for gearbox fluid from a leaky hydraulic cylinder. We drip grease on the farm's roads to guide us back to the shop. For more fluid.

Can't wait for the boys to get out of school for the summer. Josh and August. Bat-Wing and Robin. Child labor a farm father's edge.

Monday, May 29

You could spend a whole day watching foals. There's Sunshine in Paris' colt. So leggy. Oh, if he can run like his mom. She might have won a stakes had she not met Fleet Renee at the top of her game, one race before Keeneland's Ashland Stakes. Sunshine's colt is a cracker.

And there's Conradley's colt. January foal. Almost ready to wean. Balance. That's what he has. Balance.

These foals lay flat out on the hillside, as still as bales of straw in a field, these cool late spring days before flies hatch out to disrupt sleep. You can't get any work done when you're watching foals. Except you are working. It's all observation. That's the beauty of this job. It doesn't always feel like work.

Tuesday, May 30

The Mexican men want to speak to me, I'm told. Such group discussions can be tricky. These are complex men, away from beloved families many months at a time. These are men of varied ages, from 25-to-40 years old. These are men who live in close quarters. Only two of eight have the freedom a driver's license carries.

They are the finest fellows I've ever worked with. I will speak to them individually. It has been a longer season for them.

Wednesday, May 31

Last-man-on-the-farm walk this evening.

Meittinis' ultrasound today: Merryland Monroe's tendon healed! Stout filly splashes through the stream in her field. All as it should be.

Need dropboards at end of yearling barn, in case of a breakout. Get brass snaps for screens instead of these brittle nickel snaps. Who's that banging the wall in the training barn? The bulb's burned out in that stall. Replace it tomorrow. Who *is* that rockin' the barn? This pitchfork should be put away. Oh, no! That's Spectacular Malibu down. She's cast.

She's OK. Sound. Nothing broken.

Compulsion not such a bad thing. Not driven by imaginary breezes. This farm sails along on attention to all things small.

June

Thursday, June 1

Climb to the edge of the woods. Just far enough away that the farm becomes a postcard. Stand back from it. Breathe. My, what a lovely city for horses is Merryland.

From here, you understand: It can't all be fixed at once. In time, replace the post. Flash the shingles. Patch the road. Level the stalls.

Renovation is one part inspiration, nine parts perspiration. Find enough distance to keep perspective.

Friday, June 2

Stillness on a horse farm is an illusion. Like a reflection in a lake.

Cell phone rings. Trainer's name on the screen. Concentric circles ripple the lake. Trainers don't always give bad news, but that is my first thought.

Saturday, June 3

A poster-sized, black-and-white photo of the old Bel Air Race Track covers a wall in the crabcake restaurant. Step into that photo. It's the 1950s. Children are brought to the fair meet at the half-mile track. They stand in awe by wooden rails as waves of racehorses thunder by, jockeys in rainbow silks shouting for room on tightly banked turns. Some children never get the thunder out of their ears.

A Great Oak in the infield. Station wagons parked along the rail. Smell of fresh bread from the clubhouse restaurant. A hand reaches down, lifts you off the steps of the grandstand. Hold that hand, near a barn. Hot horses circling under a tree. Your father talking to another man. You stare up at a water tower. Smell of liniments in the air near the barn. Gone on the wind. Just a photo on a wall. Of a grandstand with bunting draped from finish-line boxes.

Sunday, June 4

It's a 12-minute drive from Country Life to Merryland. Just enough time to refresh your mind. A jazz groove plays on the radio.

It's a Sunday visit to the hospital wing. To look in on the lay-ups. In these 10 courtyard stalls: bows, splints, tears, breaks. Bad throats and bleeders. All with faces pushed through the yoke-screens. Pet me! Pet me! Lines from a Statue of Liberty for horses: "Give me your tired … yearning to breathe free … send these … tempest-tossed to me."

Their owners dreamed of sure things. There are no sure things. There is no golden door.

Monday, June 5

Every age has its own unease.

"During the Cold War," Mom says as we drive north from the city, "there were Nike missile sites over the hill from Merryland, right below the white mansion Jerome Bonaparte built overlooking the valley."

On top of Harford Road a mile from Merryland, white columns of the Bonaparte mansion sit atop a hillside where silos weren't for silage. You shake your head and hang on to the raft floating down history. Enlightened by Mom's lesson for the day. Very glad to be one hill over, in the timeless beauty of a long green valley.

Tuesday, June 6

At Merryland with six teenagers from Indiana. On their visit to Washington, D.C., with the Future Farmers of America. Officially: The National FFA Organization. Their instructor, Byron, and his 6-year-old son, Heath, are rabid horseplayers. We eat lunch watching TVG coverage of River Downs, in southern Ohio, which Byron can reach from home in just under three hours.

"Just under three hours," Heath emphasizes, then hollers at the TV: "Go six! Go six!"

The older kids, who are meeting this week with their legislators, know nothing about horses. Only Heath, and only because of his father.

I wonder if the FFA and the NTRA have ever done lunch? To keep something going, generation after generation, seems like you've got to keep the kids involved.

Wednesday, June 7

Glancing up the brick aisle at quitting time. Water on the floor in front of Jenkin Jones' stall. That's odd! The rascal probably just kicking his bucket.

At his door. He's upside down. In a cold sweat. Colicking. *Trying to kick the bucket, all right.* Get him to his feet.

Call J.R. Blast of Banamine. Dose of Rompum. Walk him. Pain eases.

"I'll come back in two hours," J.R. says. "That's when the drugs'll wear off. Need to know if the pain returns."

It does. Scott Alexander, the van man, rushes JJ to Leesburg. Midnight phone call from the vet: "He's in pretty bad shape. Need permission for abdominal surgery."

Who could say no? I lie awake thinking about water on red bricks. Only clue the horse gods gave.

Thursday, June 8

Awaken where the bad dream left off: JJ.

They would have called if he died. I fear that he has been sliced stem to stern, his colon resected, his career over.

Cell-phone message. The clinic: "Unusual thing. Had the entire staff here after midnight. Ready to operate. Sedated him. As we shaved his belly for surgery, he became less painful. Passed some gas. We decided to wait him out. He seems fine this morning. It's like he *knew*. Hope you don't mind we shaved him."

JJ with a summer crew cut. The hard way. The only way he knows.

Friday, June 9

On a farm, take help where you find it.

"Mom, want to drive to Leesburg?"

"Let me pack some sandwiches."

Sunset after a storm. Cross the Potomac at Point of Rocks, Maryland. Rise up onto the magnificent Piedmont farms of northern Virginia. Run straight into the colonial brick town of Leesburg. You couldn't ask for a lovelier evening with your mother, even if she is doubling as van attendant.

JJ strides out of the clinic with girls on each arm. He rolls his white eye at me as I take the shank and lead him onto the van. We unload after midnight at Merryland, moments into another day of farm life.

Saturday, June 10

The buildings of Merryland. Monuments, really. A machinery shed. Four bays, double deep. Eight huge parking spaces for essential farm equipment. Under a roof tall enough for the highest tractor-muffler.

In Merryland's gilded age, when ownership carried the Guggenheim touch, the vast shed doubled as an orchestra band shell. They'd park the equipment in the back lane. Hose off the blacktop floor. Elevate the stage so summer music banked out across a natural amphitheater of babbling brook and soft hills. Under a bowl of stars.

Oh, if only these walls could talk …

Sunday, June 11

Flint's on the phone: "P. J. Indy can't walk this morning. I left him at Charles Town. Remember when he hit that horse in February? Damaged his coronet band. Now it's a quarter crack. Probably an abscess under it. Why don't you bring him home to Merryland?"

Into the van again. Outside Harpers Ferry, kayaks climb the limestone ledges of the Shenandoah River as whitewater rafters run the rapids of the mighty Potomac. Son Josh and I sit on ancient bridges. Snarled in Sunday traffic. Absorbed in the sights of the bright waters.

Meanwhile, P. J. is rocking the van. "My foot hurts. Let me out of here." Two hours later, he runs down the ramp at Merryland. Suddenly sound. Abscess oozing blood at the coronet. Clinic doctors tell of therapeutic rides for colic cases: "Van ride cured him!" Apparently, good for abscesses, too.

Monday, June 12

Discharge Report from New Bolton Center.

Subject: Case No. 073217. MAJOR MALIBU. 2004 Thoroughbred Gelding.

I cannot begin the report without thinking of Uncle Johnny's oft-quoted quip, borrowed from W.C. Fields:

"Never give a sucker an even break."

Two months ago, X-rays showed Major Malibu's knees still "open." We prudently interrupted his training. Should have kept the sucker going instead of giving him a break. He thanked us for turning him out by ripping a 10-inch gash in his shoulder and chest. Turning 2-year-olds out in a paddock? You can kill them with such kindness.

New Bolton vet lingo: "25 cm laceration to left pectoral and medial radius. Arthrocentesis of elbow joint; normal synovial fluid. Debridement, lavage and local block. Penrose drain. Skin reapposed using 2/0 Fluorofil. Radiographs. No abnormalities. Local wound therapy. Cold hosing. Scarlet Oil. Significant improvement. Continue trimethoprim sulfa. Discharged."

A minor setback for Major Malibu, that silly sucker.

Tuesday, June 13

With summer help swelling the ranks, we intend to power wash the machinery shed. To squeegee away decades of sand, carried in on tractor tires, soiled by leaking oil pans. To wash away years of neglect. To polish the dance hall floor.

Wednesday, June 14

Cousins in Carolina heard from cousins in Annapolis: "Hey, what's this on the news about a trailer accident on 95. Dead horses on the interstate. Tell us it wasn't your horses!"

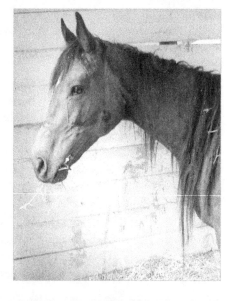

"No, thank goodness. Guy in a SUV rolled his trailer. Helicopter shots on the evening news. Traffic's backed up 20 miles around the beltway."

An hour later, a towing company hauls an emergency trailer into the courtyard at Country Life. Two mares step off the ramp. Their injuries are not life-threatening. Val cleans their wounds as Richard comforts them. Dr. Jacobson sutures tears in their thin skin: "The other two didn't make it."

The mares spend the night in deeply bedded courtyard stalls. They look at me with the blank eyes of refugees, then return to their hay.

Thursday, June 15

Channel 13 News sends a film crew. It's a big story on the local stations. But the mares are picked up before the news crew arrives. They set up cameras and interview the vet anyway. We do not care to see the footage on the nightly news. The mares were not well taken care of before the accident. We had that hollow feeling, like giving a lost dog back to a bad home. We brush it off and get back to the breeding season.

Friday, June 16

A mile from Merryland, a cattle operation straddles the rural Long Green Road. The farmer practices "interval grazing." Walks his cattle back and forth across Long Green Road between strands of electric fence. Always fresh ground on the rebound. You expect to see actor Robert Duvall in a worn cowboy hat, like in *Lonesome Dove*, rolling a stalk of prairie grass in his teeth, thanking you for stopping.

Cows brown and black and buff-colored. Up close. Just a few feet away on the blacktop. The road wet with mud and manure in a thin trail that washes away in the next sudden shower. Cows pass onto grassland that retails for thousands an acre. A culture of farming, a way of life, stubbornly maintained. You nod farmer-like to the man playing Robert Duvall and drive on to busy Baltimore.

Saturday, June 17

Tim broke his back in April. In a fall at the hunt races. Wore a brace. Threw it away.

Mark broke through the rail in May. Lay unconscious amid lengths of white-plastic PVC pipe. In grass as emerald green as the Ireland of his birth.

Tim and Mark singsong by me as I stand at the rail. Trading tips on the horses underneath them. Tim blusters a challenge to race. Mark replies, but on the wind I can't make out what he said. I call to him: *"What?"*

Irish accent on the wind as they gallop away. *"I said, 'No joyridin' roun' 'ere.' "*

Mark fakes a serious side. He wants you to think it's all just hard work. It's not. They *are* joyriding around here. On sunny summer days. On well-broke horses. On

a freshly harrowed track. These folks who ride, they enjoy it. They couldn't do it otherwise.

Sunday, June 18

Son Josh has reached a point of diminishing returns on power washing the cavernous machinery shed. Maurilio, standing nearby, sees the light at the end of the shed. Takes the nozzle from Josh.

"Very good job, Josh," he tells him in the same soft Mexican accent I've heard him use to reward good horses. "Very good job. You start. I finish. OK? OK."

Monday, June 19

The way Rachael, upon receiving a leg up, lowers down into the saddle. Almost hydraulic. The way Cindy passes a hand, palm down, under the throat latch of the bridle, to gauge a proper fit. Loose enough — but not too loose. The way J.R. trots Timmy the lead pony up alongside a set of babies. The way Fabian backs a blowing breezer into the wash stall. It's a hypnotic jazz tune. Watching skillful people in rhythm is akin to music.

Tuesday, June 20

The 2-year-olds file down from the training barn in a mock post parade, J.R. leading them to the track. So powerful is the urge to identify the best prospect. To make a bet. To be *right*.

The definitive text on the illusions of horse racing was written by Brendan Boyd (*Racing Days*, 1987, published by Viking). Alongside dreamlike black-and-white photos by Henry Horenstein that sear into the mind's eye, Boyd wrote:

"The post parade lets us get up close, feign expertise, sell our brains on what our hearts have already bought for us."

Wednesday, June 21

Last cover of the year for Hookedonjoy today. Sometimes maiden mares just don't want to get in foal their first year. Sometimes the best mares are the worst producers. I grabbed down from my grandfather's shelves a leather binder published by H.P. Whitney in 1926. His private stud book. In it was listed the produce record for the great racemare Artful, the only horse to defeat champion Sysonby. Artful was an awful producer. Barren. Barren. Barren. Six cold scarlet letters, over and over on her page. If you like a mare, and she's barren, you still keep her. You suspend hope for a year. Nothing is new in this game.

Thursday, June 22

Headline on newsstands at train station: "Job-Related Traveling Stresses Families."

The mobility of today's business workers. Not a world a horse farmer sees every day. Husband on cell phone to wife "... I don't want him using my computer for that stuff! Amtrak's late again. I'll be home at nine." Everyone on train now knows his private business. His itinerary.

I can't help it. I couldn't do it. I don't care if most yearlings don't X-ray clean and most racehorses don't run fast and most stallions don't hit and maiden mares go barren. A guy hosing a sore horse on a rundown backstretch at any two-bit racetrack in this country has a sunnier disposition than most of the people on this hot old train.

Friday, June 23

Dramatic summer thunderstorm over the valley of the James River below Richmond. Beach traffic snarling I-64. Evasive maneuvers to reach Colonial Downs. Find the old Williamsburg Road abandoned, almost underwater. Think of summer reading: *To the Gates of Richmond: The Peninsula Campaign*, by Stephen W. Sears.

"Stragglers always brought up the rear of any army on attack ..."

Dash into the grandstand in time to see East Jet whipped by Yankee shippers. "Skulkers led the way in retreat back to Richmond."

Williamsburg Road so dark at dusk. Rain dripping from canopy of ancient oaks, from green-black pines. So what if she lost? Quit your skulking. She took you over historic countryside. If you measure the journey of a racehorse only in dollars and cents, you shortchange the whole deal.

Saturday, June 24

In the thunderstorm last night, a tree fell, smashing down on the aluminum stock trailer. Rip of a tree trunk. Sudden crash. A mare in a courtyard stall thought the sky was falling. Slammed through her stall screen. Broke the Dutch door. Spent the night grazing in a side yard. Discovered at dawn by sister Alice, up early, a nurse at Johns Hopkins. She summoned authorities for the escapee.

This evening, three inches of rain fell in three hours.

Sunday, June 25

Delaware Park clubhouse. Weight-bearing beams wrapped in wood paneling. Old cold walls now a techno-tapestry of flat-screened TVs.

Glowing with races from outer spaces.

You're lost at the carnival. A barker calls out today's changes.

"In the seventh race: Scratch the one. Take out the eleven."

Lifers in cubicles scribble madly. Like keeping a bingo card.

You should be at the yearling show at Timonium. Chose a long ride instead.

Watch as Dancer in the Citi slides in the slop. Lost in the flood. Still, a firsthand report for partners. Double doors to the casino swing open and close. Slot machine bells a mindless siren to the masses. Their quarters are our purses. A marriage for money.

Fifty miles away, the farm crew at the yearling show stands up to a downpour. Cell phone rings. And the winner of the Amateur Judging Contest? Two years in a row: impish son August.

Today was spent at a little distance from myself.

Monday, June 26

A half-mile from Country Life. On double-long trailers on freshly paved car lots. Bundles of floodlight poles. A chill. Like seeing a stack of caskets. Something's about to die: our night sky. The end of stars.

Tuesday, June 27

Last stop on the 2-year-old sales season today at Timonium. Like an auto auction. Who wrecked earlier on the sales calendar? Who wrecked yesterday in workouts over a washed-out, frantically replenished racing surface?

Bent frames visible in repository. Before you get behind the wheel of a good deal, check the X-rays.

Wednesday, June 28

The rest of this summer will be known as "After the Big Rains."

Trees fell, rootball and all. Over electric lines on Glenarm Road. Power to Merryland so vulnerable. Horses can't go without water. Gas-engine generators hum the pumps alive in the wells. Water to the barns. Water to the houses.

Flotsam and jetsam. Deadwood poured out of the cutover. Dammed the culvert pipes. Sent floodwater overtop earthen bridges. Driftwood in the spindles on J.R.'s bridge. A new high-water mark.

Fifteen inches of rain in five days. Today, first day of clearing.

Thursday, June 29

He grew up in a stucco house on Glenarm Road. In those days, so open he rode his broodmare to Merryland to be bred. After snowstorms, he rode in a horse-drawn sleigh down these same roads.

"This area has hardly changed," he said on arrival, having flashbacked in time, jogged by the sight of the stone house at the corner of Williams where once lived Nancy Boyce, popular cartoonist of the *Maryland Horse* magazine. He stood in the tidy two-stall stallion barn. Recalled the day 20 years ago when he received word the sire in which he owned a share had been killed in a stallion fight.

"It's double fenced now," I lightened his momentary gloom.

Then he smiled as he captured lost memories. "If this place could speak …" his voice trailed off.

Friday, June 30

Cousins are pouring in for a family reunion this Fourth of July weekend, 100 strong. We are bound by descent from an immigrant vintner who arrived in the 1880s. It's a thin thread, but it's enough in this modern world.

They will think the farm is Shangri-la. The place all mowed and spruced up. Yet so foreign is agriculture to them. There's not a Future Farmer of America in the throng. There are a few *former* farmers; they ride the train now, driven to it by economics.

Entertainments on a farm are few, though. We hurry to replace the frayed plywood basketball backboard. With new plywood. Capital improvement, farm style. I expect they will want tours of Merryland, of Country Life, second cousins and their girlfriends. In perfect rote, I play with phrasing in my mind, playing the host: "Welcome to the Alamo."

It can be difficult, in an afternoon, to describe what happens on a horse farm.

SUMMER
2006

July

Saturday, July 1

One hundred relatives on the front lawn. Family reunion. Connecticut. Carolina. New Hampshire. New Jersey. Genetic link to an urbane French horseman.

Narrative to family from afar:

In the midst of the Great Depression, Adolphe Adrien Pons phased out his Thoroughbred consulting business in New York City. Bought a farm north of Baltimore. Named it for a station stop on the Long Island Railroad, echo of his dream: Country Life.

Without him? No silhouettes of mares on dark green hillsides tonight. No adrenaline pulse at the sight of new foals each spring. No winner's circles. No stallions. No Merryland for the next generation. No roller-coasting disappointments with horses either. But mostly: No life in the country.

Certainly, no family reunion on a graceful old horse farm. Maybe at some swim club? Maybe at some riverside park? But not on a farm.

For that privilege, someone once took a great chance.

Sunday, July 2

When Grandfather arrived in Maryland in 1933, he needed a farm accessible to roads that would take him to racetracks in Havre de Grace and Baltimore, or to the train station for trips to New York City for business. He discovered 100 acres for sale, on well-traveled U.S. Route 1. Protected by hills. Graced by a welcoming home. He bought the place for $20,000.

Monday, July 3

Hitler sullied the name forever. Adolphe, pronounced as the French would, rolls off with a soft *A*. Say "apple." Say "Adolphe." A gentle name.

It fit him.

Grandfather was born in Montpellier, France, in 1883. In letters, he tells he arrived at age five. In Ellis Island records, his entire family arrives for good in 1894. He would have been 11 years old. Grandfather's first son was born in 1913, Adolphe Jr. Older brother to Dad and Uncle Johnny, the two who ran this farm for 50 years.

At the reunion. A photo of a youthful Uncle Addie, circa 1935. *Watching* a stallion in the front field. Not *holding* it. He's the Marx Brother who left the act. I'm not sure why. Horses are not for everyone. It's a speculative life, replete with physical danger. Dad nearly lost his life to a savage stallion.

Uncle Addie went into the auto parts business.

His descendants stared into the photograph. Saw their ancestor on this very ground. None of them have anything to do with horses, but they cheer farm victories with the spirit of devoted alumni. Empathize with the losses.

SUMMER 2006

Tuesday, July 4

This hill over Route 1 tonight. Backlit by fireworks from the football fields of Bel Air High, two miles away. Outlines of the farm flash into view with every rocket, then fall back into the night. Black sky explodes into red sparks, pink streams, white light. Foals startle at the bombardment, then resign themselves to grazing beside indifferent dams. Implacable behavior Tesio observed on his farm in Italy, during World War I shelling.

This hill, where 40 years ago cousin John refused to let go of the shanks on the spooked mare Mimika and her fractious foal as they bolted downhill on rain-slicked grass. He skied between them for 200 yards.

"I was afraid to let go!" He smiled as he relived the story this past weekend. He chose a walk of life in another field. Banking in New England. Horses are not for everyone.

On this hill last March, each of us gave some of Dad's ashes to the wind. Tonight, foals graze in bursts of light, then fall back into the night.

Wednesday, July 5

Romance of farm life evaporates quickly. Pressure is on to find the source of the water break that left houses and barns dry on the Fourth. Hoses strung from secondary lines quenched the horses. But no water for houses. Showers a memory. Tempers fray.

Country Boy Carl, of the A-1 Plumbing Service:

"That old galvanized line that fed the milking parlor must've burst. This was a cattle barn when your grandfather bought this place. I'm gonna abandon the old line. Take some photos as I trench a new line. Keep a folder. The next poor sonofabug will have a clue where to look."

Thursday, July 6

Penn National just demolished the old grandstand. Architect's vision of the coming facility? Viva Las Vegas.

Every few years, track operators will wonder why they bother with racing — the mountain of maintenance, the liability to jocks, starting gate crews, exercise riders. Legislators will ask: Why so much to horsemen? Why not redraw the formulas?

A vicious circle. Built on the backs of brown horses running.

In the glow of the backstretch overlook, we dropped off P.J. Indy at Flint's barn. The track floated below, unmoored from the anchor of the vanished grandstand. Ephemeral. Elemental. Here, in the blue mountains of Pennsylvania, for this one moment in time, just brown horses running.

It looked like a team practice. Under lights.

Soon our cunning sibling in the gambling trade, Brother Slots, will take over the family business. Woody Allen joked: My brother thinks he's a chicken. I let him, because I need the eggs.

We let Brother Slots pose as a benevolent chicken, because we need his eggs. But he's really a fox in what will be our new henhouse, the casino. We need the eggs.

Friday, July 7

Is state ownership of a racetrack a better model than private hands? Ask Monmouth, closed these last two days because the governor shut down all state offices considered "nonessential." Trainer, to his grooms: "No paycheck this week. You're nonessential." To his owners: "It's not that the race didn't go. It's more like, 'the races didn't go.'"

Saturday, July 8

"When's 'Butterbean' run next?" I ask Larry about East Jet. Our one-horse stable comprises a corpulent filly nicknamed by the Merryland crew. She runs in Larry's "Winners Run Farm" silks, a play on our shared riparian boundary, Winters Run. Larry often phones the trainer, suggests races, proffers feed supplements. Butterbean's been on omega-3 fatty acids for six weeks now. It's a dollar a day. If she feels better, he feels better. He came into the sport with 5 percent of the filly Mrs. Vanderbilt, older sister of Sagamoon and Mr. Vanderbilt.

Deference doesn't last long in racing, where happenstance often determines success. Beginners sense this. Think they can do as well. Remarkably, they *often* do. A spike of good fortune in the harsh actuarial graph.

"Listen, Earl!" he barks at me. "I just got off the phone with the trainer. There's a race on Tuesday for her for 25. I told him, 'Let's run!'"

Butterbean cost $7,000 at Timonium. Owes us nothing. Enriches our lives. A great diversion. That's racing.

Sunday, July 9

Self-dramatization is endemic in a diary about life on a family farm. It's a stakes race. You have to be nominated. It costs to enter. It costs to start. Stakes are high.

Success is an umbilical cord that nourishes. Failure is a companion. I can stand at a mirror and see my dad at 52. That was about the time four mares got loose on Route 1. I can hear Uncle Johnny: "You take a horse to a sale, don't come home with it. You can't eat horses."

Lighten up by reading a master writer:

"One school of theological reflection holds that the trials of this life ... are designed to strengthen us for a more comfortable life to come. For such as pass this testing, there is a reward. It is a green and pleasant heaven, shaded by lofty elms. It has a slow leisured pace — in the daytime — and sometimes cool winds bellying down from the Adirondacks. Sure enough, here we are at Saratoga."

From *This Was Racing*, by Joe Palmer. Wherever fine old horse books are sold.

Monday, July 10

Potentially big weekend ahead. Malibu Mint in a grade I for farm sire; Wahoo Moon at Colonial. Soon, Sagamoon ships to Saratoga.

Meanwhile, at Merryland, 2-year-olds go round and round. Building sand castles on the training track. Beautiful. Fleeting. Hypnotic. Like a day at the beach.

Tuesday, July 11

Butterbean a good third tonight at Colonial. Purse of $17,000, with an additional $8,500 available to Virginia-breds. For $25,000 claimers. She earned $2,805.

Every race is the same: one winner, trailed by a field of losers. Some lucky enough to offset their training costs. Thirds are fine. Thirds are like singles in baseball. Enough of them, you stay in the game. That's racing.

Wednesday, July 12

On the phone with New Bolton:

"I'm trying to reach the veterinarian who did check ligament surgery on a foal of ours last year. She's in the yearling sale in Kentucky next week. I think I need a letter to disclose the surgery for the repository."

Thursday, July 13

As a foal, the filly developed a clubby-looking foot. Severe enough to warrant surgery. Corrective shoeing a follow-up. A year later, this faxed summation from New Bolton: "... there is a good to excellent prognosis for life and athletic soundness."

Friday, July 14

E-mail to partners:

"On the issue of the check ligament surgery performed last July. It was not 'invasive joint surgery' and does not require disclosure under the conditions of sale. However, if you're the buyer, and the morning after, you notice a slight thickening below the knee, and you ultrasound it, and you discover that somebody had been in there with a scalpel a year ago ...

"Undisclosed, the matter could go to arbitration. We would prevail, but arbitration is never a happy experience. So we submitted New Bolton's letter yesterday. And a leading Kentucky veterinarian just ultrasounded the filly, took some images, for inclusion in the repository as well.

"This is a beautiful filly with a fine page. We'll wait to discuss a reserve until prospective buyers have checked the repository."

Saturday, July 15

A New Jersey client in the farm office yesterday, with a tip on Joey P. against overwhelming favorite Lost in the Fog at Calder. I type in my TVG account password and make his bet. Lost in the Fog loses to a bunch of ordinary Joes.

I check the odds on Malibu Mint for the Princess Rooney. She's 20-something to 1 against 1-5 Dubai Escapade. What the heck? Favorites get beat two-thirds of the time. I put $2 across the board. The bridge jumper who dropped a hundred grand on Dubai Escapade leaps into the Atlantic when she stops. Show pool is *huge*. Malibu Mint pays $49 to win, $26 to place, $79 *to show*. Two across earns $154!

Farm sire gets his second grade I winner. His first, Declan's Moon, returned to the game today, after 16 months. He played like a quarterback coming off the disabled list. Overconfidently. Lost by a nose. An illusion. Just being *back* is a win.

Racing gods smile down, move on to the next needy fellow in Horseland. "That's enough for you," I hear them say. Thank you very much.

Sunday, July 16

Kentucky Ted's observation on the insatiable appetite of horsemen: "It's never enough."

Trainers feel this the most. Leaving the winner's circle, owners ask: "What's next for her?"

Mare has a nice foal. Owner commands: "Breed her on her foal heat!" Nine days from the most physical act imaginable.

Full book for a stallion was 20 mares when Grandfather arrived in '33. Full book was 40 when Dad and Uncle Johnny stood Saggy, sire of '61 Derby and Preakness winner Carry Back. It takes 100 mares now to produce enough first-crop runners to propel a young stallion onto the freshman sire list. He misses "The List"; he's on the boat out.

"It's never enough" is a trap.

Yesterday was enough for me.

Monday, July 17

At Delaware Park. Partners in 3-year-old maiden Dancer in the Citi lunch in a dining room where crown molding is hung with the silks of owners who've won the famous Delaware Handicap. Busanda. Flower Bowl. Straight Deal. Obeah. Susan's Girl. Late Bloomer. Relaxing. And a favorite: Urbane, by Citidancer, sire of Dancer in the Citi.

The partners rush outside for the $16,000 claiming event. Dash to the winner's circle. Order extra prints of the win photo. Breathe relief when no one leads her back to a different barn. Run back inside to watch the replay.

After eight starts, a maiden no more. Winner's purse of $10,350 the first big installment against months of expenses. Delaware-certified awards to boot.

This all took about an hour. The win, though, had been in the planning for two years. To a first-time owner, as big a deal as the Del 'Cap.

Tuesday, July 18

The yearling filly in Kentucky brought half the average. Mike phoned:

"Fellow bought her as a broodmare prospect. Said he'd run her first. The check ligament issue didn't stop him. Said her ovaries were worth the bid."

So she's gone. A card laid is a card played. A fellow goes to a yearling sale to buy a broodmare prospect. Happenstance. You can't win if you don't play.

Wednesday, July 19

Next order of business. J.R. on the phone: "Merryland Monroe's doing great. Back in light training. Tendon looks good on ultrasound."

Merryland Monroe is a half sister to the Kentucky filly. She's our broodmare prospect. In training. Once more.

Thursday, July 20

Delaware Park canceled its card Tuesday. Too hot to race. Good thing Dancer in the Citi ran on Monday. Happenstance happened on Tuesday.

Friday, July 21

First capital improvement five years ago was a "walking machine" for Training Barn #1. A/k/a: Training Mill. Eurociser. Free Walker.

As its name varies, so does fencing for the circle of sand over which the horses freely walk/trot/canter. Fencing options: Woven wire. Solid oak. Soft plywood. Our choice? Five bands of rubber the width of fence boards. Allows horses to see the farm. Stay cool. Not without hazard, though. Leg over the rubber sometimes. One idiotic horse in a 100 and you second-guess yourself.

An old friend brought us the rubber bands he opted not to install with his machine. Training Barn #2 could use a walker. Expense sends me running. But a couple hundred dollars of free fence? Maybe the first step to the next capital-intensive, capital improvement project.

Saturday, July 22

The grade I win a week ago is a balm that soothes the actuarial table of horse misfortunes. Yearlings that bring only half the average. A racing stable depleted. Jenkin Jones, sore back. P.J. Indy, quarter crack. Two-year-olds already layups: Moon Drive, chip. Tina's Prospect, shins.

Breed for speed. Soundness secondary. You'd like to hit a bunch of singles, but home runs pay for all the horses that can't get to first base. Racing stables, yearling sellers, pinhookers, stallion farms, all depend on home run horses. Everyone looking for "The Big Horse."

On deck: Sagamoon at Saratoga. A race in the book August 11.

Sunday, July 23

Niece Catherine is an exercise rider in Virginia. She fell and hurt her back recently. Her mom, Doris, is in a walking cast from an Irish hunter who props.

Motorcycles. Horses. Hand grenades. Parachutes. It's not "if." It's "when."

Granny's bookshelf in Richmond holds an original copy of *Lee's Lieutenants: A Study in Command*, signed by the author, Douglas Southall Freeman. A passage recounts the battle of South Mountain, near Frederick, Maryland. Local folk, sympathetic to the Southern Cause, presented Confederate general Stonewall Jackson with a gift horse. Beholden to no man, Stonewall paid for the horse. It promptly reared and flipped over on him. He lay on the ground. Spinal injury was feared. Spent days riding in an ambulance.

Down the ages. "Rider beware." But they all get back on. Horses are not for everyone, but if that blood flows in your veins …

Monday, July 24

Sampling of "Sire Result Scanning" column, from fax of weekend races. Runners by the sire finished:

8th in a 10-horse field.
2nd in an 8-horse field.
Scratched.
3rd in a 12-horse field.
Won.

Lots of losers. One winner. And these are the lucky ones that stand training. That aren't on the disabled list. It's a fax on the facts of racing.

Tuesday, July 25

Mares bang the floats in the automatic water tank. This evening, happy hour doesn't sound too happy. Dominant mares back their rumps to any who approach. What? No water? Somehow, the rubber clean-out plug has been kicked loose. Water slides out the hole at the base.

Automation has a downside. The assumption that everything works, doesn't work — where horses are involved. Assume nothing. See for yourself.

Wednesday, July 26

She's been working bullets in the morning, but in the afternoons, large fields of maidens scramble her. Memo to partners:

"Wahoo Moon ran her best race last night at Colonial, breaking good and running right behind the leaders. She finished sixth, only beaten 1½ lengths. She earned her first paycheck: $480."

I don't think she's a morning glory. I think she hasn't bloomed.

Thursday, July 27

Laptop computer holds roster of horse inventory. Asks me: *"Are you sure you want to delete this horse?"*

You're a little late asking: We sold her in Kentucky.

Still, I pause to second-guess, to reflect. She was the last filly out of a grade I producer. By a favorite sire. And she had the look, the attitude. The way she dragged handlers to her field every morning. The way she skidded to stops after galloping full bore. The way you thought she might be "The Big Horse."

My fingers pause over the delete button. *Yes*. I think yes. *Yes. Yes. Yes.* I can't be a collector. I have to make decisions. *Yes.* I can't look back. We have her sister. I can't collect horses. *Yes.* She was appraised by the market. She sold. We did the right thing.

YES! I want to delete her. Please don't ask me again.

I will lie in wait for years, for her to cycle back through, a retread broodmare in some distant auction.

Friday, July 28

Preparing report of mares bred for Aug. 1 deadline. Four stallions. The freshman bred 100 mares; veterans bred 60, 45, a dozen. Two hundred mares, many with foals, processed through here in the past five months. Report card from another semester in the School of Equine Agriculture.

Saturday, July 29

Such a great circle, the lovely nuances of this little-understood game of brown horses running. Sagamoon is at Saratoga. She's a New York-bred by Malibu Moon.

Alfred G. Vanderbilt, master of Sagamore Farm in Maryland, bred the family. Sagamoon's dam is named Hey Up There, because her mother is Tall Glass O'Water, her father Cormorant, named for a high-flying sea bird. *Hey up there!*

Vanderbilt's way with a name. Tall Glass O'Water was by Thin Slice, out of Water Baby, out of Tot, out of Cup of Tea, out of Teahouse, full sister to Native Dancer, foundation sire of Sagamore Farm. Native Dancer's dam was by Discovery, who raced at Saratoga in Grandfather's silks in 1933. That year, Vanderbilt bought Discovery for $25,000. And Grandfather bought Country Life.

Same as it ever was. Gray, red, bay, brown horses running. Circle of a country life.

Sunday, July 30

Summer reading, from another master, Kent Hollingsworth, first author of the tongue-in-cheekily-titled editorial column "What's Going On Here." At once, a question and an answer.

Inscription in his book *The Kentucky Thoroughbred*, to brother Mike, who was moonlighting as a night-school instructor on the horse industry:

"To Michael — Understand you are teaching under cover of darkness, schooling incipient Meadowlands players. Teach them that in racing, one must win as a gentleman, lose as a man; it applies in all endeavours."

Night school for Meadowlands players!

Then off the cuff, at a moment's notice, he scribbled all anyone need know about racing. About life. An entire lesson in 20 words. To apply in all endeavours.

Monday, July 31

Sagamoon sleeps two doors down from budding superhorse Bernardini in Barn 24 at Saratoga. A friend whispers:

"Why don't you sneak her down the shedrow and let him cover her?"

Like Joe Palmer's story about a racemare named Annie G.:

"Halfway down the stretch, the boy felt the saddle slip, pulled her to the outside fence. That mare stopped over there and she had a foal. I'd bred her the year before but I thought she hadn't caught. Well, gentlemen, Annie G. won that race by three open lengths. And the foal ran second. That's what I call a horse with class."

With a work in :49 and change over the main track, Sagamoon is more likely to break her maiden on the *afternoon* of Aug. 11 than under a cover in darkness, in night school, in Barn 24 at Saratoga. She's got class.

August

Tuesday, August 1

As nostalgic as a 1930s postcard, Merryland Farm is changeless. By virtue of her beauty, certainly. But also by covenant. A deed of conservation easement — 21 pages of prohibited and restricted activities. Each year the farm is inspected by the Maryland Environmental Trust, along with its co-grantee, the Long Green Valley Conservancy.

Renovate all you want, they say. Just don't step out of the original footprints. They mean the foundations of buildings. Square footage. But from the *word* footprints, I feel emanations of those who once stepped lively around here. Vibrations of powerful ghosts. Free-willed equines and a cast of colorful caretakers. Stretching back through time.

Five years ago this month, we began to watch over this preserve. It's an easy anniversary to remember. Three weeks before 9/11.

The world may change, but Merryland may not. Except cosmetically. In the freshened-up aisle of the bank barn, hunter-green screens, tan grain of oak under hand-hewn beams.

Wednesday, August 2

Guiding light behind Merryland for five decades, Betty Shea Miller celebrated her 90th birthday today at the Mercy Ridge retirement home. In the farm biography in the 1990s, after the farm had passed to Baltimore County as a "horse park," Betty wrote:

"My husband Danny Shea bought this farm in 1939 for $20,000. Nothing less than World War II could interrupt Danny's zealous efforts to transform Merryland into a busy Thoroughbred training center."

Merryland was a place of merriment, where the annual yearling trials were a popular tradition.

The conservation easement states "public events associated with racing on the track shall be subject to the approval of the Grantees."

But the trials were private. Precedence is on our side. Walking in their footsteps, hoofprints, whatever.

Thursday, August 3

In 1802, the state of New York passed *An Act To Prevent Horse-Racing:*
"All racing, pacing, or trotting of horses, for any bet or stakes, shall be declared to be common and public nuisances."
Same temperate view as Merryland's easement.

Friday, August 4

Lady Suffolk, the great gray mare who ran 162 races over a 16-year career, trotted into Saratoga Springs in 1847. A new racecourse lay just outside village jurisdiction, finessing the public nuisance issue.

On August 14, 1847, a race: "For a purse of $250. Mile heats. Best three in five, for which David Bryan enters gr. m. Lady Suffolk in skeleton-wagon. James Whelpley enters b. g. Moscow to sulky."

Lady Suffolk won by a neck, and horse racing — well, harness racing, to be precise — had come to Saratoga. Sixteen years later, in 1863, the Civil War disrupted horse racing down South, and owners of flat runners sought sanctuary at the Spa.

SUMMER 2006

Saturday, August 5

Photo of the Saratoga grandstand in the 1870s. Very modest. Just an empty old viewing stand. Like standing on a Civil War battlefield, then reading *The Red Badge of Courage.*

Sure, there was a race.

Sure, there was a battle.

But what did it *feel* like?

Sunday, August 6

Imagine the whipped-up crowd in that wooden grandstand the summer of 1872. For the 2¼-mile Saratoga Cup. A battle between "King of the Turf" Longfellow and rival Harry Bassett.

Going to the post, 17-hand Longfellow twisted his left front shoe. His rider, unaware, felt the horse faltering in the race. Went to the whip. Longfellow answered with a surge, the crowd screaming for their favorite. But he could not overtake Harry Bassett. The twisted shoe had embedded in Longfellow's frog. He hobbled off the track on three legs.

Longfellow ran 18 furlongs with a shoe bent double into the sole of his foot. How did *that* feel? Bandaged foot. Bloody-red badge of courage. Longfellow's career over that day. Cheers of admiration ringing from the grandstand as he struggled back to his barn.

Monday, August 7

The "silks" room at Saratoga. Full-length observation windows on a room the length of a railroad car.

Bettors with baby carriages stare at the silks, overwhelmed by the limitless whimsy of the horsey set. Chevrons. Diamonds. Bands. Lightning bolts. Epaulets and gold braids. Like a rich lady's closet.

How *hard* could it be to run a horse at Saratoga if thousands of silks are on pegs inside?

It's a trick. The illusion is that so many silks somehow diminish the achievement of seeing just one particular set of silks at Saratoga.

Yours.

Listen to any owner who has never raced there:

"Before I die, I'd like to own a horse good enough to run in my silks at Saratoga."

Tuesday, August 8

The New York breeding program makes such fantasy accessible. A state-bred maiden special weight for 2-year-old fillies comes up Friday. Sagamoon might run.

And so … we've sent our silks to Saratoga.

Restrictive rules (breed-back, residency, etc.) limit quality but not quantity. New York-breds are everywhere at Saratoga. It's like in-state admission to a top college. Preferential treatment. Sense of entitlement. You don't have to score high on the SAT test to run on a FRI at the SPA — if you're a NY-bred. But you have to draw in. With so many matriculating, that's where the trouble starts.

Wednesday, August 9

In 2004, the mare Hey Up There foaled Sagamoon on Jan and Sandy's tidy little Jansan Farm above Fort Edward. To fulfill breed-back rules, Hey Up There was sent to the late New York sire Distinctive Pro; her 2005 colt was from his last crop. We named him Mr. Vanderbilt.

Just a few years of planning. With one goal in mind: To have a set of silks lifted off the pegs and set on the jockeys' changing table. For the next race at Saratoga.

Sagamoon drew in.

Thursday, August 10

In a bittersweet ritual all families face, clothes have been handed down. Dad's seersucker made such frequent appearances at one Saratoga meet that Kentucky Ted quipped:

"Hey, Joe! You're runnin' that suit back pretty quick!"

Not worn since last August, still on a hanger, his plaid shirt jumped into my duffle. He used to laugh and say: "First time I came to Saratoga, I was *in utero.*"

Somehow, my wearing his shirt will keep his streak alive.

Friday, August 11

Honestly, we only own 15 percent of her, but who's counting at a moment like this? (A button pops off the plaid shirt.)

Cornelio Velasquez stands in the farm's orange silks. Sagamoon circles under the number six tree. Her name a play on Vanderbilt's Sagamore Farm breeding. Under ancient maples, in seersucker suits, ghost of Alfred G. bends in conversation with

ghost of Joe P. I'm in my own private graveyard of champions. It's all too good. It's all too symmetrical. Grandchildren in his footsteps.

Tom Durkin's voice: *"And Sagamoon is on the move."* For a moment so thrilling, we look like a winner. At Saratoga. In the orange silks. With a favorite filly. For wonderful partners.

But Prado slips by on the rail. We finish second. Jockeys return through the clubhouse on a painted lane. Trainers absorb excuses, then repeat them.

"Cornelio says she was just looking around."

The replay fills a giant screen in the caverns of the great grandstand. In Dad's memory, a ginger ale in the Jim Dandy Bar. Hoofprints of that exemplar of longshots; the 100-1 winner of the 1930 Travers. We watch the replay another three times. "Right there! I thought we had it!"

When they close the casket someday, the kids will mutter: "Remember that day at Saratoga?"

Saturday, August 12

Racehorses in the tan barns of Saratoga's training grounds known as "Oklahoma" must be ridden across the four lanes of Union Avenue to train on the main track. Cars halt as sets of 6, 8, 10 horses stride across the famous boulevard. Past wrought-iron gates.

Horses step onto the main track at a gap on the outside rail. Down the stretch, Saratoga's fantastic "grand stand." An ocean liner of white wood, red awnings. A colossal display of a simple peppermint theme. Like a circus tent in a summer field.

Spell broken by a siren, by flashing lights. Loose horse on the track! Stirrups swinging, a wild-eyed colt flees to the gap. Instincts pulsing directions back to Oklahoma.

Crossing guards spring from stools.

"Close the gates!"

But the loose horse is upon them. He ducks left. Finds himself cornered where the open gate hinges to the iron fence. Out of the frightened crowd, the colt's trainer materializes. Seizes the reins.

Surreal timing. Horse unscathed. No fan trampled. No car crash. Catastrophe averted.

Sunday, August 13

In the quiet of an Oklahoma afternoon, the Phipps horses each graze for 20 minutes in their walking rings. Some cooling out from races, white sheets pulled halfway back, gathered on their loins. Soaking up vitamin D. Whetting the appetite for the steaming mash carted in wheelbarrows to their dinner tubs.

Under TVs in trees, fans stare up at Hall of Fame jockey Jerry Bailey as he is honored:

"And I want to thank God, who got me through *rocky* spots in my personal life, and *tight* spots on the rail."

Artist Peter Williams, on a canvas in the paddock, transforms what you *see* into what you *feel*. But no soundtrack. At that moment, a lone trumpet searches into Billy Joel's "New York State of Mind."

Horn notes captured in the trees. A blanket of music over the chorus of handicappers.

Monday, August 14

Horsemen's Relations finds four seats on a tranquil Monday. Sons Josh and August watch me fumble with a debit card for the touch-screen betting monitor in the box.

Through the afternoon, underage touts of the video-game generation roll a show pool. Initial balance of $40 becomes $22. Balloons back to $44. Settles finally at $39 by the last race.

"That's the most fun we've ever had at the track, Dad."

Redeeming the betting card at the windows, I gush to the clerk:

"My kids had fun today. Those monitors in the boxes are great for young fans, aren't they?"

"Some people love them," he says, shoving $39 through the window. Bitter tone. Teeth clenched. "Some people *hate* them."

Then it dawns on me: Monitors have taken the jobs of mutuel clerks.

Tuesday, August 15

Some owners aren't satisfied unless their horse, ready to run or not, is *stabled* at Saratoga.

"Where's my horse?" irritated owner asks an assistant trainer.

"At Aqueduct."

"Get 'im up here. Bug your boss."

Stalls so tight, racehorses are stabled on the backs of Oklahoma barns. In pony pens. Fenced by pairs of drop bars. The day rate is $100, and drum-tight racehorses in white standing-bandages poke heads through $2-worth of drop bars. You see a trainer on his pony on the main track. Galloping to the gap. Cell phone to his ear. Riding one-handed. Preoccupied.

New York trainer's state of mind.

Wednesday, August 16

The sport of polo attempts to come down off its high horse at Saratoga. Haves and have-nots meet at halftime. An engaging announcer blurs class distinctions. Exhorting bleacher bums and boxholders to stomp divots on a 300-yard lawn pocked by hooves of polo ponies.

The announcer reports iconic trainer Allen Jerkens is in the throng. I climb down from the bleachers, hoping to pass him at a divot. To mumble "Hey, Chief" to him, like some flippant Mohawk brave in a tribal Sundance.

Thursday, August 17

Metaphor for success in the rules of polo. The players are always trying to "find the line." An invisible tangent. A straight line in the spinning wheel of pony paths.

As we left Saratoga for home, the line pierced the arc of summer. Decision-time awaits. Yearlings to sell at Keeneland. Mares to enter in fall sales. Foals to wean; some to cull. Racing stock who've underperformed to be claimed, or sold. Animal husbandry lessons simple as a 4-H manual.

Water the flowers. Cut the weeds.

Trying to find the line.

Friday, August 18

Today, I saw an empty packet of Prolixin in the tack room. An antipsychotic in humans; a long-term tranquilizer in horses. At the racetrack, trainers can't reliably train on Prolixin. Withdrawal time uncertain. Purses lost. *Owners* psychotic. But on a training farm, another tool. Like Ritalin for equine attention deficit.

On a certifiably dangerous horse, a balancing act ensues: Put the bad actor on Prolixin and safely school or risk putting a rider on a helicopter.

Saturday, August 19

Watching a set work at Merryland. One horse a problem child. He works sandwiched among other horses because of his history of 180-degree turns. A nickel horse that turns on a dime. Drops riders. In the stretch, the silly horse spots a glassy bar of sand under the rail, where the track was sealed and the harrow missed it. Ten feet long, a foot wide. On a 3,000-foot-long track. He spooks. Bangs into the horse working next to him.

"Good thing the rider wasn't changing goggles at that moment," said J.R.

Sunday, August 20

Evenings in Saratoga. Fiddlers on Broadway played a lively reel. Hard to get the music of Saratoga out of your head. Mornings, I stood near the starting gate and

listened to the percussion of the gates swinging open.

Back at home these nights, I listen to the music of summer sounds. Tree frogs and cicadas.

Monday, August 21

Another arrow in the New York-bred quiver. Promising 3-year-old New York Moon shipped up from Aqueduct. In the last race today. Orange silks loom boldly at the sixteenth pole before the cavalry charge on the turf course swallows him up.

Almost a Jim Dandy Day ...

Tuesday, August 22

At Saratoga, I watched a Claiborne filly named Nunnery rear in the paddock. Sent young star Fernando Jara skyward. Trainer Billy Mott stepped in quickly. Took Nunnery's reins. Led her around the walking ring. On the track, Nunnery dumped Jara again. Out-maneuvered outriders. Nunnery headed for Church Street, but found faith in the eyes of a bearded railbird, who gently reached over and held her till help arrived.

Loose horses, anywhere, spin material for nightmares. Tonight as I made my rounds, I double-checked chains on gates. Vigilance versus the odds.

Wednesday, August 23

Three horses in three claimers today. None taken. Partners relieved, but sooner or later, they learn: You forfeit the grand chance of The Big Horse if you collect claimers.

Try this: Think of cut day in the NFL. Familiar names, draft picks, injured veterans, thrown into the marked-down bin. Then think of the playoffs: Who's there? The teams that cut the weeds, watered the flowers, made decisions.

Thursday, August 24

Mexico is about one-fifth the size of the United States, but it produces virtually the entire equine labor force of this country. Or so it seems. Our men are homesick. Their work visas don't expire for a few more weeks, but they want to go home. Soon.

In my office, the men gesture about phone calls from their wives. These are men in their 30s and 40s, and they worry that someday they will be worn out from work. They mimic being old and crippled, rocking imaginary canes in their hands.

Friday, August 25

Imagine this cycle. Home in Mexico for three months. Away in the States for nine. Sending salary home by debit card. Every year, the same. Work and return. While children grow, then bear children of their own. Scant hope of anything more than a seasonal work visa. Green card a lottery. Citizenship the remotest of chance. The oldest of our men are about to be grandfathers. They come from a culture of family. The word "sacrifice" is not abstract.

Saturday, August 26

Reading *Roads to Gettysburg,* a parent's diversion at the wildly popular Battlefield Soccer Tournament.

Local elections draw battle lines. Roads to Gettysburg full of lawn signs for www. nocasinogettysburg.com.

A Civil War rages as son August and thousands of 13-year-olds fight on. Young men oblivious to politics. What footsteps they fill on this ground!

Sunday, August 27

On Cemetery Hill, where Lincoln delivered the Gettysburg Address, rebel yells from soccer games carry on the wind. Life imitating life. Battle on a battlefield. On the Taneytown Road, we meet the head of the Gettysburg Equestrian Historical Society, Richard R. Fait Jr.

"Casinos aren't going to bring in tourists. They're going to bring in gamblers. Casinos'll give 'em free food. They'll make huge parking lots with hookups for RVs.

They'll build hotels. They don't want their gamblers coming into town. They don't want them to leave the casino grounds.

"It's all up to the Gaming Commission now. Zoning in place. All that's needed is a license to gamble. This is sacred ground. *Casinos* shouldn't be here."

Monday, August 28

Merryland's vast back fields soon to be home to the weanling crop. That great 1940s photo of 19 babies barreling down the hills of Merryland. How racehorses used to be raised.

At Vanderbilt's Sagamore Farm in the '40s and '50s, manager Ralph Kercheval raised yearlings on hills above the barns. With great success. In later years, yearlings stayed below, for accessibility to farm help. But the poorly drained bottom fields yielded soft runners. Either that, or Native Dancer's influence waned. Whatever. This year's foal crop is running back in time, into the hoofprints of a '40s crop.

Tuesday, August 29

Stood in the back of the van today, as Ambrose shuttled Allenda's Moon from Merryland to Pimlico. Like being 16 again, inside a van sailing past road cuts on the Northway to Saratoga. Circus on the move from Belmont. Pulled my hands in from the window bars, as we cornered off Nelson Avenue onto the backstretch, trees reaching for the van's side.

Inside the box, anxious racehorses rattled chain tethers. Out the windows spread the great glacial plain of Saratoga Springs. The brooding grandstand anchoring all.

Wednesday, August 30

So a friend says: "Hey, 'ja hear Larry LaPrise died? The guy who wrote the 'Hokey Pokey'! Traumatic moment for his family, when they went to put him in the coffin. Couldn't get his left foot in."

That joke popped into mind as I wrote an e-mail for New York Moon, who ran once at Saratoga, and now can't get back in until other New York-breds have done the Hokey Pokey.

Ran him once at the Spa. Now, can't even get his left foot in.

Thursday, August 31

To the lasting confusion of travel agents, *Sarasota,* Florida, is not *Saratoga,* New York. But through E.B. White's eyes in 1956, more than the names were similar. When Sarasota was still the winter home of the Ringling circus, White recorded the scene as a girl stood atop a bareback horse, training in the ring. In his essay *The Ring of Time,* he might have been describing training at Saratoga, or horses in training anywhere, for that matter.

"Enchantment grew … out of something that seemed to go round and around and around, a steady gleam in the shape of a circle — a ring of ambition, of happiness, of youth. Time itself began running in circles, and so the beginning was where the end was, and the two were the same."

September

Friday, September 1

9 a.m., backstretch Laurel.

First raindrops of Hurricane Ernesto drum down on the old wooden barns. Trainers crack orders in the half-light of shedrows. Jockeys jump off one set, hop on the next. Saturday's breeze horses are moved up to today.

Horses sense the storm. New excuse to resist the starting gate: It's a lightning rod.

At the rail, a trainer tattles on another trainer's use of steroids. Winstrol V, Equipoise. Testosterone products.

"He gives 10ccs to every horse every month. What's that do to a horse's mind? To a horse's body? Racing doesn't penalize for anabolic steroids. Why not?"

The word "equipoise" means an equal distribution of weight, of balance. But it doesn't feel equal at the track this morning. Starting gate crew hollers, "Get tied on!" to guileless riders as the question hangs in the warm air.

Saturday, September 2

9 a.m., backstretch Timonium.

Carried on Ernesto's wave last night, the track's cushion of sand has migrated downslope to the rail, exposing the stone-dust base on the high-banked turns. Small gray stones mix in a slurry of sand. A slippery soup of stones to fly back into the lungs and eyes of horses and riders this afternoon, when East Jet should steal the

lead against $10,000 claimers, when Surf Light should rate off the pace in the $50,000 Alma North Stakes.

Two days ago, sunny skies at the state fair. Parents held children up to the hurricane fence to watch the merry-go-round of racehorses. Today, though, it's Sophie's Choice for our horses: Which baby to risk? Surf Light? Last year's Maryland Million heroine on Laurel's grass course is set for auction in November. My head tells me to run East Jet, scratch Surfie. My guilty heart acquiesces. Not a flattering admission.

Get over it. This may look like a carnival, but it's still business.

Sunday, September 3

9 a.m., backstretch Merryland.

Raining still. We know that four hours after the last drop, this good old track will have shaken itself dry. Impervious clay base stays as hard and tight as a clay tennis court. The base of Merryland's track is tilted a gentle two degrees on straightaways; pitched at four degrees on the two turns. Precisely graded by long-dead engineers. We stand in the barn door like we're under the grandstand at Wimbledon, waiting out a rain delay.

SUMMER 2006

Monday, September 4

10 p.m., backstretch Country Life.

Ernesto rains on. End-of-summer reading. Excerpts from *The Honest Rainmaker*, A.J. Leibling's comic take on New York racing in the 1930s.

"Here at Belmont Park this season," Mrs. Harriman said, "we're confronted by a severe Depression, and a continued period of rain could ruin us. I thought you experts might be able to prevent it."

Colonel Stingo: "The most modern method of meteorological control will be utilized."

Fall asleep to rain on the roof, entranced by Leibling's magic: "My latest apparatus has proved as efficacious in driving away rain as in inducing it."

I dream of Sagamoon at Belmont. On "Big Sandy." On a dry track. Betting that The Honest Rainmaker has a reversal of form.

Tuesday, September 5

10 p.m., farm office.

TV hung sports bar-style, suspended high in a corner. I watch as Haldy runs way last against $7,500 claimers. Stay for the replay. Same finish. Damn!

Head for the car. Message on cell phone:

"This is Flint. Call me. Haldy collapsed on the track after we unsaddled him. He died. I think he ruptured an artery. I think he bled out."

Now I'm filled with shame for swearing at his poor effort. I go back into the office. Call Flint. His voice is uneven. He has just watched an animal die. Haldy's body is on the track. Under those harsh lights. Like a sacrifice on that grandstand-less foothill.

The insurance company will need a vet certificate, I remind Flint. He replies:

"Anytime a racehorse dies on the track, state vet does an autopsy."

Equibase chart notes read:

"Haldy stopped."

Unmatched brevity. My late-night e-mail to partners is not so succinct. I hit "Send" as I comprehend: This is a deadly sport.

Wednesday, September 6

3 p.m., Laurel Paddock.

Jockey Rodney Soodeen strides out of the jocks' room in slick black rain pants for Wahoo Moon's race. Color of mourning. Just a coincidence. In this theater of sport, each race is a one-act play. Last night a tragedy. Today a comedy, a surprise ending. Shouts from the winner's circle as $40 win tickets are fished for: "Wahoooo!"

Thursday, September 7

9 p.m., Country Life hillside.

Orange moon above the watershed. A wahoo moon?

248

Such a double-barreled sport. Torn between affection for good horses and divestment of bad ones. By auction, claim box, attrition. Accountants caution against accumulation. Good ones pay for bad ones you didn't know were bad on that sunny day you signed for them. Before performance made the line so clear. Before margin notes on the inventory list pondered their fate: Keep or sell?

Friday, September 8

Grand plans for Pennsylvania-bred Haldy to win slots-enhanced purses fell victim first to bureaucratic delays, then to cruel fate. Only solace now is modest mortality insurance, tied to his lowest claiming price. Oh, how those underwriters understand this sport! Gelded claimers are exposed to double barrels of exacting forces: Owners aiming to unload, and racetracks shooting for full fields.

Saturday, September 9

History of the horse. From *A Strange and Blighted Land: Gettysburg, The Aftermath of a Battle*.

"At least 3,000 horses were killed outright. Injured horses were herded to a field near Rock Creek on the Union Army's old right flank, and shot. One informer underscored the offensiveness of these dead horses, which 'lie thick wherever the fight was hot. Some have been burned, others had earth heaped over them.' Eyewitnesses called the whole ground, for miles around, 'a vast charnel house.' "

At Merryland, J.R. sees horses fast and slow, good and bad. He has a stock line for owners insistent on progress.

"The horse does everything we ask of him."

There is a lot of history in that line. Good and bad.

Sunday, September 10

Springsteen grew up near Monmouth Park. A mom-and-pop trailer outfit from New Jersey once told me he helped them unload a riding horse for his family. They asked him if he owned racehorses.

"No."

Monday, September 11

Keep or sell? Second opinion called for. Local racetrack vets at a disadvantage to sales vets when interpreting yearling X-rays. Digital pictures e-mailed to vet at Keeneland.

"Get that colt down here. That old chip will scare away some pinhookers, but he'll still sell fine. Won't know unless you try. Hell, he's in Book Three. Sells Sunday? Better drive him down here."

Tuesday, September 12

Last dance for Dancer in the Citi tonight, as Flint suggests we retire the brave but sore-ankled filly who struggled home fifth against $7,500 claimers at Penn. Don't punish her. The last dollar on racing's table is bad business. The December mixed sale closes this week. She didn't make the broodmare team. Sell.

Wednesday, September 13

Front seat of a horse van. New perspective. The eyes of van drivers unfamiliar with the area, but who, over the decades, have found these farms from all directions.

Roads and towns inspired by the Bible. Jericho. Jerusalem. Joppa. Wilna.

Chesapeake Bay tributaries shouldering the blacktop. Little Gunpowder River. Big Gunpowder. Winters Run.

Covered bridges. Mill houses. Rock walls. My home ground.

Out the lane at 11 p.m. Into the night. Bound for ol' Kaintuck. From fieldstone to limestone. A 12-hour journey straddling Appalachia. Tree branches thwack van mirrors. Slap the peak of the box. Startle the red yearling.

High adventure awaits.

Thursday, September 14

Down into the great basin of West Virginia. Tired mind playing tricks. Orange running lights on cab seem like the rising sun. Pull over. Sleep for an hour on bench seat.

Road sign: 5 percent grade next 4 miles.

No one at weigh station at 4 a.m.

Next sign: If brakes fail, don't take exit ramp, 7 percent grade there. Use the runaway truck ramp farther downhill. Sure.

Safe at last on the valley floor. Orange sky above red cliff walls.

Awakening in the half-light halfway to Lexington, the red yearling colt rocks the box. Six hours later, he's sleeping in Barn 15 at Keeneland, white noise of the auctioneer's chant droning on.

Friday, September 15

In the adventure of travel, nothing is guaranteed. Driving the van to Leesburg earlier this week. Construction on the Dulles Toll Road. Narrowed lanes, defined by Jersey walls. A worker hopped onto the concrete wall. Almost lost his balance. Swung his arms back to save himself from falling into my lane. Just driving a mare to a clinic and I'm 30 feet from killing a man.

Saturday, September 16

Hemingway cliché: If you are lucky enough to have lived in Lexington as a young man, then wherever you go for the rest of your life it stays with you, for Lexington is a moveable feast.

Actually, he wrote "in Paris," but not Paris, Kentucky. Never mind. It works.

Drive the ancient back roads at sunset. Find the real Kentucky. Not opulence but sustenance. Herd of Black Angus on bluegrass in orange light. You are immersed in Kentucky, in full cinematic effect.

Profit in the horse business isn't just from the final bid, or the winner's purse. It is also found in its sense of place.

Sunday, September 17

Rolex clocks on the wall above the summary board give the time in Sydney. In Tokyo. In London. In Dubai.

In Lexington.

Where they give you two minutes. Five thousand yearlings. Thirty yearlings an hour. Fourteen days in two-minute time trials. Keep or sell?

As bidding winds down on the red colt, I think of the sport of lacrosse, where a timekeeper runs onto the field with the official clock when time is running out. Adrenaline sounds an old alarm: "Clock's on the field!"

That was then. This time around, clock's on the wall. Reserve met. Game over. Sold.

Rush over to the Northern Dancer bar at Keeneland for simulcast of Sagamoon's race at Belmont. Counting on good vibes of famous Maryland stallion for an edge. "The Honest Rainmaker" kept rain away. Dry track. She gets beat a dirty nose. Oh, well . . .

Double-barreled action today.

Monday, September 18

Food court in the Keeneland sale pavilion. A lady on crutches swings a white ankle-cast and it occurs to me: It's like a ski lodge. Noisy in a great hollow way. Filled with folks taking a break from strenuous sport. Overpriced food for a captive crowd. Suddenly, I've been too long at the fair.

Tuesday, September 19

Got halfway home last night. Alone in an empty van. A year ago, Dad was my co-pilot. He liked to stop before he left the Bluegrass. For an authentic box of Kentucky Fried Chicken. For Richard, for Monday Night Football.

This time around, I couldn't drive the whole way. Stopped at a Ramada Inn, where salesmen at a termite-control convention kept the bar open late. When Dad quit drinking at age 57, suddenly there was a choice. For both of us. Now I gratefully go about my father's business, spared from an unfulfilling career in another line of work.

Wednesday, September 20

Climb to 2,610 feet in western Maryland and fall off the Eastern Continental Divide. Surrounded by mini-Alps that give way to terraces of blue-ridged mountains. You decompress on the beauty of Maryland's cows and cornfields. All the way back into Baltimore, where screaming traffic dissipates all reverie. Where farms are few. And far between.

Thursday, September 21

Leafing through photographs of Merryland in the time of Betty Shea Miller. There! That's the one! From the 1970s! She's leading a busload of inner-city children on a tour of Merryland. Doesn't she look happy surrounded by all those kids? Doesn't she look proud of her farm? And look at the stallion barn behind them. Perfectly painted. Weathervane atop the cupola. Cedar tree shading all. That's the photo to run in the farm ad this month. That's the way to remember Betty.

Friday, September 22

Reached home too late for last Monday's celebration of Betty's life. At the Keeneland sales that day, Kentucky Ted had said: "We'll raise a toast here just as the party at Merryland is starting. It'll be Miller time in two states!"

So ahead of her time. She persuaded her neighbors to place their farms in preservation. These days, handsome green markers quietly inform passersby that these properties are protected by the Long Green Valley Conservancy. A quiet legacy.

Saturday, September 23

9 a.m., backstretch Laurel.

"We'll take the filly to the gate this morning. If she breaks good, we'll run her Wednesday."

Spectacular Malibu fidgets behind the starting gate until she decides it's time to go in. Stands patiently as the starting crew waits for a break in the stream of galloping horses.

"Get tied on!"

Th-waanngg!!!

Springs of the gate reverberate in the morning air. Specky's hindquarters uncoil. She launches out cleanly. Sails past. Three furlongs later, disappears into a point.

"OK. We'll enter for Wednesday." 5 p.m., backstretch Pimlico.

A three-story bandstand towers over the infield as Wahoo Moon listens to the bombardment of electric guitars from who's left of The Who. We ask these horses to do anything, everything.

Sunday, September 24

Trainer Ferris Allen walks down his shedrow. Ducking into each stall. Running his hands like a chiropractor down the spines of every horse. Feeling feet. Touching tendons. An assistant carries a notepad.

"Put the magnetic blanket on this filly," the trainer says.

About a veteran gelding: "Better get him in ice. Don't underestimate ice."

Next stall. "Claimed this horse in Florida last winter. Bowed in first start for us. Chance of coming back? Fifty-fifty. Maybe less. That happens …"

On barn help: "Nobody appreciates how many people it takes. Jock's agent bought lunch for the crew. Food was gone in four minutes. Hotwalkers. Grooms. Assistants. Exercise riders. It's an army of labor. You'd think a jock's agent, here every day, would know how many mouths we feed."

"Hell, nobody knows, 'cept payroll. Payroll knows."

Monday, September 25

In mind today are seamless improvements we saw at Keeneland. Limestone quarried from similar veins. Magnolias 25-feet high along a widened outside rail, like they've been there forever (but dogwoods gone). A tote board scaled to Times Square. And Polytrack. Last Saturday, over Turfway's Polytrack in a prep stakes for Keeneland, Malibu Mint bounced out in 1:08 and something.

Times squared.

SUMMER 2006

Tuesday, September 26

Excerpt from J.R.'s Unauthorized Diary, in which he writes about the owner of a 4-year-old maiden:

See you got a check last out. Fifth, huh? That's good.

"He run fourth," owner responds. I saw the chart, can't help but wonder. Thinking DQ. Or bad test on the winner. After a moment of awkward silence, owner says, "I don't care what they say. He run fourth for a ways. He run fourth."

I apply his placing system to other areas of my life. To my savings account. And under this new system, I was fast in the 440 in junior high. Basketball shots that hit the rim went in. In this reality, his horse was on the lead until they popped the latch.

Wednesday, September 27

Spectacular Malibu didn't know why she should walk instead of run on the track as Juan led her to the paddock this afternoon. So instead of stepping nicely onto the backstretch for the long walk over, she struck out. A sharp blow to Juan's ankle. She was *this* close to getting loose. He couldn't walk her without help. Used his cell phone to call the trainer in the paddock: Could you send a pony over?

She arrived late. Refused to let the track identifier lift her lip. He OK'ed her on her markings, not her tattoo. She sized up her rivals and snorted a warning.

In the aftermath of her spectacular first start, I am astounded again at the thin line. She's cooling out in the testing barn. But hell, if Juan had let her go, we'd be headed to New Bolton instead.

Thursday, September 28

It's a long way to Tipperary.

The quarantine farm of that name on the Mt. Horeb Pike outside Lexington was waiting. An all-day drive to deliver two weanlings to prep for the November sale.

Across the pike roll the historic grounds of J.R. Keene's Castleton Farm — the most prominent Thoroughbred nursery in the world at one time. Bred or owned by Keene from 1893 to 1912: Sysonby, Peter Pan, Colin, Maskette, Black Toney, Domino.

It's quitting time, and I don't want to wear out my welcome. So I just nod in thanks toward the Castleton stallion barn, where Malibu Moon has no clue that he sired a spectacular winner yesterday.

Friday, September 29

Driving the van on Winchester Road. Kent Hollingsworth's lively treatise *The Kentucky Thoroughbred* on the bench seat. Fresh in my mind is the chapter on Hamburg, champion 2-year-old colt in 1897.

These days, Lexington is eating Hamburg Place, John Madden's once-vast savannah of Thoroughbred success. Madden's splendid bluegrass now prey to invasive cloverleaf of I-75. But the story of the farm's namesake lives on through Hollingsworth's hand:

"Young man, do you own that colt?"

"That depends on whether you want to buy him or attach him," replied John Madden.

"What's your price?"

"Fifty thousand dollars."

The highest price ever paid for a racehorse was $40,000, when Leonard Jerome purchased champion Kentucky as a sire prospect.

The stranger offered $40,000. Madden seemed tempted, but then shook his head. The stranger thereupon wrote out a Wells-Fargo draft for $40,000, took a silver dollar from his vest pocket, and flipped it into the air. Madden caught the coin, and the deal was made, at $40,001. Subject of the trade was Hamburg.

Saturday, September 30

Hurrying home for horse sales. A mountain of entries, as 1,000 yearlings go on the block at Timonium, beginning Monday.

First, though, the mountains of Maryland. Rest Stop at Sideling Hill. Spectacular roadcut exposing a 340-foot-deep history of the world. Air warmer than the land. Mist climbing off the valley floor, blowing over me in a gentle jetstream. I slide a quarter into one of those Mt. Rushmore binocular machines. Look out over the edge of a once-great sea that extended west. When Lexington, beyond the zone of eroding silt and sand, would have been under a shallow ocean, full of shells and skeletons of marine animals. To the east, the terraced Piedmont, the Shenandoah Valley that concealed the northward march of Lee's Army into Pennsylvania.

Trucks gear down. Roar like dinosaurs through the eons of rock. In the parking lot, a driver towing a gooseneck horse-trailer eases to a stop. Heading west. Climbs out of his truck. Hitches up his pants. Looks in the slat windows of his trailer, checking on the horses. They are resigned to his plans.

You don't rest at Sideling Hill unless you are on a long adventure. Emerson said: "Events are in the saddle. We're along for the ride."

And what an adventurous ride these horses give us. They do everything we ask of them.

FALL
2006

October

Sunday, October 1

The number is so round: 1,000 horses. All for sale at Timonium over the next three days. Half the herd in tents in the infield. The largest yearling sale ever in Maryland.

Such a perfect number evokes ancient history. Mongol horsemen of the 13th century were decimal dependent. Marco Polo wrote:

"Great Tartar chiefs appoint an officer to every 10 horsemen. Ten companies of a hundred men were a thousand-strong." The size of Mongol brigades that sacked cities. A Mongol "horde" meant simply a camp, from their word "ordu."

Tomorrow morning, unaware commuters snarled in York Road traffic will stare down onto a vast valley of white tents, wondering what horde has encamped near their village, as 1,000 Mongol ponies parade over the grounds.

At stake: the mysterious culture of the horse.

Monday, October 2

Autumn in the trees on the drive home. Dramatic October sunsets. Irish fiddle music on the radio as the mind replays images from the sale. I saw the best yearling by a farm stallion break loose, race down the tents, past colorful banners. A loose charger in a medieval tournament. She bolted left and disappeared into a tent. So did everyone in pursuit of her. Fear of losing her in maintenance areas, where steel spikes anchor the canvas.

To stand in the path of a runaway horse is reckless. And yet every horseman and horsewoman on two good legs waved and coaxed the filly into submission. It's a high sense of sportsmanship that saves another man's horse at the risk of personal injury.

Ingrained in the culture. No one hangs separately. Everyone hangs together.

Tuesday, October 3

In the moment before declaring "no bid" on an offered yearling at the Fasig-Tipton Midlantic yearling sale, the auctioneer suspends the gavel in midair. Hesitant to confess failure. For the auction house. The breeder. The agent. The industry.

The auctioneer shudders. Suddenly, his gavel cracks out the guilty verdict.

Wednesday, October 4

The elevator stops at many floors in this business. Where do you want to get off? That was the question posed today to partners in Spectacular Malibu. If we accept the offer, she'll run in the Maryland Million in someone else's silks. Pre-entries close today. If we decline the offer, we may be turning down more than she'll ever be worth again.

The elevator paused to count votes, then resumed its climb.

Thursday, October 5

To qualify foals as state-breds, Pennsylvania requires out-of-state mares to arrive by Nov. 1 this year, even earlier next year, by October 1. Construction crews at Philadelphia Park have been told to finish up ASAP. Slot machines are en route.

Year-round mare owners boarding in Maryland politely request that their mares be sent to Pennsylvania by the end of this month. As yearlings arrive from the sales, mares leave.

Friday, October 6

Perfect Moon is a reminder of this sport's quirky sense of *noblesse oblige*. Colorful California trainer Mel Stute won with Perfect Moon's sire, highborn Malibu Moon, in May of his 2-year-old year, 1999. For 24 hours, the colt was the best juvenile in California. But he'd broken his knee in his maiden win. The day after, he was *hors de combat*, a 2-year-old stallion prospect.

At Timonium this year, Mel bought a vanload of yearlings, with hopes that one of them will turn out like Mel's $4,700 Timonium yearling of 2002 — stakes winner Perfect Moon, from the first crop of the colt with unfulfilled promise.

These days, from his driveway paddock, lovable Perfect Moon poses like a silly sentry at the gates of Merryland, a standing invitation to the unpredictable world of Thoroughbred ownership.

Saturday, October 7

In the debris field of sales-week paperwork lay a dusty green folder of drawings by C.W. Anderson. An impulse buy for $30 at a knick-knack auction near the Fasig-Tipton ring. Anderson's pencil drawings from the 1940s form a visual link between the alpha-and-omega horse books of Farley's *The Black Stallion* and McCarthy's *All The Pretty Horses*.

Captions capture the subjects: Man o' War at 21; Young hopeful; The salt block; Four of a kind; Blood will tell.

It's not a complete set, but it's a circle of horse portraits that begins and ends without the messy complications of people in the pictures. Such a simple sport when it's just about black stallions and pretty horses.

Sunday, October 8

The ash tree will blaze red for three days, then lose its leaves before the maple knows the month. Merryland's hill will fill with deer. When next you look, it's empty. As you drive up Bottom Road, the great earthen bank of the racetrack runs your eye to the white rail, where a black horse in a workout is silhouetted at full speed, as though in a Muybridge animation.

People are peripheral. Extras. Location is the star. A standing ovation for the brilliant performance of the clear cold stream that flows through the farm.

Monday, October 9

A book of C.W. Anderson's pencil drawings rests on a hall table in the big house. "A gift from the artist," Uncle Johnny once told me. "I helped him out of a jam."

Vague mention of a driving infraction coming through the county.

The book only moves from its sacred spot at Christmastime, when the tree crowds the corner. Once a year for as long as I can remember, those drawings have arrested my attention.

Tuesday, October 10

"Sid and Shirley. Karl and JoAnne. Dick and Carol. John and Marcia. Welcome to Merryland. Today is Jenkin Jones' first day on the track in four months. We gave him the summer off. His back was bothering him. In the old days, before year-round racing, Merryland was famous as a resting place for weary racehorses. These days, trainers don't stop on a horse. They just medicate and keep on going. Or lose them in claiming races when they get sore. They hate to send horses to farms. Afraid the horse won't return in good shape. Or, the owner will decide to change trainers. But just look at JJ bouncing around. Horses need a break. Old-time trainers ran 'em hard, but gave them a few months off to recharge."

Wednesday, October 11

9 a.m. Laurel backstretch.

Spectacular Malibu jogs the wrong direction along the outside rail. Just "backing up." She swings around at the far turn, comes towards us at a gallop. A horse breezing along the rail blows past her. Specky attempts to run off, to race the other filly. It is a moment of sheer instinct. Jockey Julian Pimentel quickly reins her back to a controlled gallop as they near the half-mile pole. Then he leans forward in the tiny exercise saddle, giving her the signal. She disappears around the turn, reappears far away in the distant homestretch.

"I got her in :48," trainer Mike Trombetta says. An hour later, he drops her name in the entries for Saturday's Maryland Million Lassie.

261

FALL 2006

Thursday, October 12

He died a year ago today. No one says it, but everyone knows it. Then comes a call from cousin Rick, for whom best-man Dad made a memorable wedding toast: "To Denise, and de' nephew."

Months ago, a puppy wandered along the farm lane. No owner to be found. Now the size of a Buick, Ouida opens doors in Mom's house and in her heart. Reincarnation is a stretch, but thank you to whoever sent this dog.

Friday, October 13

After seven days of side reining at Merryland, the yearling filly was ready to have a rider on her back. While running in her paddock two days ago, she tried to jump the fence. Didn't clear it. Hind legs hung. Knocked new fence down. At first we thought pulled muscle. Then too lame to walk. Leesburg X-rays revealed fractured pelvis. Career as racehorse over before it started. Everyone glum with today's sad news.

How do these horses hurt themselves? They just do.

Saturday, October 14

Before her first race 17 days ago, she tried to break loose from her groom on the walk over. Today, Spectacular Malibu was led over for the Maryland Million Lassie with a groom on each side and a lead pony as escort. She argued again with the track identifier trying to read her lip tattoo. Ah, well. That's our girl. A horde of friends gathered in the winner's circle as Spectacular Malibu snorted at defeated rivals walking home behind her.

We're riding that elevator.

Sunday, October 15

In olden days, yearling trials were the feature of some famous parties at Merryland. The tradition lives on, with a new wrinkle.

For our "Autumn Day in the Country," the farm's most precocious yearling is selected to wear the saddle cloth of a farm Maryland Million winner. Last year, budding star Spectacular Malibu galloped around in Surf Light's winning saddle cloth.

Today, burly Daniel Moon wore Spectacular Malibu's winning cloth.

Monday, October 16

Merryland on the day after a fabulous open house is resplendent still, as though a happy wedding reception was hosted yesterday. Grass mowed. Hedges trimmed. Track harrowed. Horses clean.

Lawn chairs stacked against trees awaiting the catering truck. Colorful tablecloths taped down. Leftover pies waiting in the fridge.

It's post-traumatic dress syndrome, this sigh of relief after the big show. I look around to thank the farm crew, but they are busy tacking up today's sets for the track. How did so many things go right these past few days?

Tuesday, October 17

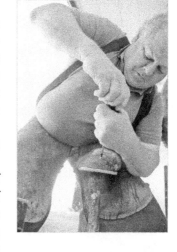

Burly boutique blacksmith Butch Wheeler carved out the dead tissue in P.J. Indy's quarter-cracked hoof. The bed of Butch's pickup is lined with splatterings of fiberglass patches from prior patients. P.J. was lightly tranquilized, but not senseless as Butch tapped and drilled a dozen short screws into the gelding's hoof.

"If he can't feel, you can't tell," Butch explained about how deep to drill.

He heated up a strong-smelling concoction of resin and glue, into which he dipped strands of fiberglass thinner than angel hair spaghetti. He slapped gooey globs of his home-made patching material onto the screws in P. J.'s hoof, took a break to let it set up, then rasped it down to conform with the curvature of the hoof.

P.J. is going back to work, thanks to Butch.

Wednesday, October 18

Romance of a training barn is spellbinding. In the tack room, racks and racks of saddles, a cavalry outfitter. A simple set of orange blinkers on a hook becomes a still life.

For farm guests last Sunday, resident artists Ellen and Laurie latticed the wash stall in flowers and photos, ceramics and shirts. They did a brisk business in their makeshift gift shop. Enthralled with equine memorabilia, guests snatched up souvenirs of their day in the country. Romance of a horse farm to carry home.

Thursday, October 19

Equine nutritionist Steve Jackson examined the condition of the high-maintenance elderly mares in Val's care. Survivors of founder, of dystocias, of ruptured arteries, of foal after foal after foal. These dowager matrons are sentimental strongholds.

"I wouldn't change a thing," he observed, "except maybe rock the toe back on this one mare. Might have a little navicular."

He began a Ph.D. discussion on how bursitis erodes the navicular bone, from pressure of the deep flexor tendon. He concluded his visit with a question on the pH of the pastures.

Friday, October 20

Everyone calls them the "Stucco Boys." They drywall the farm's old houses. In exchange, we train their young horses. Heavy-metal rock music, 12-packs of beer, and ribald stories accompany the Stucco Boys to the job.

Today they howled about a Louisiana bush track straight out of the movie *Casey's Shadow*. One of the Stucco Boys had been a jockey. He once hopped on a fireball sprinter in a two-stall starting gate and saw a chicken strapped to the saddle of the other horse.

"Always bet the chicken," the former jock advised, in case the chance arose. "They don't weigh nothin'. Chicken'll win every time."

The Stucco Boys fell off their kitchen bar stools laughing at the absurd truth of horse racing.

Saturday, October 21

Sagamoon got the big sandy track she needed today at Belmont. Mike phoned Mom from the winner's circle: "I'm standing on hallowed ground."

It's not just the win. It's the saga of Sagamoon's lineage that prompts Mike's hyperbole. He is seeing strands of time you can only see when a win, like morning dew on a spider web, highlights it. History is firing Mike's imagination.

Grandfather Pons, for the absent August Belmont II at the 1918 Saratoga yearling sale, advises Samuel Riddle to bid on Man o' War. He sires American Flag, who sires Lady Glory, from whom Grandfather breeds Raise You in '46. She sells at Saratoga in '47. In '61, she produces Raise a Native, by Native Dancer, Alfred Vanderbilt's great gray sire who stood at Maryland's Sagamore Farm.

Sagamoon's sire is Malibu Moon, whose broodmare sire is Mr. Prospector, by Raise a Native. Sagamoon's dam is the last mare Vanderbilt owned.

It's a web, sewn into a tidy winner's circle moment today in the vastness of historic Belmont Park.

Sunday, October 22

Racing at Keeneland on a cold autumn Sunday. Frenchmen in black coats saddle a filly for the grass stakes. Behind her ears, an odd attachment is clipped. I find out later that it was a pull string for two white cotton earplugs the jockey yanked free when he asked the excitable filly for her run down the homestretch.

Racing at Keeneland on a cold autumn Sunday. All alone. Only the sound of your own heart pounding.

Monday, October 23

For the second time this month, 1,000 yearlings for sale. This time around, in Lexington. Commercial Kentucky breeders more aggressive than regional horsemen with conformation of young foals. A consignor warned: "Somehow her growth plates fused while she had wires on her knees. She'll never be right."

They say that legendary Calumet trainer Ben Jones would recommend putting down the farm's bad foals. And famous English yards shot slow racehorses. What do you do with a yearling with fused growth plates? Breed it?

It's the damnedest thing sometimes, not to walk face-first into the spider webs of history.

Tuesday, October 24

At stake: the culture of the horse. Preserved nowhere else as at Keeneland. In memorabilia, in photographs, in warm restaurants on the first floor. The very first race run at Keeneland, 1936. Vision of a few hardboots. Like a long drive in a tight football game. Calling plays on the run. For the program for that first race, the secretary handwrote names of jockeys. Some entries didn't have a rider listed. The program might have been printed an hour before.

They made it up as they went along, Hancock and Haggin and Beard and Whitney and Headley and Combs and who else. The first race was for 2-year-old fillies. Some Sagamoon of that day took the prize. The winner's circle is hallowed ground now. It wasn't always. It was just a gleam in a few guys' eyes.

Wednesday, October 25

It's not that the thrill is gone. It's just that the road is long. Limestone greets you on the drive in. On the drive out, it falls from eroded perches to mine the shoulders with

boulders. This time around, only the oak leaves cleave to the trees in the Daniel Boone National Forest. The maples have fallen into the river, brewing a weak tea.

Deep into the night in the mountains of western Maryland, snow dances on the roadway. Kentucky recedes like the tide that once washed over her.

Thursday, October 26

Over a three-day sale, 47 yearlings failed to draw a single bid. Summary sheet said: Not Sold ($1,000). No one draws up a plan that aims for this end. It just happens. Stud fee *in* doesn't mean stud fee *out*. The median price was $7,500. The Repository was a book of revelations. Everyone raises bad horses. It is a great courtesy of the sales company to provide a marketplace. And some very good racehorses will come out of this sale … but I drove an empty van home. Haven't an eye good enough to spot the cat in the picture.

Friday, October 27

Life in the time of cholera. Again. Equine herpes virus is back. Monmouth closed. As a precaution against shippers bringing in the plague, Philadelphia Park shut its gates to incoming horses.

Last night, Penn National did likewise.

Surf Light had been stabled at Penn but came home after the Maryland Million. She is set for auction at Keeneland in two weeks. It boggles the mind to think of the impact the herpes virus could have on 5,000 horses moving through the Keeneland sales grounds.

Saturday, October 28

T Bone Burnett sings a song about Marilyn Monroe called "Fatally Beautiful." I don't play it around the filly we cheekily named Merryland Monroe. She is auditioning for a starring role at Laurel, working bullets for a racing debut around the time of Mike's birthday in mid-November. The only song we want to teach Merryland Monroe is "Happy Birthday."

Sunday, October 29

"She's throwing exercise riders around like they're bug boys. Aqueduct's got a five-horse field for a grade III. The Breeders' Cup next week sucked up a bunch of the 2-year-old fillies."

Leaving Laurel at 2 a.m. as gale winds howled through the hardwoods, Spectacular Malibu tempted fate for a race-and-return in the Tempted Stakes.

At betting windows over in the art-deco clubhouse, we placed our feet in red-painted silhouettes of shoes that show big winners where to stand for their IRS portrait. But A.J. Liebling's characters from *The Honest Rainmaker* were unleashing wind instead of rain today. After jockeys in the first race couldn't control their horses, the card was canceled. All bets were off. The Tempted reset for this Friday. Shoeless Joe on the road home.

Monday, October 30

Two schools of Thoroughbred ownership. The first is the private school. The breed-and-hold school. Married to your horses. Hold them until they die. Bury them on the hill. The second is the public school. Correctly guess the moment in a horse's life when the public will pay the highest price; then sell.

The dissolution of partnerships pits the two schools against each other.

Tuesday, October 31

Two weeks from now at Keeneland, we sell 15-year-old Prospective Joy. Nicknamed "Queenie" by the farm staff in homage to her status, she is the only mare to produce a grade I winner for this farm. She peaked in value about seven years ago, when her daughter Hookedonthefeelin won the grade I La Brea Stakes. But now, to dissolve a partnership, she boards our van in two days. Bound for Kentucky.

Traveling with her will be Surf Light, winner of Maryland Million Ladies so spectacularly, so sentimentally, three days after Dad died.

By Keeneland standards, these are not spectacular offerings. By family farm standards, they represent our finest stock. No reserves when partnerships are being dissolved. Strategy unfolds in two minutes in the auction ring.

Preparing the van for a long ride is usually like packing for vacation. This time around, it feels very different.

November

Wednesday, November 1

They arrive in a fleet of ridden-hard cars. Around noon. Straight from Pimlico, where they've breezed racehorses all morning. They read J.R.'s training chart on the dry-erase board. Spend time in the stall with their yearling. Hop on. Take a lap around the shedrow. Gather in a set for the long hack down to the track.

J.R. on Timmy the Lead Pony maps it out from noon to 3 p.m.: "Two and a half times around, Mark. Des and Milan, meet you over at the gate. You're just jogging, Lauren."

Riders know each yearling by name. Or by sire. Or by dam. By something. The name gets passed along. This is risky business. No such thing as a garden-variety yearling. You don't want to be the last to know a quirk. Courage is not absence of fear. It's resistance to it. Good riders quiet their fear.

It's a contest. They don't expect to stay on, all the time. A good-sized yearling colt weighs 1,100 pounds. If he says it's time to go?

"Rider off," J.R. calls out.

Thursday, November 2

"What track we headed for today?"

Innocent question the 5-year-old race mare Surf Light seemed to ask as she climbed into the van at 4 a.m. Prospective Joy's attitude at 15 years of age: "I'll do whatever you ask."

I don't know what'll happen when we drop the ramp in Kentucky for the sales. I don't know who'll be coming home. If any. Dissolving partnerships requires market appraisal. It takes a hard heart. Tough guys like John Madden ... they went into and out of partnerships same as joining or leaving a card game. The glorious uncertainty of the Turf, Madden called the whole business.

It's not so glorious after all. This uncertainty.

Friday, November 3

Kentucky moments. Heading west on I-64. Smell of fermenting grain from distilleries. Like bread in the oven.

Morning workouts at Churchill. Day before the Breeders' Cup.

Afternoon spent watching simulcast of Aqueduct's Tempted Stakes from inside a Churchill mini-theater. Spectacular Malibu leans into the lead but is outrun to the wire. Still, she's second in a grade III!

Stop at Fasig-Tipton to see Hookedonthefeelin. Sold her at Timonium 10 years ago. On Sunday night, she sells again.

Over to Keeneland, where we sell Hookedonthefeelin's weanling half sister this Tuesday. On deck for Thursday's sale is their dam, Prospective Joy.

Big week at hand.

Drink it all in.

Saturday, November 4

You hear at dinner that Breeders' Cup handle was somewhere around $120 million, maybe more. We didn't live in the golden age of racing. But today, we lived in a golden moment of racing, if handle equals gold. It appears that while not everyone watched the Breeders' Cup, everyone bet it.

Sunday, November 5

Announcer Terence Collier picks up the narrative of Hookedonthefeelin:

"This mare won the grade I La Brea Stakes. Her first foal is Pussycat Doll, who also won the La Brea."

If this were fiction, that script would be dismissed as improbable.

Auctioneer Walt Robertson: "Million five. Million seven."

A lady from Pennsylvania versus a man from California.

"Two million eight. Three million? Two million nine. Is that what you wanna do? Two million nine. Three million?"

Robertson drops the hammer: "Two million nine."

For two hours, Hookedonthefeelin is the high price of the sale. Then some filly straight off the track steals the headline.

Monday, November 6

Lunging ring at the stallion's farm. Gazebo roof. Daylight between rafters and walls. Door thick as a castle's.

Stallion headmaster Wayne Howard tutors the pupil, Malibu Moon. A whip merely a prop. Wood-chip footing an excitable sound as the stallion, free from his shank, begins the exercise routine at a canter.

"Ho, ho. Just trot. Steady. Good boy. Steady. Trot on. Good boy. Ho, ho. Walk. Wha-lk. *Huh-hoooo.* Wha-lk."

And so the lesson goes. Interspersed with playful antics. A dash or two across the middle to scatter tight-knit observers. Flash of bell boots and polos. Assumption of risk.

"Gotta get it right. Good boy. Walk once, and that's it. And we'll call it a day. Ah! Ah! Ah! Ah! Gotta finish on a good note. Now walk. Wha-lk. And stand. *Stand.* And stand. That's it. Good boy."

Tuesday, November 7

If pinhookers don't like your horse, *you'd* better. The disconnect of resale versus racing. A beauty contest versus a talent show.

Race is a four-letter word to pinhookers — and to most commercial breeders. Sales are the game. Racing is for someone else. Someone who can face death by two years of monthly bills.

"What's driving prices for weanlings?" a major consignor is asked.

He answers: "Luckily for us, it's not racing."

Hookedonthefeelin's weanling half sister didn't make the pinhookers' short list. But she made ours.

Wednesday, November 8

She's covered in straw. Half-asleep. Exhausted. I groom her with my hands. Pick the straw out of her tail. Discover a tiny leather tag clip-tied against her tailbone. Hip number punched into the leather: 496. A tiny affidavit to buyers in due course, and to stable-release personnel. Meanwhile, her mom's up in Barn 45. Tag in her tail, too. Sells tomorrow.

The filly expels a short burst of gas. I put my head on her flanks and listen for gut sounds. Lots of noise. That's good. Things are working in there. No colic. Horses a most perishable commodity.

Thursday, November 9

The market for elderly mares is what you make it. Mike was underbidder on the 15-year-old mare today. Lost her to a gal intent on acquiring a good old mare for a nice young stallion. Back home at the farm are two younger sisters. And soon, the weanling daughter.

Mike says: "Kind of like we're the manager for Gladys Knight and the Pips. Gladys signed with another label. All we've got are the Pips."

FALL 2006

Friday, November 10

Groom snaps a shank on a weanling. Vet approaches. Endoscope like a scarf around his neck.

"Put that twitch on lightly."

He eases the fiber optic snake up the filly's nostril. Examining her epiglottis. Her arytenoids. Her pharynx. As he withdraws the scope, he swabs mucus off it with a cloth. Stuffs the cloth into a test tube.

"Just cells. For a DNA sample."

In the event of a racing injury someday. To regenerate tissue. Straight from the factory. Like car parts. Torn tendons same as bent bumpers. Fixable. Someday.

Saturday, November 11

Drizzling. A soft, warm rain on the beautifully stark Kentucky landscape. Washing away lingering sadness about having sold a favorite mare two days ago. Mike always thought we'd be burying her next to her sire someday.

So this friend tells him a story about a foal who'd escaped from a barn fire. Scorched half to death.

"And he lived?" Mike asked. "What'd you name him?"

"Bernie."

Mike fell off his chair laughing. "You named him *Bernie*?"

Sunday, November 12

I saw an auctioneer on break. Pacing in valet parking. Chanting numbers. Like a man having a nervous breakdown.

I saw a bid spotter make a mistake. Holler "Hep!" to the auctioneer's chant. For a number higher than the bidder intended. The auctioneer chided the bid spotter who, with wounded pride, smiled bravely. In servitude to his boss way up there like a god.

I saw an empty shoe-shine stand. Heard a fellow say: "I'm gonna hop up there and charge $10 to listen to woes of the horse business. Limit 10 minutes."

Sale at its halfway mark today.

Monday, November 13

"Kill all your darlings."

It's a coarse phrase meant to shock. Attributed to William Faulkner. As advice to writers unable to delete pet phrases. Change it to: "Sell all your darlings." Then it's advice to horse owners unable to delete pet horses when the market is right. Still, a piece of you dies when you sell a darling horse.

After Prospective Joy sold, I phoned the farm. Spoke to Mom. Ellen. Val. Cheryl. Left word for Richard:

"We bid as far as made sense."

Maybe it's a necessary desensitization. Thick skin a prerequisite. We are farmers. Horses are livestock.

No, they're not. Thank goodness, they're not. They'd be as memorable as cattle. We'd have no darlings.

Tuesday, November 14

Race mare Surf Light sold yesterday. We only owned a quarter of her, but there she goes anyway. The filly who graced Christmas photos. Covers of sale catalogs. Covers of racing programs. The filly who won the Maryland Million Ladies at laughable odds three days after Dad died.

Our darling Surf Light.

The market is so strong for young mares. It was the right thing to do. They're horses. We have people to think of. Anyway, given the never-ending nature of horse sales these days, both mares could cycle back through in a year's time.

Wednesday, November 15

The great rock wall of Xalapa Farm. On North Middletown Road heading from Paris to Mt. Sterling. Taller than a man. Miles long.

Repaired sections show insets of fresh limestone. Unweathered. Still cream-colored from the quarry.

You can't look at Xalapa's wall and not consider the men who built it. Stone by backbreaking stone. It is the pyramid of the Bluegrass. A wonder of the horse world. Right there on the van drive home.

Thursday, November 16

In trips past, a riverside pasture 30 miles from Ashland has been the site of a revival tent. This time around, all I see are poles that supported the tent, some bleachers that stood like pews in a roofless church, cows indifferent to the echo of long-gone sermons.

The tent, like the sycamore, has lost its cover. Winter's coming. Let's git this filly on home.

Ellen rings: "Where are you?"

FALL 2006

Friday, November 17

Grade-school children lined the sidewalk outside St. Agnes School in Atlantic Highlands of New Jersey. In a touching salute to the funeral procession for Charlie Hesse.

He was Merryland's first client five years ago. In his honor, we stopped at Monmouth Park on the ride home to buy a *Form*. His dad built the racing surface for the modern Monmouth in 1945. Charlie redid it in 1978.

Long before new stadiums featured luxury suites, Monmouth had flowers draped from three decks of parterre boxes overlooking the track. It's what heaven looks like to a horseman.

Saturday, November 18

At Laurel, Merryland Monroe went wire to wire today. It's November. A 3-year-old making her debut. Patience paid off. From torn tendon to overnight sensation. Ombeleevobul!

Meanwhile, in New York, Sagamoon and Edgar Prado made it look so easy on TV. In the quiet aftermath, I consider: First time in farm history we've won two races in a single day.

Sunday, November 19

In Grandfather's terse diaries, he seldom chronicled his own children.

"John and Joe day off."

For this diary, let the record reflect that today, August was singled out by his soccer coach after the Fallston Cup final. Captain of his last game. Three years on the same team. Lost today on a sudden-death kick.

"I know you're upset about leaving your friends, August," the coach said, "but not as upset as I am. You're moving on to high school."

Horse business like soccer. Lot of running. Not much scoring. Random chances.

If it's your choice someday to play this game, son, remember the Fallston Cup. A little luck here and there, it goes your way. But dammit, it can just as easy go the other way.

Monday, November 20

History junkies find each other. Sue Stephenson is curator of the Selima Room at the Prince Georges County Memorial Library in Bowie, which houses the Turf library of William Woodward. She sends me clippings of old Maryland farms. Sepia-toned ads from Danny Shea's days at Merryland. Obits that chronicle careers. Xeroxes of magazine covers. As entrancing as classic movies. You look back and are propelled forward. You understand the dedication of lives before you. Renew your vows.

Tuesday, November 21

If I could, I'd be a red leaf flattened in the pages of the 1932 book *Maryland and the Thoroughbred*, by D. Sterett Gittings. Published by the Maryland Horse Breeders Association. Aerial photos of horse farms. Narrative rich as Maury loam. Foreword by Governor Ritchie:

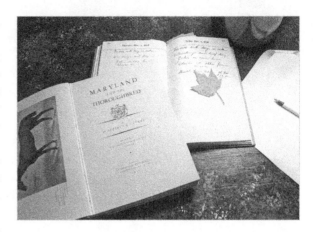

"... carrying on this most important industry of raising Thoroughbreds ... should have the unqualified support of the State."

New Maryland governor elected this month. So what? We're pressed meat in a slots sandwich. Delaware east. West Virginia west. Pennsylvania north. Soon, New York will toothpick it all together, pricking through at the Mason-Dixon line.

Grandfather came to Maryland to live in 1933, perhaps influenced by this book. He had to have read it. Today, he'd probably pick Pennsylvania.

Wednesday, November 22

Maintenance at Merryland deferred by prior owners. Frayed asphalt shingles on the training barn. Leaky roof circuit hard to escape. Estimates arrive.

I wish I could open a slots parlor in the kitchen here. To defray bills for roofs and tractors. For sand and septics. For workers' comp and complimentary tickets home for the Mexican crew for Christmas.

Thursday, November 23

Yesterday, I watched the grooms at Merryland ferry saddles and bridles from one training barn to another. Tacking up fresh sets of yearlings. An assembly line. Fifty horses a day. Racehorses learn best if they learn in company.

At a time in Maryland when breeders are abandoning the field for gold in Pennsylvania, it's great fun to have a going concern in this training center.

Makes us thankful for these and all our blessings.

Friday, November 24

Dug up and replanted trees today on the farm. A dozen tough-to-kill cedars that'd volunteered along fence rows. Tied blue tape on each seedling to mimic expensive nursery stock. From the pickup came the sweet sounds of Garrison Keillor's Hopeful

Gospel Quartet, as we laid out a line of trees that someday we hope will absorb the sound and sight of cars.

Why is it that you never forget planting a tree?

Saturday, November 25

Call at 9 a.m. from trainer. Spectacular Malibu had a bout of colic last night.

"We don't keep syringes around, but we have Banamine in paste. We dosed her with that, just to get something on board. Hardest part was getting a vet out on Friday night of Thanksgiving weekend. This morning she seems fine."

And so Saturday starts off by dodging a bullet I didn't even know had been fired. Thanks given to Trombetta and his good team at the track.

Sunday, November 26

Wahoooo!

What? Jockey's objection? Watch the JumboTron. Replay of Wahoo Moon floating wide for racing room. Such a bull she can be. Recall the smashed gate at Merryland from yearling days.

In football, video replay must present irrefutable evidence to overturn a call on the field. In racing, referees aren't on the field. They're three stories up. All they have is video. Those stewards. Way up there. Invisible as gods.

We stood paired up with partners in the winner's circle, watching a JumboTron of two horses as the gods made us crazy. Finally: Wahoooo!

Monday, November 27

Deer hunter.

"So it's private property. I know a horse from a deer. I'm just following the blood trail of a buck I shot next farm over."

Sure enough, on a brown maple leaf at my feet, a bright-red drop of fresh blood.

"Must a hit him behind the rib cage. Probably in the liver."

He needed the rack for bragging rights. I couldn't find fault with his tracking ability. He must wound many a fine buck. I pointed to where I thought a deer would go to die in these tranquil woods.

Tuesday, November 28

A sight I can't shake. Two weeks ago, I watched as an out-of-control racehorse barreled upstream against the flow of morning workouts. Rider clinging. Unable to steer.

Trainers hollered to their jocks: "Turn and go the same direction!"

Only a collision could stop this bus. That, or physical exhaustion.

Spectacular Malibu had just come off the track. Merryland Monroe was just coming on. They dodged the backward bullet work.

Football. Baseball. When will racing do something about steroids?

Wednesday, November 29

Signs on the Jersey Turnpike:

"Gridlock alert day. Use mass transit."

No. Gotta make the sixth at Aqueduct.

Sign on the Belt Parkway leaving Brooklyn: "Fogettaboutit."

Hard right into the vast parking lots of the Big A. A casino mogul's dream.

Into the tunnels. Belly of the beast. Horseman's bookkeeper. At a racetrack in bankruptcy. Sagamoon's track sheet reflects cost of doing business in New York. Everything deducted.

Racing Form handicapper: "Mark this down. Worst field of New York-bred maidens. Timid choice is disappointing New York Moon."

In winner's circle, trainer motions me aside.

"It's about Tina's Prospect. She stress fractured this morning."

Even when you win, you lose. A day in the life of New York racing. Hard to fogettaboutit.

Thursday, November 30

Dad followed progeny of farm stallions into winner's circles across the land. "Photo Joe," ol' Tom Patterson used to call him. Kentucky Ted suggested we get a cardboard cutout of him: "Joe on the Go." Pull him out for win photos.

He certainly was missed this month. It's irreverent enough to think about a cardboard cutout. No, I'm fine with just his spirit. Impossible to fogettaboutim in these moments.

December

Friday, December 1

Bookended on either flank by resistant hills, Merryland Farm is an inviting bowl of bottom land. Pierced by a fast-flowing stream. Embarrassingly picturesque. A storybook farm.

Native Americans wrote the first chapter. Paths through woods are moccasin made. Game abundant under cover of beech and poplar until farmers flowed north from Baltimore. The Ma and Pa Railroad ferried goods out of the well-watered land. Horsemen succeeded the farmers. Idyllic flat setting for a racetrack. Sweeping upland stretches of Piedmont on which to raise young horses.

A happy ending is assured for this land. Ironclad easements lock it in preservation.

Contentedly, my stream of daily entries, two years running come New Year's Eve, ends this month. My study is a tottering tangle of reference materials. Somewhere in the stacks are E.B. White's diary entries of farm life. A city friend had cautioned him: "I trust you will spare the reading public your little adventures in contentment."

Saturday, December 2

Laurel's Toddler Stakes was written as a prep for the year-end Maryland Juvenile Filly Championship. But Spectacular Malibu scared off opposition. Racing office tried to entice trainers: "What if we wrote it at six furlongs instead of seven? And put it back up for Sunday?"

"Nope. We're ducking that filly."

The Toddler didn't go. No one to play with, Spectacular Malibu will train up to the local championship.

Sunday, December 3

Announcer Terence Collier halted in surprise on his way to the auction stand in the Timonium sales pavilion. Over the loudspeaker, his cohorts cued up the song "Hitchin' a Ride," which talented Terence sang for a 1970s pop band named Vanity Fair.

A moment of merriment before obligatory announcements. Soon the sale company was briskly posting summary sheets awash with "Not Sold" and "Reserve Not Attained." A bazaar of private negotiation ensued as vanity vanished. Mares hitched a ride home any way they could.

Breeders limped off into the night, the expense of feeding marginal stock clamped like a trap on their legs.

Monday, December 4

Bad karma. Some horses get sideways with you. Bad luck follows them. Finds you. We sold a disagreeable mare who specialized in pinned ears and late cover dates. Her parting gift was her weanling filly. Pre-sale X-rays four days ago. Chip in one hind ankle. OCD in the other. Dreamgirl gone in two photos. Pinhookers took a pass. We closed our eyes. We can't race every foal.

Discipline. Sit on your hands. Discipline.

Our partner bought us out. Now the weanling is certain to become a stakes winner. His daughter wrapped her arms around the filly and the LLC dissolved on a sweet note.

Tuesday, December 5

In the mail arrives an invitation for an open house at Philadelphia Park. Welcome slots players. Welcome horsemen. Come shake hands with the 800-pound gorilla. King Kong has arrived in Pennsylvania.

The Maryland legislature feigns an allergy to gambling. Meanwhile, the state's latest lottery bait is a simulated horse race game called Racetrax. It plays on TV screens behind gas-station counters as we fill up the farm's pickups. Our image. Our sport. Our livelihood. Their game.

Disclaimer on back of Racetrax playslip reveals the chasm:

"The Maryland Lottery encourages responsible play. Remember, Racetrax is only a game."

Wednesday, December 6

Trainer Mike Trombetta to the exercise rider:

"Make sure you get her attention the last sixteenth. Make sure she finishes up. Two and change will be fine."

Trainer to the clocker: "You got her in 1:01?"

He keeps right on talking.

"A quicker five-eighths than I wanted, but I gotta train her. She's going a mile. We'll train right up to the Championship, but she needs to work. It'll be two months since her second in that New York stakes."

Thursday, December 7

Following Laurel trainer Ferris Allen stall to stall on morning rounds.

"Filly arrived from Delaware Park. Ninety minutes up the road, but weeks ahead of our winter. Look at that long hair-coat. Already needs clipping."

He ducks under a webbing. Lifts a blanket off a 2-year-old colt.

"If the training farm says he's ready to work six furlongs, I'll breeze him a half-mile. Any time a horse comes into a new barn, even older horses, they face change. New track. New surface. New riders. New training style."

Training racehorses is close work. At 10 a.m., out on the track, a grader pulls sand back from the rail. Quickening the cushion. It's a new track between morning work-outs and afternoon races.

Friday, December 8

Double headache. Just get it over with. Hard phone calls to tell two owners that the humane thing is to put down their yearlings.

"She's got EPM. She's a hazard to herself and others. The treatment had no effect."

"The filly that fractured her pelvis in October is still suffering."

Permission granted.

Saturday, December 9

Seconds after administering the pink shot to the first filly, the veterinarian takes her gently by the halter. When the barbiturate overdose takes sudden hold, she collapses backward. He's in a tug-of-war to let her fall softly. Releases at a moment timed from hundreds of euthanasias. A dignity to his method.

The Valley Protein driver wouldn't get out of his truck until he'd been paid. Crossly, he asked: "You didn't say you had two horses. You got two checks? All right then."

This is nasty work. But it has to be done. On every farm. Don't kid yourself.

Ellen phoned. "Wanna go to a movie?"

Please, just drive me out of this one.

Sunday, December 10

In Kentucky last month, I saw a 3-year-old colt just retired to stud. Baby teeth still intact. Were Man o' War's baby teeth intact when he was retired at 3? And why didn't Man o' War run at 4?

Turf writer Joe Palmer, from *This Was Racing*:

Mr. Riddle asked what weight Mr. Walter Vosburgh would put on Man o' War at four.

"If he wins his first race," the handicapper for The Jockey Club said, "I'll put the heaviest weight on him that any horse has carried in my lifetime."

Man o' War bred mares as a four-year-old. Of his first 92 foals, 26 won stakes. That's 28 percent stakes winners. That's a record with teeth. Palmer's editor Joe Estes penned the poem beneath Herbert Haseltine's bronze of Man o' War at the Kentucky Horse Park:

"Dream and hope and yearn,
For there's never a man among you,
But waits for his return."

Monday, December 11

Type "family farm" into a search engine. Buzz words leap out. *Traditional. Rural. Idyllic. Endangered.*

The conclusion? *Must use remaining knowledge and expertise as framework for "new family farm."*

Five years ago, the business plan for the purchase of Merryland's 159 acres tilted heavily on boarding mares for a healthy Maryland breeding industry. That suited us. Danny Shea's racetrack was in such disrepair that it appeared anachronistic.

Skip ahead in the book: The renovated racetrack is now the farm's economic engine. Slots in neighboring states have sucked local mares away. Still, their babies have to go to school somewhere. Some apply to the University of Merryland.

An example of a "new family farm." It's Agricultural Darwinism.

Tuesday, December 12

Out of the tack room stepped a rider, young and brave, but hunched and stiff from a fall two days ago. You could almost hear the bones in his back pop when he straightened his shoulders.

As he bent his knee for a leg up, I recalled a business bromide: "There are old pilots. And there are bold pilots. But there are no old, bold pilots."

Wednesday, December 13

Vanned a yearling filly to a Delaware farm today to begin 90 days of certification. We run two horse hotels in Maryland, but send our babies to grow up in other states, and our mares to foal away from home. And we buy out-of-state-bred yearlings by our sires.

Major Malibu lives at Penn National. Aiming for a January debut at Philly Park for Pennsylvania-breds.

Sagamoon lives at Belmont. She's 2 for 4 against New York-breds. Looking for a stakes.

Spectacular Malibu lives at Laurel, but spent 90 days in Delaware to become eligible for certified bonuses of 30 percent of purse money.

Harpo's Fairy, of course, lives in West Virginia. At Charles Town. Looking for West Virginia-bred maiden money.

We reach for low-hanging fruit on the subsidy trees of other states. To keep our farms in Maryland, we support out-of-state businesses. It's Darwinism. Check one: adapt or perish.

Racetrax is only a game to legislators.

Thursday, December 14

A select corps of Maryland trainers ship divisions to Florida, where grooms are plentiful in the warm climate. This time of year, the local help situation is dire. Being home for Christmas means home in sunny Mexico. These days at Laurel, it's not deck the halls. It's all hands on deck.

Trainers turn left around their shedrows. Hot-walking shank in one hand; cell phone in the other. Florida on the line. On their mind.

Friday, December 15

The Delaware Thoroughbred Horsemen's Association made a deal. The money paid by mushroom growers for horse manure at the track would come to the horsemen. In the range of a half-million dollars a year for soiled straw.

Delaware Park kept its backstretch open this winter. More than 300 horses there. Nomadic trainers, who might have gone to Fair Grounds or Oaklawn, winter at home with their families. Bolster the local tax rolls. Van to races at Laurel, Aqueduct, Philadelphia Park. The track charges $8 a day stall rent. But a $3-a-day contribution from the manure fund knocks the rent down to $5.

Charlie Whittingham's line that owners should be treated like mushrooms. Kept in the dark. Covered in horse manure.

Who would've thought there's gold in them thar' hills of manure?

Saturday, December 16

Jackie Wilson is about to make his racing debut. Hot walkers with soul laugh at his name. "Jackie Wilson! I loved Jackie Wilson!" They break into bars of "Lonely Teardrops" and "Higher and Higher" as they circle the shedrow.

One-part showman, two-parts show horse, Jackie Wilson sticks out his tongue on demand. He cocks his head over his webbing like a singer in the spotlight.

But he is not very fast in his workouts. And perhaps too pleasantly tempered to fight racing's wars. Maiden claiming beckons.

Sunday, December 17

Philadelphia Park cuts the ribbon on their slots parlor today.

This is not the Maryland Miracle era of the late 1980s. When our tracks were renovated. When sports palaces glitzed at Laurel and Pimlico. No, this is the era of the Philly Phenom.

Sense of dread that as Pennsylvania climbs, Maryland will decline.

Monday, December 18

Meanwhile, it's 80 degrees today. Feels like a California Christmas. Thoughts of champion Declan's Moon at Hollywood Park. Working bullets, but running like his powder is wet. His breeder, Brice Ridgely, mused at the ups and downs of horses, of horse farming.

"Sad thing is, I don't know anything else," Brice said. "Like the joke about that farmer who wins the lottery. His friends ask him: 'Whacha' gonna do now?' He says, 'Guess I'll keep on farming till the money runs out.'"

Tuesday, December 19

The resorbed foal. The chipped yearling. The bleeding racehorse. The impregnable mare.

At the Timonium sale two weeks ago, I saw horsemen get up and go out of the business. With land in Maryland so valuable, why does anyone persist in farming? Torn between two powerful pulls. Desire for a way of life; desire to make a living.

Wednesday, December 20

From what I've seen of desire, I favor the fireplace in the big house, hung today with pine boughs from trees in the lane. And I favor chevrons of geese skimming the big hill at dusk as weanlings pose like shadow cutouts. And I favor Mom's amateur family photos, famously double-exposed so that spirits of Christmas Past inadvertently appear year after year.

Pink sunrise. Orange sunset.

Dinner sounds from an aisle of mares chewing through their hay.

Garlands of holiday decorations on the farm gate.

It's a world through rose-colored glasses. Really rosy when you win a race.

Thursday, December 21

On a coffee table at Merryland, a back issue of the *Maryland Horse* magazine: November 1964.

Cover photo of a flaming barn: "34 Horses Destroyed As Laurel Barn Burns to Ground." That photo kindles vigilance in fire prevention.

We've upgraded electricity in barns and houses at Merryland. An expensive priority.

But that's easy, compared to No Smoking. For it was cigarettes to blame at Laurel in '64. So many people still smoke near, or in, a barn. Look at the ground outside a barn door. You can always find a crushed cigarette butt. Sometimes a spent match. How timeless, how ubiquitous, this dangerous habit.

Friday, December 22

Christmas party in the track kitchen at Merryland. Like the Day Room in *One Flew Over the Cuckoo's Nest*. Television high in the corner, piping in races from anywhere. Bar stools spinning as pizza boxes are passed.

It's a Broadway casting call for racetrackers. Teenage girls with that horse fetish. Spanish-speaking men at a table by them-

selves, isolated by the language barrier. Office gals in reindeer antlers. Exercise riders in Santa Claus suits. Older men hard as washboards from miles of hot-walking. Carpenters with hands bent from a lifetime of shimming. All mildly eccentric, slightly peculiar. But withal, an unmatched platoon of the finest soldiers.

In spot-on observations in his book *Racing Days*, Brendan Boyd described a character: "There's a guy you only see around the track."

Or the kitchen at Merryland.

Saturday, December 23

Year-end recaps from local newspaper headlines:

Hearing Examiner denies request for school near horse farm, citing unsafe access. (Maybe it was testimony about horses coupling.)

Base Realignment and Closure program, known as BRAC, to add 100,000 to the county's population. (Did they really say 100,000?)

Land Preservation Efforts: $400 million diverted from Program Open Space. (Luckily, Merryland was put into easement under an earlier administration.)

Sunday, December 24

A farm pickup truck doesn't usually last 13 years without a dent, but Brice found us a clean-bodied old Ford for a young man's Christmas present.

"Just leave the farm tags on it and you won't have to get it inspected."

But, Brice, the gas tank leaks.

"Oh."

Inspected on Thursday. Titled on Friday. Hosed out in the breeding shed on Saturday.

And parked down by the culvert tonight, so 16-year-old son Josh won't see it until he unwraps the keychain on Christmas morning. He gets his license in three weeks. He gets his first set of wheels tomorrow. The only farm truck without a dent.

Monday, December 25

Christmas present from Ellen. A photo album with a list of the things we carried to Merryland five years ago:

Aug. 16, 2001. We came full of enthusiasm. The rest we brought.
Cups. Plates. Chairs. Brooms.
Fertilizer. Lime. Bat-Wing.
Blade. Bolt. Lawn mower.
Screwdrivers. Stall screens.
Buckets. Shanks.
Lock. Key. Latch.
Paint. Spackle. Concrete.
Level. Transit.
Primer. Caulk. Roller.
Sump pump. Fuel pump.
Snow plow. Salt.
Hammer.

I remember so clearly the day we bought the farm. It didn't have so much as a hammer on it. What a great Christmas present, Ellen. Your photos. Your list. Your memory of that first hammer!

Tuesday, December 26

Home from college for the holidays, Mike's son Philip joined brother David and cousin Josh at creekside this morning. They dragged the water-logged body of a deer up into the sand. No one asked them to dig a grave, but they did. Before covering him, though, they hack-sawed off the rack the hunter was searching for last month. Eight points. Perfect as Mother Nature can make.

Of course I know there are too many deer. That doesn't diminish the perfection of this one. Or the understanding of his death 100 yards upstream, wounded by a hunter who then couldn't track him.

Lessons from farm life. Unfair world sometimes.

Wednesday, December 27

New York Moon cut his lip in his stall. To stitch him, vets numbed him with Novocain. A prohibited substance in his bloodstream now. So today, no New York Moon in lucrative New York-bred race at Aqueduct. No favorite in a "non-winners-of-one-other-than."

Thursday, December 28

E.B. White wrote of a fictive trip to Walden Pond with sanctimonious Senator Joe McCarthy.

"I gave him a draught of undiluted morning air. Perspiration broke from his neck and forehead. The morning air, taken neat, had been overpowering."

I'd like to bring state legislators to Merryland. But the wholesomeness of Maryland's farms seems anathematic to Annapolis men. The farm life, taken neat, is taken for granted.

Friday, December 29

"Merryland Monroe! She's a beauty!" called Laurel track announcer Dave Rodman as the filly crossed under the wire 3½ lengths on top. Win Number 300 this year for jockey Anna R. ("Don't call me Rosie") Napravnik.

One race earlier, the heart-shaped star on St. Mary's Citi shone like a miner's lamp in a crowded four-horse finish. Second. By a half-length.

Laurel has two finish lines. I watched as Merryland Monroe and St. Mary's Citi dashed to the first finish line. Tomorrow, Specky needs to continue on past for another sixteenth. To the second finish. For a one-turn mile.

Saturday, December 30

Today, the racing gods giveth odds of 1-5 on Spectacular Malibu. And they taketh away the win in the final stride. First, under the first finish line. Second, under the second. Two months was too long between starts. Lost by a neck.

Losing partners walked slowly out of the track. Savoring the "what if?" Politely desirous of another chance. Came up two feet short of a win in a 5,280-foot race.

Her groom stroked her neck as they walked home past someone else's winner's circle. Of everyone there, he seemed most able to appreciate her gallant effort.

"Oh, well, that's racing," I said to myself, loud enough for newcomers to overhear. It didn't feel hollow. It felt true. That *is* racing. You can lose at 1-5. Hell, you can cut your lip and never even start.

Sunday, December 31

Sometimes it's not good luck you need. Sometimes just an absence of bad luck is enough. I think back to unloading Spectacular Malibu as a yearling in a thunderstorm at Merryland. She could have broken loose that night. Or on the walk from the backstretch before her first race, when she struck her groom.

In what other business are dreams secured merely by the snap on a shank? Or the courage of a groom just kicked by a 1,200-pound animal?

Oh, well. That's racing.

At midnight tonight, this diary of Merryland, this journal of characters four-legged and two, flows back underground. It surfaced somewhat accidentally. Two years ago, a draft of a January diary was under consideration on an editor's desk, when suddenly a lengthy feature on Declan's Moon had to be scratched. The Kentucky Derby favorite had been injured. What to do with those open pages? How 'bout that diary idea?

And somehow one month became 24. Tonight, fireworks and frying pans will bang in the New Year. Tomorrow, I'll begin straightening up my study, after two years of whimsically recording little adventures in contentment on a lovely farm named Merryland.

ABOUT THE AUTHOR

Josh Pons got one A in college. In English. In short-story writing, to be precise. He took that as a life sign to stick with the short narrative form. A day at a time is all he can muster. His first published work, not counting seven years as a reporter for *The Blood-Horse* magazine, was *Country Life Diary: Three Years in the Life of a Horse Farm*. His second book is *Merryland: Two Years in the Life of a Racing Stable*. His third book, *Letters from Country Life*, tells the story of his grandfather, Adolphe Pons, establishing the family farm in Maryland in 1933 after a quarter-century as the personal secretary for Man o' War's breeder, August Belmont II. His writings have earned two Eclipse Awards. He lives with his wife, Ellen, a professional photographer and artist, on Country Life Farm near Bel Air, Maryland. They have two sons, Josh and August. His grandfather, Adolphe A. Pons, founded Country Life in 1933. It is Maryland's oldest Thoroughbred breeding farm. Merryland Farm is the state's oldest Thoroughbred training farm. They are both appropriately named.